SULTANS OF STYLE

By the same author:

In Vogue

SULTANS OF STYLE

Thirty Years of Fashion and Passion 1960-90

Georgina Howell

EBURY PRESS
London

For Tom

First published by Ebury Press
an imprint of the Random Century Group
Random Century House
20 Vauxhall Bridge Road
London SW1V 2SA

British Library Cataloguing in Publication Data
Howell, Georgina 1942 -
    Sultans of style: thirty years of fashion and passion,
    1960–90.
    1. Fashion designers – Biographies – Collections
    I. Title
    746.920922

    ISBN 0-85223-914-9

Typeset in Trump Mediaeval by Tek Art Limited, Croydon
Printed and bound in Great Britain by Mackays of Chatham, PLC, Kent

Contents

Acknowledgements

My grateful thanks to the following:

Philip Clarke, Editor of *The Sunday Times Magazine*, and Anna Wintour, Editor-in-Chief of American *Vogue*, for their encouragement and permission to use the majority of the pieces in this book.

American *HG*, British *Vogue*, and *The Correspondent Magazine* for allowing me to use the other features, especially Miles Chapman of *The Correspondent Magazine* for his help and advice.

Michael Roberts for being the first person to suggest publishing these pieces as a book, and Gail Rebuck of Random Century and Rowena Webb, my editor there, for actually doing so.

My mother who has made it possible for me to go to New York, Milan or Paris at a day's notice.

Snowdon for allowing me to use his photographs on the cover, and for the great pleasure of working with him.

Michael Boodro, Senior Features Editor of American *Vogue*, for his sympathetic guidance and robust calm.

Philip Norman, who occasionally put his own work on hold to read mine.

Richard Godfrey for his invaluable advice re Porkinson sausages.

Lastly, a very special thanks to David Robson, the editor for whom I wrote a third of the features in this book, and from whom I learned better self-editing along the way.

Introduction

*I*F designers have seemed exceptionally stressed during the recent decade – weird, unbalanced, exhibiting odd behavioural patterns – it has not been just because commercial pressures were fierce. It is because fashion is no longer a question of long or short, of action and reaction, or even of role-playing. Fashion itself is debunked and style has become personalized: fashion as in fashion victim, style as in *Style Trial*. The public is cynical, and every move made by designers, whether of clothes, décor or buildings, has come under derisive media scrutiny.

Advertising directors have turned their backs on the study of the needs and desires of the once all-important consumer to study the philosophy and living habits of the designer. Once a shadowy figure behind the clothes, he now spends much of his time on view, making videos and in-store appearances and hosting charity galas. The press documents his social life, photographs his houses, dissects his private affairs and even speculates whether he has AIDS. No personal style? No publicity, no payola. If there is a conflict between the designer's life and the designer's image, it is real life that must be rewritten.

Rock Svengali Malcolm McLaren was one of the first to take for granted the contemporary triumph of form over content. Manager of the Sex Pistols and Adam and the Ants, he put style to groups, then groups to style. 'As long as the band has the right look,' he said – we were talking in his Wardour Street office in 1983 – 'the music doesn't matter too much.'

At one end of the style spectrum are the Beau Brummells, who take the view that 'If John Bull turns round to look after you, you are not well-dressed.' At the other end are the exhibitionists, who would parade the streets, like the Marchesa Casati, in a tigerskin top hat with a couple of leopards in front and a Tunisian slave behind. But McLaren's design protégée Vivienne Westwood was something new. She created confrontational nose-thumbing costume for people with a terror of passing unremarked. Her inspiration came from pornography and materials that might have been found blowing around a broken-down housing estate. Lately she has discovered the one remaining source of inspiration with the power to annoy us: the Queen and her crown, ermine trimmings and button-up twinsets. As fashion, they're schlock. As style, they're 100 per cent effective.

For more than a decade Ralph Lauren's advertisements, presented in ten- to twenty-page portfolios, have documented the same cast of characters lounging over tennis courts and polo fields, cashmere sweaters thrown over their shoulders, living vicariously for the hard-working professionals who can afford the clothes. What is extraordinary is the watertight completeness of the vision. In the museum-piece Polo store in Manhattan, four-poster beds and handmade quilts are sold from chintzy bedroom settings eerily complete with bath towel, turned down sheet and fresh flowers – with silver-framed family photographs of those familiar faces on the bedside table. The fiction, the style, is so persuasive it has overtaken real life. The Prince and Princess of Wales buy Polo.

'I'm not an artist working alone in his studio, designing the perfect armhole,' explained Ralph Lauren, equipped for a day in the office in denims and cowboy boots. His stone-washed blue eyes grew dreamy. 'I was the guy looking at the magazines and movies, saying "Wow, *that's* where I'd like to be." The way I see it, you've got to paint the environment. It's not just the car, it's where you're going in that car. I'm trying to paint a wonderful world, a life that makes you feel good. Maybe I'm redefining a life we lost. That's my movie. What's yours?'

Lauren, with his static vision of an America that never was, and Calvin Klein, steadily packaging classics that could have come from a 1930s' *Tatler*, produce clothes but design and sell Attitude. Which is just what Vivienne Westwood does – only, of course, it's a different Attitude.

Style has extended the limits of taste beyond the fashionable. After three decades of épater la bourgeoisie and leading from the ground, it is in the international couture that the prolonged shake-up in garment culture has resolved itself.

'I want to get back to the position where the couture becomes a kind of laboratory for ideas,' said Frenchman Christian Lacroix at his début in 1987. 'Everything must be a kind of caricature to register, everything must be larger than life. The new couture should be all about theatre.'

Casually juggling the famous components of the Coco Chanel formula, the German Karl Lagerfeld excels in impertinent parody and inversion while producing the one and only uniform of the last decade, the new Chanel suit and its thousand-and-one copies. 'Good taste is like a red light,' he told me. 'Everything stops dead!'

Issey Miyake says from Japan, 'The only thing I ask Snowdon is I don't want pictures that look like the photographs in fashion magazines. I don't want to do decoration. I believe in questioning.'

The Tunisian Azzedine Alaïa, although the nearest modern equivalent to Balenciaga, is style-crazy for the Queen Mother, boxer Mike Tyson and legendary Arab singer Oum Khalsoum.

The fifties were a time of tyrannical pronouncements from Paris. The envol line was followed by the princess line, the tulip line by the I, H and A line, each outdating everything in the average woman's wardrobe. *Vogue* told you what colours and fabrics to wear, season by season. In the sixties, the initiative came from the street. Dictatorship ended, and designers had to think out a way to snatch back the lead. They succeeded when they had something more than a set of options to offer. It took them about a decade to produce a point of view.

'Clothes should be unimportant,' said Englishwoman Jean Muir in 1978. 'Don't call me a fashion designer – self-important, pretentious term! What one does has to be a reflection of one's way of thinking.'

Pick a life and find yourself an Attitude. Over-stressed, high-powered business woman? Buy Donna Karan. Cool, low-key operator? Try Armani. Sexy global socialite? Dress Lacroix.

Even a decade ago this book would have been called *Pharaohs of Fashion* and its subject would have been limited to the kingdoms of the catwalk and the Vatican of the couture. Under the umbrella of style the fashion aristocracy find themselves in embarrassing proximity to the sartorially unobsessed, cheek to cheek between these covers with the monarch and the prime minister, a belly dancer and a media queen. None of these are high fashion contenders, but all assembled in this book have been or are sultans of personal style.

Add a handful of London charity socialites and a contingent of Arab wives, each of whom then wielded the spending power of a small country, and you have some of the poles of taste between which most of us are used to navigating our own manners and modes. So while the talk show host in his lilac shorts suit, lime shirt and gladiator sandals gets and gives a derisive look at the train-spotter in his anorak, trainers and Bri-nylon slacks, both can plot their position on the style map in relation to the Queen and a stripper.

All boundaries and divisions are blurring. Designers now plan their collections for maximum video impact. Fashion writers crouch over word processors instead of typewriters. Pattern cutters work on computer instead of card, sending the instructions straight from the screen to a numerically controlled cutter which slices through two hundred pieces of fabric at a time. Fashion photographers such as David Bailey make television commercials for cars and chemicals, while film directors such as Ridley Scott make commercials for scent. Bailey notices that young American movie audiences, raised on the remote control button, have begun to holler 'Fast forward!' in the boring bits. A flip through any fashion magazine already reveals the contrasting close-ups, action shots and changes of pace by which a movie fixes your attention for two hours, while films and novels have rapidly adapted to the shorter attention span of the video generation.

Magazines have changed in other ways. In the American edition of *Vogue* on the table beside me there are approximately 400 pages of advertising, much of it imitating the 216 pages of editorial. Alexander Liberman, editorial director of Condé Nast, says that the structure of magazines is changing in a move to regain the authority of the editorial. It can be hard to tell the difference, not only because the same photographers use the same models for editorial and commercial work, but because most sophisticated advertising has lost interest in selling a product. It now sells the image.

'Persuasion is the oldest, most boring thought in advertising,' Peter Arnell, fast-talking director of Arnell/Bickford Associates, told me in the lobby of the Royalton Hotel on an early trip to New York for American *Vogue*. Arnell is a plump, bespectacled figure whose words have trouble keeping up with his thoughts. His firm's accounts include Misty Harbor rainwear, whose ads notably failed to show raincoats, and a New York bank, EAB, whose ads displayed photos of a man crating lettuce or showed footage of a plane taking off. For no very obvious reason, EAB deposits had risen by $4 million a week since Arnell's campaign had taken hold. We were, however, talking about his campaign for Donna Karan, America's most successful woman designer. It started with an advertisement for tights that didn't show tights. It showed bare legs and sheets. Other Karen ads show a woman reading a financial newspaper in a cluttered bedroom with a baby on an unmade bed, or rising rumpled from her seat after a long plane ride, in the back of a yellow cab or shouting angrily on the phone.

'If they had a caption,' said Donna Karan, 'it would say "I know what you are going through. I understand your plight. The one thing you don't have to worry about is your clothes."'

The Karan campaign is an almost literal rendition of the designer's life, albeit with the designer impersonated by a beautiful young model, but it is only an extension of a radical change in emphasis. 'I start by recognizing that people believe magazines and newspapers more easily than they believe advertising,' said Peter Arnell. 'So I editorialize. The way I see it, if I do my job right with Donna's ads, I'm doing reportage on the designer and what she's doing and feeling. What is important now is how real you can get.'

The eighties was the action decade in which fashion finally got its act together and became one enormous, fully-stretched international conglomerate. High finance moved into the luxury goods market, Yves Saint Laurent became a public company, we got the first new Paris couture house in twenty-five years. Venerable designers toppled, brand-new designers toppled, AIDS thinned the ranks of talent worldwide. Survivors took on more than they could handle and designers quivered under the strain of up to twenty collections a year. Italians and Japanese established beachheads in Paris, the top models were black, white or Asian, and the same ideas emerged simultaneously in all quarters of the globe like a crop of overnight mushrooms. Mass-market fashion and catalogues got a lot better. Couturiers decided to rip themselves off for a change and started a score of less expensive lines.

This was the decade when every woman did a job. Physicists, film studio presidents and fund-raisers defined themselves through their work rather than their relationships. Melanie Griffith summed it all up in 1988's *Working Girl* when she said, 'I've got a head for business . . . and a body for sin.' But just when women were supposed to have some of the answers at last, they were actually living a schizophrenic fashion life, changing as many times a day as Marie Antoinette. Get up, get dressed, jog; change, office; change, play with the baby; change, out for dinner. If the schedule had slipped they would have found themselves in a leotard, headband and leg-warmers in the board room, wearing a power suit with the baby, or in a coatdress with Dallas shoulders at the gym.

In the end it was these women who drew the line. The woman getting dressed today has maybe ten minutes. She doesn't have time to be bewildered by fashion or good taste or self-decoration. Luckily, none of that counts for much any more.

As long as we've got some style, the clothes don't matter too much.

•

Press the rewind button thirty years and witness a seventeen-year-old copywriter composing her first fashion caption for *Vogue*. I still have it: fifty words entitled 'Vogue Patterns – Cottoning on to summer'.

Georgina Boosey, the copy editor and later a friend, warned me to re-read my words carefully. She told me that recently a headline for straw hats had had to be changed at the last moment and at great expense because no one had noticed its implications. It headed a regular feature called 'Why not?'

'Why not', it asked in Bodoni Bold typeface, 'spend the summer under a big black sailor?'

When my father died, the RAF Benevolent Fund had offered to help with fees for a secretarial course. Full of envy for friends at art school, I had dragged myself sulkily to the London College of Secretaries. There teachers with hairy legs took me to task for wearing black stockings. The only stylish figure I encountered during these few months was John Betjeman, who gave a hilarious speech to those few of us assembled on the journalism course.

At the end of this he had put one foot in front of the other, joined his hands as if in prayer, and added, 'My dear girls, I ask you one thing. Please, whatever you do, don't become secretaries.' Then he read to us from his poem called 'Business Girls'.

> From the geyser ventilators
> Autumn winds are blowing down
> On a thousand business women
> Having baths in Camden Town . . .
>
> Rest you there, poor unbelov'd ones,
> Lap your loneliness in heat.
> All too soon the tiny breakfast,
> Trolley bus and windy street.

The teaching staff had escorted him from the platform with faces like thunder.

I entered *Vogue*'s annual Talent Contest at sixteen because my mother told me to. She had triumphed in many competitions herself, collecting four iced cakes one Christmas, a weekend in Paris for a winning slogan and theatre tickets for being the owner of the oldest vacuum cleaner in Kensington. In 1958 *Vogue* had sent my mother a bottle of Lenthéric's Lotus d'Or for identifying the silhouettes of twenty scent bottles. She had no doubt that if I entered the Talent Contest I would win the job and the £50, and consequently was not the least surprised when I did.

I had written my autobiography in 300 words, picked a summer wardrobe from the magazine and described the life I would lead on a desert island. Through that round, the contestants proceeded to the Hyde Park Hotel for lunch with the *Vogue* editors. Nervous in a hat and borrowed suit, I was disconcerted by the suggestion of the features editor, John Davenport, that we should hide under the table together. The telegram had arrived later the same afternoon. It said, 'We are delighted to announce that you are the winner of our talent contest congratulations please telephone Miss Hodge for photographic appointment soonest possible.'

At Condé Nast I was put to work first for Peter Coats, *House and Garden*'s distinguished garden editor whose demanding social round permitted few visits to the office. My job was to water his plants and take his messages.

'Out again?' said the Duchess of Westminster. 'Tell Peter I *must* have my feather boa back by Saturday.'

I had been given a small red paper-bound book entitled *So You Have Joined Condé Nast*. It told me to wear a plain dark costume to the office, not to wear jewellery other than a string of pearls, and to have a hat and gloves for the journey to and from the office. It also warned me on no account to discuss my salary. The dark costume was no problem. I generally wore black, with a great deal more black round the eyes, and hoped to be mistaken for Juliette Greco. I failed to follow the rest of the instructions. Turning to my nearest neighbour, I said, 'I get £9 a week. How much do you get?' In the escalating debate that followed most of the office joined in and a senior fashion editor, realizing that her secretary was earning more than she was, stalked into the editor's office and threatened to resign.

For a few months more John Davenport, a lovable man who suffered from bouts of ill-temper, enlivened the office. He had once tossed a small person who was irritating him on to a high mantelshelf at the Garrick. At the magazine he had already punched a messenger and proposed to most of the staff. Once he walked into the fashion room with his trousers round his ankles and accosted the supremely elegant Sheila Wetton, once Captain Molyneux's favourite mannequin, with: 'You're supposed to know about clothes. Sew a button on my flies, will you, dear?'

I joined *Vogue* at just the moment when the old guard was giving way to the new. Unity Barnes represented the old guard, a decidedly hatted and gloved lady responsible for the creation of the monstrously genteel Mrs Exeter, a fictional character created to prevent older readers from feeling neglected. Mrs Exeter was perpetually attending a spring wedding in navy shantung with touches of white, or going cruising in a greige silk duster coat.

Lady Rendlesham was her opposite number, the editor of a new section called Young Idea and the first Sultan of Style I was to meet at *Vogue*: years later she became the *directrice* of Yves Saint Laurent in London. Clare Rendlesham was a prime example of a type well represented in the fashion world, whose fragile physique fails to prepare you for an abrasive manner and gigantic effrontery. From day to day you never knew how she would treat you. Some days she'd whistle for me – 'Bonzo! Here, boy, here!' – and sweep me into Young Jaeger to pick me garments I couldn't afford. On others, she propelled me into the editor's office at fingerpoint to demand my dismissal. She changed style like a chameleon. At the time I first remember her she had just seen Jeanne Moreau in *Jules et Jim* and was wearing round wire spectacles, elastic-fronted gym shoes, long striped sweaters and short pleated skirts. The tone of the first Young Idea pictures was arch: a model sat cross-legged on a London pavement fishing through an open manhole. I was sent to buy the fish.

The antique modes of the previous decade were still in force. The wording of the annual Model Contest, for instance, had remained largely unchanged since 1952:

Don't think, because no whistled tributes are forthcoming from corner boys, that you can't be a model . . . You can reassure your father, your husband or your son, on one point: modelling is terribly respectable. Whatever you do you will always be exemplarily clothed, and excessively chaperoned – by photographer, photographer's assistant, fashion editor (*stickler* for form), fashion editor's secretary and studio girl.

And then along came Bailey, who represents some of the passion in fashion promised on the cover of this book. He described the beginning of his career to Francis Wyndham in the following words: 'I had a choice at this time, age sixteen, time Monday, 4.30 in the afternoon. I could either be a jazz musician, an actor, or a car thief . . . They – from Mars or wherever they are – said I wouldn't be a fashion photographer because I didn't have my head in a cloud of pink chiffon. They forgot about one thing. I love to look at all women.'

When Beatrix Miller, ex-features editor of *Queen*, took over as editor in '64, *Vogue* became a modern magazine. Her manner was abrupt and provocative. One of her office walls was covered in felt and on this she pinned a large notice which said: 'If we hurry, we'll be late.' Beside it was a haiku penned by our exquisite art editor, Barney Wan.

Before the perfect white inviolate chrysanthemum,
The scissors hesitate.

She pretended to be impossible – 'A revolution, by yesterday!' was a routine demand – and with her amputative style of editing she taught me basic writing rules: who, what, where, when and why, and the constantly reiterated question: 'What are you actually trying to say?'

I was buying my clothes from Biba, first by mail order and then from the two-room premises off Kensington High Street, a dark and glittering cave of affordable treasure. In 1966, for £15, the price of a Mary Quant Bazaar party dress, you could walk out of Biba in a new coat, dress, shoes, petticoat and hat. When Biba took over Derry & Toms, Barbara Hulanicki and her husband Stephen Fitz-Simon played generous hosts at wonderful parties in the Rainbow Room or in the roof garden, where rock bands played while our children ran wild in the toy department.

Before long Mrs Exeter was only a memory. Instead we got lorry driver's daughter Zandra Rhodes of the Pentel Pen make-up and the emerald hair. In the Fulham Road Clothes Shop days her partner had pleaded: 'Stay away from here! You'll frighten the customers.' She designed her first commercial prints around Daz packets, zebra crossings and light bulbs, then cut dresses out around the prints. She also loved the pretty and the conventional. 'You can't beat *The Archers*!' she would say, interrupting any conversation to switch on the radio. 'It's an everyday story of country folk!'

'Showmanship *is* the business,' she told me. 'The difference between good and bad taste is, with bad taste you're not pretending. Bad taste is just good taste a bit earlier or later. All opposites are poles of the same thing.'

She enjoyed found objects, was always rummaging in council skips, and I once saw her drag a whole tree out of a rubbish dump. Decorated with chains of safety pins and wisps of chiffon, it ended up in the window of her Bond Street boutique.

Being startling was a male occupation in the sixties, too. Christopher Gibbs urged *Vogue* readers of both sexes to buy and wear the Diaghilev ballet costumes being sold at Sotheby's. Asked about clothes, Tom Wolfe, suited in a vanilla three-piece, pointed into the windows of a Jermyn Street tailor and said, 'If that shirt and that shirt were running a race, that shirt would win.'

I caught up later with Norman Parkinson, the tallest man in the world and the only one with a jewelled cap, a brooch at his throat and a bristling military moustache. Parks used to say that if he shaved off his moustache he would no longer be bald. 'You see, the hair all comes out halfway up. Doesn't get a chance to reach the top.'

He bred horses and became a pig farmer whose 'Porkinson' sausages sold at Fortnum & Mason. Parks lived in Tobago in an astonishing modern house where, he liked to say, he could hose down the rooms in hot weather. How he was ever mistaken for a quintessential Englishman was a mystery. He was far more like his Italian grandfather, Luigi Labache, the flamboyant opera singer who created the title role in *The Barber of Seville*. He once photographed Noël Coward, who took one look, turned aside and said, 'Parks will learn that the talented always dress like stockbrokers.'

When Condé Nast asked me to produce a book for *Vogue's* sixtieth birthday in 1975, they had a fashion book in mind. Ultimately I wrote sixty thousand words and produced 344 pages in which fashion sections were sandwiched between accounts of contemporary life from the days when the contributors had included Aldous Huxley and Nancy Cunard, Clive Bell and Cecil Beaton, Virginia Woolf, Jean Cocteau, D. H. Lawrence, Evelyn Waugh, Vita Sackville-West, the Sitwells and many more. I found the changes in women and their looks to be indivisible from everything else – theatre, film and politics, novels, music and dancing and social *mores*. Fashion's only constant property is that it changes, from person to person, group to group and day to day: a fact that makes it virtually useless to the theorist. Concentrate on it and you're left with a fragmentary image. Catch it off-centre, as part of the whole scene, and you may have captured something more substantial.

On the first stop of the American publicity tour in 1975 I met Diana Vreeland, legendary former editor of American *Vogue* and empress of the Metropolitan Museum of Art's Costume Institute. 'She pushed a certain excess,' wrote Alexander Liberman, Condé Nast's editorial director, 'because she understood that you have to pass the stage lights and reach out beyond to your audience.' Part of the excess was to have three-hour conversations about espadrilles with André Leon Talley, *Vogue's* current creative director, part to eat peanut butter with a silver spoon off K'ang Hsi porcelain plates. About to deliver an epigram, the Aztec head would turn, the crimson lips would part and the *basso profundo* voice would utter like an oracle. Pink, she said, is the navy blue of India. The bikini is the most exciting thing since the atom bomb. To me, a very junior voguette, she was enormously kind, showing me her scarlet apartment ('I wanted it red as hell!') and feeding me sandwiches and coffee at her desk at the Met.

The formidable Ernestine Carter, who occupied a comparable position in this country as fashion editor of the *Sunday Times*, was very different. Even when I was her somewhat inexperienced opposite number at the *Observer* she never acknowledged me, being too busy keeping her eyes on the ball. Her effervescent blonde assistant, Brigid Keenan, once told me that at a certain collection in Paris a woman in the second row keeled over and was presently found to be dead. Mrs Carter's arm went up. Beckoning over the PR, she told her, 'You'll find my assistant standing at the entrance. Now there is a chair vacant, perhaps you would be good enough to seat her.'

I went to the *Observer* as fashion editor from 1965 until the birth of my son Thomas in 1967, following Mary Holland, who came after Katharine Whitehorn, and preceding Shirley Conran. In twenty-four months I met the editor, David Astor, twice. When I arrived and when I left I went to his office and both times found him, feet up on the desk, eating Smarties. I have a clearer memory of the traveller and charmer Eric Newby, author of *A Short Walk in the Hindu Kush*, who would ride his bicycle in the main doors, down the steps of the reception area and into the lift, exit on the third floor, cruise in a circle round the fashion room and on down the corridor to his distant office.

One day a willowy eighteen-year-old was brought in to meet me. He had just won the J. Walter Thompson travel scholarship for fashion drawing. He hung tenaciously round the office, but I couldn't think of anything for him to do. I should have tried harder. He soon surfaced alongside Molly Parkin in the *Sunday Times*. It was Michael Roberts, transforming himself from an art student into the most anarchic of fashion critics.

We met up again in 1979 at *Tatler*, the magazine that *shall* go to the ball, where Tina Brown had unerringly picked a handful of jostling journalistic talent including the urbane Nicolas Coleridge; Miles Chapman, perfecting the art of turning Morris Minor copy into Exocet missiles; the informer and generator of ideas, Gabe Doppelt; and Brian Sewell, whose art criticism frequently corresponds to Dryden's definition of satire, 'The fineness of a stroke that separates the head from the body, and leaves it standing in its place'.

On our tiny budget of £6000 an issue we wrung features out of thin air. Tina Brown took class-consciousness out of the cupboard where it had been relegated by the sixties, dusted it off and injected it with her own brand of life-giving serum. Her method was to give her victim lots of rope and let him hang himself. We used for the Bystander party pages the very pictures that other magazines would have trashed. The élite passed out under tables, threw up and rogered their girlfriends on the billiard table. Debs lifted up their skirts and showed their bottoms. We revealed the names of Mayfair matrons who didn't pay their bills. We photographed the most attainable of crumpet as the Madonna. Tina Brown introduced the Gentleman Hack to the gallery of English literary types and routinely brutalized eligible men in Rosie Boot's Guide to London Bachelors. She told you what they were worth, their nasty little habits and where to find them hanging out on their own.

Last orders now for Nicholas de Rothschild! . . .
Isn't it time somebody bagged Lord Burghersh? . . .
Martin Amis, the tiny ironist . . . his girlfriends are startled to find their pillow-talk parodied on the lips of some fresh sexual grotesque in his latest novel. . . .
For proletarian appeal, there's always Frank Johnson. 'Come round to my place, I've got some mince I want to finish off' is typical of Johnson's courtship style. If you're a toff, don't rule out the thinking woman's boff. . . .

And courtesy of frocks 'n' shocks merchant Michael Roberts and his extraordinary series of lookalikes, we even had the Princess of Wales modelling piefrill blouses.

A brief spell as woman's editor of the *Mail on Sunday* paid off my son's school fees and allowed me to become a freelance writer. I settled to a run of features at the *Sunday Times Magazine* for which, if I was very lucky, the photographer might be Snowdon.

Snowdon sittings are minefields of tension. Sometimes you may not speak a single word to the subject, sometimes you're required to make easy conversation. The stress occasionally releases itself in fits of laughter. There is absolutely nothing that he does not notice. After greeting his resoundingly famous subject for a few minutes, he will draw you to one side and murmur, 'There's a tiny little hair protruding at a right angle from the left nostril. Would you be very kind and deal with it.'

I would sometimes fill in for him on fashion shoots, acting as stylist. Once, after photographing wedding dresses in the snow and in a boat on a frozen lake near his house, the team was to make its way back to London in two cars. Snowdon's was enormous and crammed with cameras. Mine was old and rusty and contained me, the model, the make-up artist, a couple of hairdressers and all their equipment. I had already had one puncture and suspected I had cracked the suspension by driving into a ditch. Then Snowdon asked me to put a chesterfield sofa on the roof and bring it to his London house. I am not a timid person, but somehow I could not say no. I drove back along the motorway in a strong crosswind, dropped everyone at relevant underground stations and brought the sofa to Snowdon's door.

I knew I had been the victim of one of his practical jokes the next time I went to his house in the country and found the sofa back in place.

In New York by 1988 I was writing profiles for Tina Brown's *Vanity Fair.* I thought my fashion days were over until weeks of rumour up and down the white corridors of Condé Nast's Madison Avenue powerhouse culminated in the announcement of a new editor-in-chief for American *Vogue.*

Anna Wintour, abbreviated of skirt and diction, is the brisk manipulator of the world's most powerful style force. Her telephone conversations seldom run to more than three words. 'What's up?' she'll say, and 'Okay.' After which you know precisely where you stand. Office politics falter at her crisp, 'You'll get over it.' Operatic dramas terminate at her door. 'At the end of the day it's only a frock.' Or 'All for a bit of acetate.' So succinct has she become lately that her husband David Shaffer, head of the children's psychiatric unit of Columbia University and Hospital, told me he has watched her sit down in a restaurant and, when the waiter arrived with the menu two minutes later, ask for the bill.

She had paused sixteen months at British *Vogue* and only nine months at American *House and Garden* before taking up the job she was born to do. The first time she brought me over to New York I was ushered into her almost empty white office by a succession of secretaries who were very nearly genuflecting. Blinking in the alpine light, I first perceived only a group of enormous blue and white vases filled with a thousand dollars' worth of pink cabbage peonies. Anna Wintour sat at a white desk in a braided white Chanel suit. The skirt was somewhat shorter than the jacket and far below were navy and cream stilettos. Her pearls tangled with her gilt buttons, and her Louise Brooks hair and huge sunglasses were the only dark marks in the room.

She sprang fashion out of an arty studio phase and gave it back to girls on the street: 'I don't see many girls walking around with trees in their hair.' In Anna Wintour's *Vogue*, girls in couture frocks bop along with ghetto blasters and sit in cafés looking approachable. Sex is omnipresent. She has freed up and featurized fashion in a way more natural to a newspaper mind. Her father is Charles Wintour CBE, writer and former editor of the *Evening Standard* and *Sunday Express Magazine.* 'I hope he will like what I am doing at *Vogue,*' she told me when I first met her, 'but he's not the reader I'm aiming at. For one thing he's not deeply interested in his clothes, and I don't think he's as concerned with his beauty and health as he ought to be.'

She is remembered for arriving to edit British *Vogue* at 8.30 am on her first morning in 1984 with the question: 'Who runs a 7 am exercise class here?' In one graceful movement she revolutionized the magazine, decorated and furnished a house in Ladbroke Gardens, conducted a highly successful transatlantic marriage and had a second baby. Early visitors to the hospital found her checking profits with one arm, the baby cradled in the other.

It is hard, in this country where no editor invokes the same veneration, to convey the awe with which she is regarded in New York. When recently a messenger went missing with a pair of Chanel shoes she needed for a benefit gala, her secretary was so terrified that she consulted a psychic out of *Yellow Pages.* A neighbouring office heard the assistant breaking down in tears. 'They are very expensive shoes,' she sobbed. 'They are for someone very, very important.' After some thought the psychic divined that the shoes were on a rubbish dump in New Jersey.

Writing for magazines today means much travelling. A glamorous job? Well, yes. Also many delays in airport terminals where all the seats are made of chicken wire and you have to queue for a ticket to queue for a coffee. Days spent cabbing across foreign cities with a white face and a blank notebook. Evenings spent lying across a king-size bed moodily flicking buttons on the television hand control, waiting for the comforting rumble of the hotel dinner trolley.

Backstage reporter to the couture, I try to flatten myself against the wall while the designer and his team reach meltdown in the all night run-up to the show. Fashion designers must reinvent their product twice a year, and it is no wonder they so often break down at the finale. Most haven't slept for up to forty-eight hours.

My first American job for Anna Wintour in 1988, while she was still editing *HG,* had been to write a round-up of the top American decorators. Nothing could have formed a better introduction to *Vogue*'s Manhattan, a world of stupendous picture collections, enfilades of faux-marbres and Rothschild abundance. The power and status of American decorators had never stood so high. Over the last decade they have succeeded the painters of the sixties and the fashion designers of the seventies as the social arbiters of our times: companies such as Parish-Hadley, MAC 11, Mark Hampton and Mario Buatta are chosen for reasons far beyond the aesthetic. The choice of a designer for your Fifth Avenue triplex or country house in Connecticut is a crucial element in the struggle for acceptance into the social register. Acquiring the proper decorator confers instant pedigree and lineage simply through the writing of a massive cheque.

New York's dozen great decorators exercise their patronage with varying degrees of ruthlessness. No one is more despotic than the septuagenarian Sister Parish, the Mount Everest of the new shelter culture. In Manhattan she operates from Gloria Swanson's former Fifth Avenue ground floor maisonette: 'It's convenient for the dogs.'

What were her feelings about privilege?

A small figure in a huge black hat, she regarded me tolerantly down a patrician nose. 'It's a great help. It helped me, and when I'm employing people, I notice it.'

New money?

'We're not against it. We want to give them pleasure, make them feel comfortable.' Pause. 'And *grateful*. But remember you're starting from scratch, mentally and physically.'

A friend recalled having gone into a room that Mrs Parish had worked on. 'There was this commode between the windows that was the wrong proportion. I said, "Sister, this doesn't fit!" And she said, "Don't you know I wanted it to look as though it had been inherited, so I went out and bought it too small."'

Doesn't this, I asked, come down to snobbery?

'I do sometimes reject clients,' said Sister Parish, 'for reasons of snobbery.'

'Yours or theirs?'

'Mine.'

I looked around me. I was in an office like a tiny country drawing room in bandbox turquoise stripes, with a garden rose in a green glass vase, a blue china jug, a piece of needlepoint and a painting of dogs. Through the window, where there should have been a Wiltshire garden, skyscrapers speared the lowest clouds. A murder or mugging far below had blocked 63rd street with a dozen police cars.

What a triumph of form over content! What a Sultan of Style!

Georgina Howell, 1990

Cristobal Balenciaga: *'Je ne me prostitue pas'*

*I*N the field of Parisian couture – the art of making a metre or two of fabric into a dress which will be recognisable all over the world as the work of a certain dressmaker – no one has ever risen so high as the Spanish fisherman's son, Cristobal Balenciaga. He was acknowledged as the master by the greatest in his profession. When, in German-occupied Paris, Balenciaga exceeded the authorized yardage and was shut down for two weeks, the rest of the couture forgot their differences and joined forces to finish his collection on time. Chanel, who never had a good word for anyone, said: 'Balenciaga alone is a couturier in the truest sense of the word. The others are simply fashion designers.' The great dressmaker Madeleine Vionnet, a woman of few words who dismissed Chanel as 'that hatmaker', called him *'un vrai'* and wore the dressing gown he had made her until the day she died. Givenchy called him 'the greatest influence on my career'. Christian Dior compared the whole couture to an orchestra playing a symphony composed and conducted by Balenciaga. So what was so extraordinary about his clothes?

Pauline de Rothschild, who dressed at Balenciaga for twenty-three years, likened the construction of his skirts to the cutting of sails. 'A woman walking would displace the air so that her skirt would billow out just so much, front, back and sides would round out each in turn, imperceptibly, like a sea-swell . . . . Nothing held them out; neither whalebone cages nor petticoats gave them any support. Legs moved easily, the front of the long skirt running a little faster ahead than one's walk.' Diana Vreeland, who produced his retrospective exhibition at the Metropolitan Museum of Art in 1973, treasured her own Balenciaga with its gold paillette top shaped like a shell and its skirt with layers of grey tulle. 'As it moved, the colour changed like rolling clouds of smoke. Simply, one walked into a room and no other woman was there.'

Tina Chow's favourite Balenciaga, from the forty she has

collected since his death, is a toreador bolero. In cream faille crusted with sequins, it is 'laughably small, like two big shoulder pads with tight sleeves. In fact, it has no pads and it is as light and supple as a new leaf.' She talks about the way it feels to wear his clothes. 'Sometimes the shapes of the clothes have strong form and are so abstract that you think they must be uncomfortable. I have one of his most severe black suits, but when I take off a modern jacket and put on Balenciaga's it feels like slipping on a cashmere cardigan.'

He was ambidextrous and could draw, cut, assemble and sew equally well with either hand. He worked with astonishing speed, putting together an entire garment in one sitting. His window-dresser Janine Janet remembered him, late in the afternoon on the eve of a winter sports holiday, cutting out the anorak he would wear.

He never made headlines like Christian Dior, but as the decades passed and swept away the nostalgia that had given rise to the New Look and the young revolution that had inspired the mini, the enduring innovations of Balenciaga could be appreciated at last. His lampshade peplum, barrel jacket, rolled collar and bloused top of the forties informed every look we think of as originating in the fifties. While Yves Saint Laurent's 'smoking' trouser suits and see-through dresses stole the attention of the press in the sixties, Balenciaga evolved the sack dress, the high-waisted chemise and the seven-eighths tunic that remain staples of the modern wardrobe. Fabrics and sleeves were his obsession. Courrèges and Gloria Guinness remember him working on a single sleeve for a night and a day without food or sleep. The silhouette of the garment was always strongly graphic, so that in the thick of the crowd on a ballroom balcony or in the racing enclosure it was always the Balenciaga client you noticed first.

We know as much about the man himself as we would have in his lifetime, for he was the least accessible man in Paris, and never gave an interview until he had retired. He was born in Guetaria, a Basque fishing village on 21 January 1895, the son of the village seamstress. Apprenticed to a tailor at thirteen, by twenty-four he had opened his first dressmaking house in the fashionable summer resort of San Sebastian. His customers were the ladies of the court of Alfonso XIII: when the king was deposed in 1931, the young couturier went bankrupt. He reopened in Madrid and Barcelona, but came to Paris six years later to escape the Spanish Civil War.

He never descended from his high plane to acknowledge praise or censure. The *Harper's Bazaar* editor, Carmel Snow, was the first to register the arrival of a new master when he came to Paris in 1937, and devoted pages to 'the connoisseur's couturier'. But it made no difference: like every other journalist after 1957 she was only permitted to attend his collection if she was prepared to return to Paris one month after seeing every other fashion show. He treated the press with contempt, and even his clients fared scarcely better. At 10 Avenue George V, the audience sat blinking in the white glare while, in total silence, a parade of the ugliest models in Paris passed disdainfully from left to right carrying numbered cards, and under the strictest instructions not to smile. Every collection included a black dress made entirely by his own hands. This was the dress to watch, for it always embodied the heart of the Balenciaga adjustments for the season, minimal as these might be. Downstairs there was a shop so forbiddingly impressive and brusquely managed that few dared to enter. Upstairs the showroom was ruled by the austere and spinsterly Mademoiselle Renée with her grey chignon and black dress; and woe betide the queen, ambassador's wife or film star who arrived late for a fitting. When one client asked for an invitation to the collection for a friend who had always been curious to see the clothes, Mademoiselle Renée responded icily: 'Curious women are not welcome here.'

André Courrèges, who worked for him for a decade, compares his entry into Balenciaga's world to that of an ascetic taking holy orders. 'The atelier was pure white, unornamented, and intensely silent. People whispered and walked on tiptoe, and even the clients talked in hushed voices. Once or twice a day the door of Balenciaga's office would open, and you would hear him leave the building to go and pray in the church on the Avenue Marceau.' His parish priest, confessor and friend Father Robert Pieplu called him 'a haunted man: haunted by a great plan, a vision of the world and of the individual, and by a conception of his work'.

Unlike Madame Vionnet, who preferred to dress the great beauties of the day, Balenciaga demanded only that his customers be 'distinguished'. Oddly, he was not a snob. He declined invitations from the grandest of clients, and his friends came from all walks of life. Asked what he meant by distinguished, he would give a rare smile and paraphrase Salvador Dali: 'A distinguished woman always has a disagreeable air.'

'He meant,' translated Diana Vreeland a couple of years ago, 'that his clothes were made for triumph and spectacle and drama, not for ordinary life or ordinary women. A woman had to be able to carry the thing off, and to have somewhere to wear her Balenciagas.'

Youth, slimness, sexual attraction, he could do without. His clothes extrapolated from the body instead of following it. He could square the shoulders, straighten the back, wasp the waist, bustle the bottom until a stout dowager turned into an hour-glass, if that was his intention – but he was more likely to turn her into a pillar of jet, a walking bow or two balloons of taffeta.

The women he dressed were autocratic, wilful and spoilt. Yet he brought them to heel and schooled them into a secret masonry of devotion: women such as Mrs Paul Mellon, who had shadows painted on the floor of her New York house to give the impression that the sun was always shining, or Mona Bismarck who even had her gardening clothes made by Balenciaga; in cinnamon to match her hair and the walls of her house in Capri. From his first client, the Marquesa de Casa Torres, who apparently wore a suit he had copied for her at the age of thirteen, to Jayne Wrightsman, Sunny von Bulow, Queen Fabiola of Belgium, Mrs Alfred Hitchcock and Daisy Fellowes, they were women who could shatter opposition like glass. Yet none of them dared ask for a dress to be rushed through for an important engagement.

Balenciaga was a man with a calling far removed from the commercial imperatives of today's couture. He lived to observe the onset of the image-making, licensing and make-up tie-ups that fund the loss-making couture of today, but they are not conditions that he could ever have accepted. He certainly would have been devastated by the establishment three years ago of a Balenciaga ready-to-wear at 10 Avenue George V. '*Je ne me prostitue pas*,' he announced to the news world of ready-to-wear in the sixties, and the press dubbed him a dinosaur. He described his last years in haute couture as 'a dog's life', referring to the pressures of scheduling, the financing, the late deliveries, the falling in quality of all around him. One day in 1968, without warning, he quietly hung up the white cotton over-jacket in which he habitually worked and resigned from his vocation.

He was only four years from his death when he asked his protesting admirers: 'Why do you want me to carry on? There is no one left to dress.'

Who Do You Think You Are? David Bailey?

JUNE, 1963. Six floors above the gardens and sandwich bars of Hanover Square, high anxiety vibrates along the white corridor of Vogue Studios. An elderly man in spectacles hurries up the passage to Dressing Room Five. He joins a distinguished-looking woman with a neat chignon: art director and fashion editor confer in whispers.

Suddenly the double doors of the studio opposite are wrenched open. Glimpsed momentarily between them is Jean Shrimpton in a formal satin ballgown. Her hair is heaped on top of her head like a pile of pale brown tennis balls. Mascara-blackened tears roll down her oval face. The shaggy fringe tangles stickily with false eyelashes framing the bright blue eyes. She tugs feverishly at the narrow skirt, bundling it up to her waist, and canters down the corridor on long thin legs. The back of her gown is cruelly twisted into a five-inch metal clamp, and her hair-piece is secured with a forest of pins. With a strangled sob she reaches the women's lavatory, and runs inside. There is the sound of a key turning.

David Bailey in a black leather jacket bursts into the corridor, black eyes snapping, face diabolical. 'Sexless ratbag!' he shouts after her. 'You should never have come down from the treetops! Come back, you bitch, and we'll try one with your head in!' He finds himself nose to nose with two faces in which shock and anticipation struggle for control.

Uttering a word that only one of them has heard before, he turns on his heel and kicks the door shut.

David Bailey, choosing fashion photography over a career as a jazz musician or car thief, walked into *Vogue* in summer 1960. Before Bailey, fashion sittings had been serene, urbane experiences involving country houses and greyhounds. Photographers such as the suave Henry Clarke, the society exotic Cecil Beaton and the gentleman farmer Norman Parkinson took up their cameras to project *Vogue's* ideal – Barbara Goalen or Fiona Campbell-Walter – passing aloofly Ritz-ward with a rolled umbrella, or turning quizzically to the camera, one gloved finger to her chin.

Who would have thought that the staid intricacies of a well-made dress, the aesthetics of the fine image and the quality print, the antique aura of a snobby old magazine could be transformed into Bailey's vehicle for sex and fame and money? Almost immediately Bailey became the Elvis Presley of photography: the original, the king of the lens. Within ten months he was living with the model he would turn into a sex icon. Within another two years there was no woman in the world – not Bardot, Taylor or Monroe – who seemed more urgently desirable than his Jean Shrimpton, the self-effacing country girl who apologized if you bumped into her and hated to walk down the street alone in case someone stared or pointed.

As Bailey turned fashion pictures into portraits full of sexual imagery, the stately drawing rooms were replaced by street markets and studio floors where Jean Shrimpton sprawled, skirts thigh-high, sometimes toying with a gun or cuddling a teddy bear. The pictures, ripped out of *Vogue*, ended up in the oddest places: pinned on garage walls, in canteens and prison cells.

The momentous first meeting took place in the studio where Brian Duffy was photographing Shrimpton for a Kellogg's corn-flakes advertisement. 'He was taking the picture against a blue background,' remembers Bailey. 'It was like her blue eyes were just holes drilled through her head to the paper behind. I thought she was the most amazing thing I had ever seen. And Duffy looked at me straightaway and said, "Forget it! You don't stand a chance. She's too posh for you." And I thought, we'll see about that.'

Jean Shrimpton remembers the first time he took her out, coming down the street in his Anthony Newley bumfreezer and Cuban heeled boots, carrying a bunch of flowers. She says that Bailey is quite different from his father Bert, the East Ham tailor who was a bit of a bruiser.

'I never liked him,' says Bailey. 'And he hated me because I wouldn't go to football, I wouldn't eat meat, I went birdwatching. He *knew* I was an effin' queer! Later I met Cecil Beaton and Michael Roberts and I found I liked homosexuals. They didn't have that fake sincerity that so many of the English do. I never minded if a man fancied me.'

'Women love him, gays adore him, children and animals run to him,' says Shrimpton. 'Mothers simply dote on him. He's universally attractive, except to fathers.'

There was another group of people to whom he was not immediately lovable: the magazine staff who had to work with him when he first came to *Vogue* in 1960, eager to kick the system out of the window if it came between him and the girls he had taken up photography to meet.

When the *Sunday Times Magazine* introduced the new East End photographers to its readers in the mid-sixties, Francis Wyndham wrote that Bailey was 'a great pet of the fashion editors'.

'A pet?' asked Sheila Wetton, then *Vogue's* senior fashion editor, wonderingly. 'He was a *brute*. I worked in fashion for fifty-seven years, and in all that time I only cried twice, both times because of him.'

'The place was run like a point-to-point,' says Bailey. 'Don't forget being a Cockney was no help in the beginning – only after '65. I remember one of those women patting me on the head and saying, "Oh, doesn't he speak cute." I thought, I'll show you how cute I am, dear.'

That particular editor describes the occasion when Bailey told her to cancel a model because he wanted to photograph the wife of a friend instead. The editor complained she wasn't pretty enough, but Bailey insisted. 'She really needs this job,' he said. 'She'll be able to work anywhere with *Vogue* behind her.' On the day, he took the girl into the studio and locked the door. When they eventually came out, the editor asked, 'What the f . . . have you been doing in there?'

'Got it in one,' said Bailey. 'You needn't bother to book her again.'

By the mid-sixties the model would be shut into the studio alone with Bailey and sometimes with Mick Jagger, Terence Stamp or other cronies, to cope with whatever devilry materialized. Not that the girls were complaining.

'I pioneered Badness,' says Bailey. 'I did diabolical things. Awful. Terrible. I had this compulsion to push forward all the time. The only reason I ever did fashion was because of the girls. It was the gates of heaven. But I only wanted to photograph girls I liked. I had to have some sense of being with them or it wasn't interesting.

'I was trying to create a mood and see the whole image. And I had to cope with these women with no visual sense, getting hysterical about some amusin' little seam.'

David Puttnam, who was Bailey's agent for a forgotten year in 1962 says, 'You have to remember, it was a different world. There was a big drama once because he brought a record player into the studio. But he was trying to create an atmosphere which is the norm today.'

There was a contrast between his treatment of his girlfriends in private and in the studio which never failed to surprise the assistants who saw both sides. 'He would crucify Jean all day,' remembers one.

'Then he would stop her at the door, ask if she had enough money, check her hair was dry and tell her to take a taxi.'

When he took her home to meet his mother Gladys Bailey, sharp-tongued daughter of a second-hand car salesman, she put the model firmly in his old bed and Bailey on the sofa in the front room. Bailey was, in fact, already married, to Rosemary Bramble, a pretty seventeen-year-old copy typist he had met in the Flamingo one heady night in '59.

'Glad and I didn't get on too well,' says Jean Shrimpton. 'I was too hoity-toity for her. When I came to make up the bed I could only find one sheet, so I went to tell her. And she said, "In this house you only *get* one sheet. Who do you think you are?"'

At first Bailey avoided restaurants with foreign menus and had trouble filling out the landing cards on *Vogue's* foreign trips. Once, when he couldn't spell 'eighty' on a cheque, he had to go on buying carpets until he reached a number he could spell: but by the mid-sixties he had become an avid reader – all of Dickens, all of Jane Austen, and Mastermind games with models on long journeys, to test his memory.

The notion that anybody or anything was unobtainable was received by Bailey as a direct personal challenge. It was for a ten bob bet that he proposed to Catherine Deneuve, the most unattainable woman he had yet met.

In the spring of 1965 he flew to Paris to photograph her in the nude for *Playboy*. Bailey had perfected a gambit for these occasions. 'Don't worry, love,' he reassured her, as the sitting commenced. 'I'm a homosexual.' Two hours later Deneuve lit up a cigarette and called him a liar.

Bailey says, 'Catherine Deneuve is a toughie, like me.' For the first time in his life he was a little out of his depth. This was no half-embarrassed English girl or over-impressed model, but a self-willed, self-motivated woman who already had children by Roger Vadim and Marcello Mastroianni, both of whom she had neg-lected to marry. Everything that money, education, admiration and Yves Saint Laurent could achieve had been done to perfection. Deneuve was racy, casual, witty and given to singing heartless snatches of comic song at passionate moments. She was a respected member of the cabal of Parisian film-makers and intellectuals. She had a humour and vivacity which her enigmatic, transparent film presence never suggested.

Bailey was in Paris again to photograph the collections when his old friend Brian Duffy bet him he couldn't marry Deneuve. They drove straight to a spot on the map where she was filming, stopping only for Bailey to buy a bunch of red roses.

'Catherine ran across a ploughed field to meet us,' he says. 'I said, "Will you marry me?" She turned to Duffy and said, "Is he joking?" Then she said, "Sure," and carried on filming. We were laughing all the time.'

The wedding took place at St Pancras Register Office a few weeks later. Bailey, who four months earlier had worn a blue velvet suit to photograph the Bethnal Green wedding of Reggie Kray, wore a sweater and cord pants, while Deneuve arrived smoking and wearing what any Frenchwoman would choose for an ambiguous assignation: a throwaway little black dress. Mick Jagger outshone both in denim suit and white shoes.

Back in Bailey's house in Primrose Hill with its all-black rooms and stairways, Deneuve briefly played the role of housewife, astonishing the fashion editors by inviting them upstairs for a casserole, and even modelled for her husband. She could meet him on any level, line for line, light up the lens any way he wanted, but the differences were already apparent. She says, 'I never thought of myself as Mrs Bailey.'

Bailey liked to be the teacher, not the taught. One evening when she was reading and not bothering to reply, he snatched a copy of *La Pléiade* out of her hand and tore it in two. Before long she was back in Paris.

One day Deneuve rang Bailey and told him they were divorced. She said, 'Now we can be lovers'. The liaison had begun and ended with a joke.

When David Bailey talks about marriage it's the nearest thing to Richmal Crompton's boy hero William Brown talking about school. There is the same scowl, the same aggrieved air and the same insistent logic.

'See, we've all been conditioned by society for five thousand years that if you get married you're supposed to stay married. All right. *Where's it written?* Just tell me who wrote this rule down. Who *said* it? All these moral things about not being gay and not being lesbian. It's not in the Mesopotamian Seven Social Laws of Livin', so where'd it come from?' His spiralling laugh coincides with the cackling of one of his parrots.

'When you begin I don't think you have to say to yourself. "This marriage is going to last for ever."'

When *Vogue's* editor Beatrix Miller invited Bailey into her office one day and asked him to photograph the seventeen-year-old Penelope Tree, she warned him to be on his best behaviour – 'no swearing, no pouncing'. But hanky-panky began the moment he walked into the studio.

'It was love at first sight. I've never known anything so instant.'

Penelope Tree's shy manner and fey silences obscured her background as the daughter of a billionaire banker and a formidable mother who was US Ambassador to the United Nations. The family divided their time between New York, a palatial house in Barbados, and Florence.

Back in Primrose Hill, the sixties fizzled out in a non-stop twenty-four-hour party. Penelope brought home the Black Panthers and a Tibetan holy man. She installed a UFO detector and Bailey grew his hair.

'The house was full of hippies looking at the ceiling and saying "great!"', says Bailey. 'I'd be getting in my Rolls and there would be three of them in the back smoking joints that I had paid for and calling me a capitalist pig! And I was just trying to fight my way through and take some nice pictures.'

It was 1967 and Bailey was at the height of his fame. His love affairs were headlined in the newspapers, his vivid, brusque pronouncements flashed across the nation, the length of his hair indicated how far you could go. It was also the year of *Blow Up*, the Antonioni film with a hazy plot about a photograph which enlarges to reveal a corpse. Its portrait of a photographer remarkably similar to Bailey was based on Francis Wyndham's original piece in the *Sunday Times*, and was actually a composite of the three East Enders – Duffy, Donovan and Bailey. Fact or fiction, the film popularized the view that Bailey was a partial professional who subordinated his work to his amoral lifestyle.

Box of Pinups, the following year, provoked criticism mainly because of the inclusion of the Kray brothers, finally sentenced at the Old Bailey to thirty years' imprisonment for murder. Malcolm Muggeridge dismissed the publication for making a 'religion of narcissism', Robert Pitman of the *Sunday Express* wrote of 'tawdry values' and the *Sunday Times*, which had published an extract, received a flood of angry letters.

The body of portraits Bailey had published by the end of the decade records the moment better than any words that were written. No photographer ever caught a decade more conclusively than he did then. It's all there: Lennon towering above pretty boy McCartney; P.J. Proby in the crucifixion pose; Cecil Beaton embracing Nureyev, fluttering high camp climbing on the youth bandwagon. The sixties had come to an end, but no one will ever forget the way it looked. It's all down in black and white, gathering history as it goes.

At fifty-one David Bailey FRPS, FSIAD, is the grand old man of photography. From 18 March in Bath, *Bailey Now!* marks the 150th anniversary of the camera, while *David Bailey Photographs* from 8 May at Hamiltons Galleries offers his prints at £900 each.

Past notoriety glamorizes the bulky, genial father of two at the top of his second profession. Many things have changed, not least that 90 per cent of his time is spent in making commercials. In contrast to the crucifying photographic sittings of the past, his shoots are cheery, gregarious affairs, high scores on the chuckle meter. He says if they're not fun, they're not worth doing.

Once voted the worst-dressed man in Britain, he is a mobile killing field for clothes, a sartorial tornado whose denim shirt tussles with the maroon sweater which recoils from contact with the corduroy trousers. The last rendezvous between chin and razor is a distant memory. His hair tends to part roughly in the middle, under a farmer's hat. 'I thought it would make me look like Harrison Ford, but it makes me look like Worzel Gummidge!'

The beautiful RAF stores manager, John French's assistant who was mobbed in Smithfield for the length of his hair, the diabolical hippy and the Proustian dandy have come down to this: a grizzled Annigoni figure, a happily married roué still giving off dangerous waves of sex and charm. Under the surface there lurks the same old shoal of grudges, but they are less apparent now that he has the freedom of what must be a six-figure income. not that Bailey ever sold out. The way he sees it, the media did.

'I stopped working for magazines ten years ago, when they stopped wanting great pictures. They don't want it good any more, they want it new. Today, by the time you've learned something, you're ditched.

'Andy was wrong! People won't be famous for fifteen seconds. What's happened is they're bored in 1.5 seconds!'

The phone is ringing across the studio, but he's oblivious.

'The kids making videos just shoot and chop it to bits. You're sitting in the cinema in California and when it gets to the borin' bit the audience starts yelling "Fast Forward!" You see it in art and everything, in the hysteria that goes on for the latest model.'

'Bailey!' wails his assistant up the stairs. 'The phone! It's Valentino.'

'Everyone's trying to book a girl you won't be able to *give* away next week.'

Bailey suddenly rises lightly to his feet and crosses to the phone with deft, tiny steps. One golden evening back in the sixties he taught Nureyev to dance the Twist at the Ad Lib, and he can tap you out a Fred Astaire party number, swinging a hat and cane and singing *Everything but the girl* – perhaps the least appropriate of all theme songs for someone who for thirty years has always had someone good on the team.

'Here's me saying what's wrong with last week's model? I photographed the same girls for a decade! I was kind of faithful. In my fashion!'

Bailey picks up the phone, cackling, and conducts a brusque exchange about money, which concludes with the words: 'We're not discussin' this. I'm tellin' you. It's yes or no.' Coming back, he's grinning again. 'I wouldn't have done that ten years ago.'

He sits on the sofa, drawing up one leg beside him in a curiously feminine gesture.

'It's too bad we only get one innings, because I would like to spend a whole life on photography, one on films, another on painting, another on gardening.'

These days, when he's not working, he's turning out oil paintings, talking to his children and counting the goldfinches that congregate around his Devon farm. In the evenings he dips into Emerson, Malraux and Delacroix's journals. He likes to quote from the golden oldies.

'It's like Nietzsche said. If you've only got one life, you might as well be extraordinary.'

Sensational figures from other decades remain trapped in a time warp, prey to creeping self-parody. Bailey has kept sharp, running ahead of the tide, still ready to destroy your programmed thinking. If you ask why he gave up fashion photography he will tell you it was too difficult. That he and Terence Donovan once sat down together at a restaurant and tried to count the number of things that can go wrong and ruin a fashion picture: that they stopped when they got to 450.

He's a survivor. Terence Donovan says if Bailey had made a big thing of being a personality he wouldn't have had the stamina. 'If you don't have a self-image you can't be hurt. Bailey was always in love with photography, not with being a photographer.'

But he nearly didn't make it, all the same. There was a moment in the seventies when the world slipped from his control, when the house on Primrose Hill entered a phase of Bad Craziness. One hundred parrots gave Bailey psittacosis. The stairs were slippery with dog mess. Bailey sat in front of the television throwing apple cores and old Coke cans over his shoulder on to the carpet. Michael Roberts, who was a lodger, describes the experience as like living in some sort of fairground sideshow. There were nights when Bailey and Marie Helvin would slip a blow-up dummy into Roberts's bed, then give it a slow puncture, so that it writhed horribly under the sheet and convinced the late-returning fashion editor that he had strayed into a frame from *Nightmare on Elm Street*.

Those were the days of Bailey's photographs of women tied and trussed like oven-ready chickens, with paper bags over their heads. When they fell to Roberts's poisoned pen, in print, Bailey cut him dead for two years, then ran into him in the Paris Intercontinental lobby. 'Crashed into me,' says Michael Roberts. 'Sent me flying.' Even Bailey admits it was a low period creatively, but soon he was off and running again with another decade of images, portraits of devastation and television commercials that expand in the mind long after brand names are forgotten.

A few years ago Terence Donovan drove down to the river to take a picture that had caught his eye the previous week. He cruised his Rolls past another Rolls, and spotted Bailey taking a picture from the same bank. They are not only the most enthusiastic professionals you will ever meet, but they are part of a vivid generation of photographers who have never been challenged. Bailey, Donovan, Snowdon, David Montgomery, Donald McCullin and Terry O'Neill are all at the top today as they were nearly thirty years ago.

Bailey's women all survived, too. Jean Shrimpton is running a seaside hotel with her husband, while the free-wheeling Penelope Tree uses Sydney as a base for her forays to study the hill tribes of Thailand. There was never any doubt about Deneuve. Marie Helvin is enjoying single life in Pimlico, busy with books, television and charity work. While she was talking over the Bailey years, he happened to ring about bringing over the microwave he had bought for her birthday present. 'Hi Toots!' said Marie 'I'm being interviewed and I'm telling all horrible stuff about you! Wanna come over?' Sheer numbers of wives and girlfriends may not be the measure of a man's success with women, but perhaps good relations afterwards may be.

Bailey's women all believe he's married for good this time, to

ex-model Catherine Dyer, the quiet madonna of Devon farm and
Primrose Hill, still ringing with the vibrations of past exploits.
Much to his surprise, they say, his daughter and son have become
a great diversion.

'Paloma's a little debt I had to pay to Pablo, for showing me you
can invent reality. Fenton's thank you to Roger Fenton, my
favourite English photographer.' Bailey says he won't have any
more children. If he did, they'd probably be called Ingmar,
Dostoevsky, Delacroix and Schnabel.

Today's post included eight scripts, six of them from the USA.
David Bailey flicks through them and reads one aloud over the
phone to his agent.

'I'd love Jerry Hall to do this one. Where it says, "I was shy and
bookish. I shudder to think how many nights I spent in the
university library." I mean, *perfect* for Jerry!' Bailey's laugh is the
high-pitched cackle you hear coming from the trouble-spot at the
back of the school lavatories. 'Okay Pete, ring me!'

His commercials are often unforgettable. There's the one in
which the angry blonde throws away jewels, coat, handbag – but
keeps the car keys. There's the devastating anti-fur film of a blood-
spattered fashion show, and the haunted playground, a warning
against the dangers of nuclear waste. There are the quirky Reebok
scenarios in the USA: the bride in sneakers coming out of the
subway entrance, the man with three legs. Catherine Deneuve,
the only one of his wives who knows the business, says he's doing
too many. 'He's getting too comfortable. He needs more of a
challenge.' Perhaps they will prove to be a stepping stone to
directing movies. It nearly happened last year. The money was
lined up, Faye Dunaway was ready to go, and at the last moment
the film was hit by the writers' strike. Is he serious about leaving
the country?

'I've won so many awards the Chiat Day agency have offered to
buy me a house if I'll go and live in L.A.'

Penelope Tree says he will never leave "because he adores
England. He has two tapes he plays over and over again. One is
John Betjeman's poems on England, the other is the speeches of
Winston Churchill. He knows them by heart.'

But Bailey is off on a familiar grievance about the way the
British hate success. 'Look, you've only got to look at the honours
list. Hockney, zilch. And a f . . . cking dart player . . . . You can
just see the people who make up the list. Let's be nice to the
workers. I guarantee they'll give the OBE to Eddie the Eagle next.
For bein' such a perfect Englishman. For failing.'

Yet Bailey now is exactly where Cecil Beaton was when the boy from East Ham first brought in his portfolio to *Vogue*. Sir Roy Strong says by 2060 he will be an old master.

'Just because you're born in a stable you don't have to grow up to be a horse,' says Bailey, who never let a good line go by, and never suffered from undue modesty.

January, 1989: David Bailey is filming a twenty second TCP commercial on Stage G at Shepperton Studios. A bulky figure with a greying beard, he moves among the crowd in a bashed up leather jacket and check tweed cap with badge.

His producer, Mary, is illish in a muffler.

'All right, wimp?' asks Bailey, kindly. 'If you get anywhere near me it's down the toilet, turd.'

She turns feverish eyes on him. 'You're such a smoothie, Bailey.'

The scenario: Night, a bedroom window banging in a storm. Phone rings, Kennedy lookalike starts awake. Subliminal flash of crying baby. He picks up the phone.

Bailey is watching the monitor. 'Stuff your hair behind your ears, Mark . . . Dave . . . Nige . . . will you?'

He climbs on to the bedroom set. 'You wake up like . . . "Where did I leave my body last night?" You've felt like that, haven't you? D'you wear a condom?'

Andy takes it on the nose. He blinks, but comes back gamely.

'Yes – but only when there's a girl there!'

'Remember to take it off when you go for a pee,' Bailey advises him. 'Okay, try the lightning!' Andy, who's from Colorado, confides that Bailey is quite a colourful guy.

The addition of three babies is occupying Bailey's attention, he tells his PA, 'The one that cries gets the job.' Meanwhile, make-up artist and hairdresser stand upstage in bikers' jackets and microskirts discussing the possibility of having a baby.

'My sister says it's like pulling your top lip right back over the top of your head,' says Cheryl. Caron sticks her tongue out, crosses her eyes and makes retching noises.

'All right, girls?' says Bailey, passing.

They answer in unison, hands on hips, with a dying fall in the intonation: 'Yeah.'

Bailey loves it. He swings production assistant Annie into line and makes them do it again. Now, whenever he says, 'All right, girls?' they chorus 'Yeah' with that same fall in the voice. He turns to the crew. 'All right boys?' 'Nah,' they snarl.

Bailey is still laughing when he gets back to the inspection line, where three rosy babies snuggle in loving arms.

'I told them to cry,' he says. 'I'm not getting through to them.'

He asks the prettiest woman in the line-up, 'Does he like you?' She gives a baffled smile, 'I'm his mother.'

'Okay,' says Bailey. 'Go away!'

Nine members of the crew stand in a ring around the bed, smiling down at the baby. The baby smiles back. Bailey is disgusted.

'What's happened to the wild bunch? Suddenly it's the soft bunch. Can't you take something away from him?'

Overwhelmed with attention, the baby's eyes finally fill with tears, his lip trembles and he breaks into a small whimper. Bailey bends over the bed and gives a whoop of laughter. 'Make-up!' he shouts. 'Snot!'

Fifteen minutes later, he shakes the tiny damp paw. 'Thank you, young man.'

He summons Andy. 'Hey! Robert Redford! We've got to try that last shot once more. Remember to look first, then turn the head.' He raises his eyes to heaven. 'It's okay, I'm gettin' used to it. I've got the patience of a saint.'

Sunday Times Magazine, March 1989

Ossie Clark and the Haunted Workroom

'*I* CAN'T bear to go into Ossie's room,' says Ossie Clark's ex-wife, Celia Birtwell. 'I can't stand the atmosphere. It's throbbing with tension, the fishtank water bubbling, the poltergeist crashing around in the dirty kitchen.'

There is a ghost among the dressmaking paraphernalia. Its disturbance is just another element in the turmoil, triggering an extra eddy of movement among the piled tables, the hanging half-finished dresses, the pinned-up sketches.

His friends would know it could only happen to him, as if he were under compulsion to invoke this further level of drama into his already traumatic life. The story of Ossie Clark, deprived in the fifties, rocketed to fashion stardom in the sixties, over-indulged in the seventies and broken like a butterfly in the eighties, is the cautionary tale of extreme creativity allied to zilch business sense.

Bankrupt, busted and precariously housed as he is, his circle decimated by excess and AIDS, he is still the one and only Ossie Clark, stylist, nonpareil, the master dressmaker. Bianca Jagger, Marie Helvin, Jerry Hall, Shakira Caine know it: that is why they climb the narrow stairs into a room so confused it is hard to see, as you fight your way through Indian curtains, where his voice is coming from. 'Ossie Clark is the best we have,' says Bruce Oldfield, not usually the most generous of fashion critics. 'He ought to be where I am.'

Hollow-cheeked, with remnants of mascara clinging to his eyelashes, eyes shining under the brim of a battered brown trilby, Ossie tucks his long grizzled hair behind one ear with a thin hand. Since he was declared bankrupt on 1 May, 1983 there have been times when he has gone as long as five days without eating.

'I'm serving these seven years like a prison sentence. The day it's over I'm flying out of this country for ever. They take away your house, your means to work. They take the Rolex off your wrist.'

Twenty years ago Ossie was precisely where it was at, wherever that might be – in Santa Monica with David Hockney; in New York with Andy Warhol, Jimi Hendrix and Roy Lichtenstein; at Reddish House witn Cecil Beaton; in Odin's with Patrick Procktor and Ron Kitaj; in Villefranche with Mick and Bianca. Fashion editors let blood to get tickets for his shows on a houseboat, in the Aretusa or at the Royal Court in London. Those were events you could not miss because they were carnivals, his clothes were sex incarnate, *everyone* was there, the models stoned out of their minds, Amanda Lear and Patti Boyd modelling, Gala nearly drifting off the edge of the catwalk . . . .

'I live by barter now.' He draws up one foot in a yellow sock and tasselled sandal on to the littered bed where he sits. 'I pay my lawyer by making a dress for his wife. I pay my psychiatrist the same way. I make Wayne Sleep a hat, he pays to get my sewing machine mended. I don't even mind any more. I detest money.'

Others do not. To them, he is the goose that laid the golden egg and conceivably might again. Latest in a series of attempts to harness his runaway brilliance to commercial ends is the contract with the new Grosvenor Street boutique Evocative, financed by the Zarach family. They fund him dress by dress to make to measure for their well-heeled international clients who will pay up to £3000 for an Ossie Clark ball gown, each with its secret hallmark of a hidden pocket for scent bottle and key.

Perversely neglecting the all-important contract, he fitfully returns to far more complicated fragments of work that belong in the glass case of a costume museum.

With great generosity and love of the stylishness that can say, 'Here, darling, it's yours!' he has left himself after two and a half decades of work with nothing to show but devoted customers – not a snakeskin suit, not a chiffon dress, hardly even a photograph.

'I'm a master cutter. It's all in my brain and my fingers, and there's no one in the world to touch me. I can do everything myself. I can make a pair of gloves on a clamp between my legs, the proper way, holding a needle in each hand. I can make a bra. I can make a pair of shoes.'

Ossie Clark came to London in 1961 on a wave of talented northerners spearheaded by the likes of David Hockney. They had all the right credentials. They were clever, working-class, subversive, dedicated to their work, brilliantly entertaining. At the Royal College of Art his skills blossomed under the tutelage of Professor

Janey Ironside, head of the fashion school, and Bernard Neville, distinguished textile designer. Already he was technically the best of his year. 'There were students from Harrow and all over the place and they didn't know nothing,' he marvels. 'They didn't know how to thread a needle, hardly.'

His world expanded again in the summer of '64, when he took off to join Hockney in the USA. The first person he met in a New York gay bar was Brian Epstein, who invited him to the Plaza the following day to collect a couple of tickets for the Beatles' ultimate performance of their tour, at the Hollywood Bowl. Emerging from the plush hotel the next morning with Epstein, Ossie – twenty-one, with a funny British accent and long hair – was mobbed in the street. 'That started it. Everywhere I went that summer, they all thought I was George Harrison. In Disneyland, I had to run for my life.'

In New Mexico he taught himself how to drive. Hockney and he took the wheel in turn to burn along Route 66 through Reno and the salt flats to L.A. 'Practise braking, Ossie,' pleaded Hockney. 'Practise braking, for God's sake.'

How could America have failed to go to the head of the boy from Oswaldtwistle? At the Tumble Inn Motel, Santa Monica, their best friends all of a sudden were Bette Davis and Dennis Hopper. At night they dined with Vincent Price in his totem-pole garden lit like a Hammer horror movie. Their only problem was deciding which three of twenty parties they would attend that night, and what entrance to make.

Ossie was determined that his finals show was going to leave an indelible memory. He came back to college with a roll of black and white striped silk twill from the painter Robert Indiana. Before the phrase 'op art' had been coined, he dressed his models in dazzling mini-length quilted stripes, one in a full-length coat with electric light bulbs switched on round the collar. At the last moment, Janey Ironside had assigned to him the final slot, the place of honour. He was the only student of his year to be awarded a first-class degree.

He was invited to throw in his lot with Quorum, a shop in Chelsea's Radnor Walk run by a cool brunette called Alice Pollock, once Orson Welles's secretary, who had begun buying his designs at £10 a batch when he was still a student. 'I told her there were two conditions. An overlocker machine, and a show.'

The first Ossie Clark collection sold to Henri Bendell of New York – the first time British design had been exported rather than British wool and waterproofing. Marit Allen, then *Vogue*'s far-seeing Young Idea editor, immediately recognized in Ossie Clark a designer who was creating prototypes with each collection. She set up a *Vogue* sitting with Jean Shrimpton and Norman Parkinson, who photographed Ossie's leather motorbike jacket, gaucho pants and fluid maxi coat.

'It let me in for a series of awful encounters with the editor,' she remembers. 'She had to justify everything to Condé Nast in New York, and felt the clothes were outside high fashion. It would be the first time *Vogue* had put its weight behind radical subculture.'

Vogue published the pictures. Soon after, Yves Saint Laurent was spotted in the King's Road and followed through with his own collection of leather bomber jackets and culottes. For the first time, fashion had worked from the street up.

Quorum was beginning to be a place to be seen. Twiggy, a hairdresser from the sticks, would save her money and come in on Saturday to buy a satin blouse. Cathy McGowan rubbed shoulders with Candida Lycett-Green. Brian Jones, who lived upstairs, bought up all the women's blouses. The Quorum van driver, Dave Gilmore, later of Pink Floyd, had one of Ossie's jackets, and Peter Hinwood, Rocky of the *Rocky Horror Picture Show*, demanded another.

'I had an immediate rapport with Marianne Faithfull. She would put something on and say "That's divine". No quibbling about the bill, but a bit of a slut. She lost a lot of them. One day she said, "I've got someone very special here for you to meet." And Mick Jagger stuck his head round the curtain and waggled his tongue at me. Then he asked me to make him a leather jacket, which he wore all the time. And then there was Bianca. I love women who make demands! We used to be absolutely bosom. The times I've slept on a sofa in her bedroom!'

In the mutually massaging worlds of rock and fashion it was hard to distinguish between friendship and business. Quorum were giving away too many clothes, allowing too many to be stolen, but life was too exciting to care.

When the fit comes on him these days to revisit sixties' haunts such as San Lorenzo, forever peopled with the ghosts of legendary parties such as George Best's twenty-third birthday and Cathy McGowan's wedding reception, Ossie rattles across the park in a yellow Beetle driven by his Ugandan model friend, Aggie Klossowski.

'Once I had a Bentley Continental – ooh, what a fabulous car that Flying Spur was – and we all went to stay in Carennac. It was the last day of a French holiday, and there were 10 miles of traffic jam. I just *stepped* on the accelerator, my dear, and we *flew* past them at ninety miles an hour and *crashed* through the barrier to freedom!'

In San Lorenzo his head goes back, he flourishes his cigarette holder and blows kisses around the room. Models on all sides run to embrace him. At his favourite table, with a tremendous air, he orders a bottle of white wine that practically has to be prised from a bank vault, and settles Oscar Talullah, his King Charles spaniel, on a chair.

'Anyway, after a bit I put Celia on a plane back to Paris for a check-up because she was expecting Albert. When I got back the villa was flooded with water and completely deserted except for little Jane Kasmin, crouched in a corner like a drowned mouse. Then David Hockney came in in tears. . . . He'd driven all the way to Spain and back after his boyfriend Peter, who had run away with Eric. The next thing, we all fetched up in Cadaques, with Mark Lancaster in Duchamp's old house, and Richard Hamilton. . . . Jonathan Guinness in his medieval monastery shrouded in mist up on the mountain, the three-year-old Olivia Channon playing in the pool.'

As Ossie gestures, his starched napkin keeps falling over the dog's anxious head, obliterating his sorrowing upturned gaze.

'Then we went to Villefranche to join Mick. We got there in the middle of the night, and Bianca opened the door in a white négligée with two Persian cats. And Mick came to the door and said "What do you want?" And I said, "Two singles and a double bed."

'The next day this stylish Turk, Ahmet Ertegun, turned up and took us all out to the most expensive restaurant in the South of France. We ate on a balcony overlooking the Bay of Monte Carlo. Everyone got very over-excited. They were just seeing how far they could go. They ordered every known brand of liqueur and when it arrived Mick just put his finger on the edge of the tray and the whole lot went crash! into the garden below. Then up came another tray of drinks – crash! Then dinner arrived – crash! crash! crash! When the bill came it was more than £2000. Ertegun paid up quietly like a gentleman.'

Tickled up by these Tobasco memories, Ossie flies out suddenly at a waiter. 'I said a *green* salad. Take it away, take it away! The boy's a twit,' he says loudly, his eyes sparkling with malice.

Raymond Clark grew up as a Liverpool evacuee in Oswald-twistle, on the border between Lancashire and Yorkshire. The family moved from the moors to a concrete council house in Warrington when he was seven.

'My father was chief boots on a luxury liner. He had a fine hand, he wrote the ship's log. My mother played the mandolin. I had three sisters and two brothers – but Sammy died. Gladys does beautiful needlework. Beryl and John both run pubs. Gay is a cleaner and a jazz singer at L'Escargot.'

The story of his early life is poignant. At school his only ally was the art teacher – soon to commit suicide – who brought him American *Vogue* and French *Elle*, periodicals which were to fall apart under the boy's eager fingering.

'I was an incredibly difficult child, derided and jeered at by everyone except my mother, because I liked cats and flowers, walked a certain way, enjoyed being alone.'

When Raymond failed his eleven-plus he was sent to a secondary technical school: 'Which was a polite way of saying I would become a builder or an engineer, which was a polite way of saying a bricklayer or an engine turner.'

The boy took to geometry and construction like a duck to water, and that led to Manchester Art School and fashion design. Under the guidance of Miss Rider and Miss Tyrer, he shone. Art school was an enchantment he could hardly believe. He stayed to work until 8.30 each night, postponing his return to the one noisy, crowded sitting room in Warrington.

'In three years I'd got it. I could dream a dress and make it real.'

His skill was to bring him many good things over the next twenty years, but never wealth. The golden era lasted from '65 to '74. In '81 his business folded, owing £200,000. With his wife he had bought what was going to be their family house in Cornwall Gardens in South Kensington. In the event, beleaguered on all fronts, he retreated alone and gave up work entirely. He had been nine stone all his life but now, depending on how he mistreated his body, his weight vacillated wildly between eight stone and an unbelievable twelve stone. At the root of his unhappiness was the end of his relationship with Celia.

The story of Celia and Ossie began at the Cona Coffee Bar in Manchester, where she had been attending Salford Art School since the age of thirteen. They were introduced by Mo McDermott, later to be a key figure in David Hockney's life.

'Celia was quite the most enchanting creature,' Ossie says. 'Her mother made her clothes, all striped mini dresses with piecrust frills. We called her Beakie Birtwell and she was already a marvellous fabric designer.'

When they met up later in London she was dressing in jeans and frilly Victorian blouses, sharing a flat with the painter Pauline Boty and working as a waitress in Hades. Her first words to Ossie were: 'D'you like me fuckin' frills?'

'It was the weirdest relationship,' Celia says. 'He flounced about, you know. I had to move out of my flat all of a sudden one day and I went to stay with him. That's how it began. Beyond the sexuality, we were soulmates.'

Enormously talented, she was never a sixties drifter or social star. She moved into her own flat as soon as she could, and thought that would be the end of the affair. Hockney's borrowed flat was being turned into what Celia calls 'the usual Ossie whirlwind'. When Hockney reclaimed his studio, Ossie went straight to Celia.

The odd relationship lasted for seven years before their marriage, and five after. 'I never knew how lucky I was,' Ossie says now.

The crunch came one day – something to do with the domestic routine – and Ossie flung out, never imagining he couldn't go back but, wearily, Celia had shut a final door on their relationship.

'I've never talked about it before,' she says. 'I always say "I have an enormous admiration for his talent", and leave it at that. I believed in the art, because I'm a sucker for clever people, and he is a genius. We worked wonderfully in unison, his dresses, my fabrics. But after the children he became ruthless and impossible.'

Celia still cannot help herself concocting solutions to Ossie's problems. He should stop exciting himself, go to the country, draw for a year – he should 'disappear where we don't have to suffer for him any more. He has always been trouble, but it's all bound up together: genius and trouble.'

It was dressmaking, once again, that brought him into temporary harbour with the ex-fashion editor of the *Times*, Prudence Glyn, otherwise Lady Windlesham. Two refugees, both survivors from better days, they met again one day in the Portobello Road when Ossie was about to become homeless. A long-term admirer of his work, she took him in as a lodger, and as her resistance to the pressures of her own life grew weaker he took increasing care of her. On good days, they pored over his library of antique dressmaking books. On bad days, he left trays and stolen roses outside her bedroom door, and fed the cats. She died on 24 September, 1986.

Bound to the commitment they both felt to the art of couture dressmaking, her last words to him, which he cannot recall without breaking down, were to 'Keep up the standard'. It is, he says, her spirit in the guise of taskmaster that recalls him to his promise by provoking the occasional spark of violence in the house – a dressmaker dummy whacked across the floor, a book flying from the table.

If so it is one of the many efforts, both natural and supernatural, to make Ossie Clark pull himself together and use his God-given talents. Today, a picture flies off the wall as the afternoon sun breaks over Notting Hill rooftops, overheating a room already feverish with friends, models, assistants and animals. The Ossie Clark whirlwind is in full swing as David Montgomery, the photographer, tries to concentrate his mind on the picture and Ossie spits out that it's boring, boring, boring.

'Is this place haunted?' asks Montgomery. 'What's the matter with me? It's boiling hot in here, but I keep shivering.'

Sunday Times Magazine, July 1987

Valentino: Palazzo Power

*I*N the studio of his Renaissance palazzo near the Spanish Steps where Audrey Hepburn sat in *Roman Holiday*, Valentino is choosing fabrics for spring ready-to-wear 1989. A crowd of assistants focus on the fine brown fingers through which casefuls of textile samples pass in a matter of seconds, as though on a conveyor belt.

Romy, Valentino's exquisite junior, hardly dares breathe. Signor Bellotti, textile manufacturer from Como, fixes his sad brown eyes on the couturier's face, which wears the expression of a headmistress inspecting poor work – pursed lips, a fine line between the brows. Without the slightest hesitation the fabrics glide through into two piles. One, reject. Two, take further.

The tense silence is broken by a muffled thumping and squeaking from a raffia basket under the table. Oliver, the pug puppy whose name christens the newest line of boutiques, is gambolling in his dreams. A fond smile crosses Valentino's face, and everyone relaxes.

'You know, I am unable to think of spring without thinking of polka dots,' he says. The voice is all intimate whispers and growls, like Melina Mercouri's. 'Now, this glazed chintz. I like the weight, but I prefer always off-white to white. The print is to be enlarged, like this. Here I want to take the flowers away so we just have background. And can you make for me some Indian checks? I have marked the pages for you in this book.'

Signor Bellotti seizes the book, and his two assistants make frantic notes. Valentino buys more than 400,000 metres of fabric a year, not counting couture. If he wants the moon and stars, Signor Bellotti will get them for him, at a discount.

The Roman sunshine warms the Piranesi roofscape tangled with wisteria, while bells from a distant campanile ring out the lunch hour. Oliver, having fought himself awake, is surreptitiously peeing on a pile of flowered silks. The putti laugh down from the painted ceiling, frolicking with flowers and a twist of yellow silk. Down in the courtyard 150 seamstresses clatter down the back staircase chattering like schoolgirls as they hurry to change out of their white cotton overalls and indoor shoes.

At fifty-six, Valentino retains the glittering good looks so lavishly distributed by God in Italy, the country of male glamour and the turned-back cuff. Half a century of the fastidious cultivation of beauty has cast over the sleek profile and heavy-lidded eyes the rapt calculating expression seen on the faces of lifelong disciplinarians. He reminds you of Ninette de Valois or Balanchine. When he throws his coat over his shoulders, you expect him to rap the floor with a cane and call, 'Positions, please!'

Through a door from the studio lies another world. Putting on a pair of finely honed tortoiseshell spectacles, he whispers, 'This is where I make my private phone calls. Cosy, like home.' He sits beneath his magnificent Bronzino, with a forest of mauve orchids in a seventeenth-century jardinière on one hand, on the other an eighteenth-century marble lion at rest between Empire vases of gold and painted porcelain.

The wallpaper, hand-painted by the boys of San Patrignano to complement the dress of Bronzino's Eleanor of Toledo, casts a green gloom. It is hard to move without knocking a museum piece off its pedestal.

The king of the *alta moda* does not go in for minimalism. The very word causes shock waves: 'You ask that after a hard day's work I should not enjoy the same as my employees? A little dinner by the television, a comfortable chair, a few flowers? You ask I should be cold? Beg for a blanket?'

A row of silver frames beyond the desk wink in the gloaming, presenting a few sympathetic faces from the élite coterie of the Valentini: Princess Margaret, Nancy Reagan, Sally Aga Khan, Queen Noor of Jordan, Brooke Shields, Jackie Onassis.

Yet at the end of the day it is only Valentino and his three pugs who take the navy chauffeur-driven Bentley – upholstered in greige toile for the summer, loden for the winter – home to his classical villa beyond the catacombs of San Callisto where the butler waits on the steps and the gym instructor waits by the exercise machines. After forty minutes puffing in a grey track-suit, Valentino will shower and settle down by himself to a television dinner. True, the food will be his favourite *spaghetti al pomodoro* with *insalata verde* followed by fresh apple pie, all eaten from antique Russian china, and the film may be seen in his private screening room or on a cassette recently flown in from

New York. Tonight, watching an old movie which he slept through the first time, he stays awake to see Rupert Everett, to the finale, in *Dance with a Stranger*. Roused by his butler, he changes into his perfectly pressed white cotton Fruit of the Loom T-shirt and slips beneath the quilted grey cashmere blanket and into linen sheets, ironed on the bed each day, to sleep among his entourage of beautiful objects until 8.30 the next morning.

Born old, the ugly shocked him from the age of four. The second child of Signor Garavani, well-heeled owner of electrical supply stores, he ruled his nursery province with a will of iron.

'I asked to my mother. I obtained.'

At six, with a high fever, he asked his mother to wrap him in a blanket and carry him across town to see his cousin dressed for a ball in pink tulle. He recalls with Proustian clarity cousin Rina's mauve dress and hat with a stiff navy bow. The same year he cried until he made himself sick when his mother tried to force him to add a bow tie to his navy suit with the gold buttons.

Then, he could not sleep unless his dressing gown was folded meticulously on his bedside chair. Today he finds it hard to forgive a visitor who has broken a porcelain plate or knocked a glass of wine over a silk rug. He finds it still harder to be a guest when he needs to be at home to check if the cloisonné birds have been dusted properly, if the white linen runner has been laid down the stairs early enough, if the wicker furniture in Capri has been tucked into its fresh cottons. At work, if an apprentice seamstress so much as touches a toile with a pin, he can tell whether he wants to employ her or not.

The obsessiveness found its perfect expression in couture, perhaps the only profession in which he could have been happy.

In the eighteenth-century ballroom that is his office Giancarlo Giammetti paces the ivory-and-lavender Aubusson impatiently, while a butler hovers with a glass of mineral water on a tray. Valentino's partner, chairman and president, Giammetti gave up his architectural career twenty-eight years ago to play Pierre Bergé to the twenty-two-year-old designer. Hard-headed, a master strategist of frocks, he supervises the development of the Valentino industry that turns out two million dresses annually, employs six thousand people, and produces ninety collections a year. It was Giammetti who steered Valentino's career this far via the United States breakthrough, the deal with the GFT, the premier Italian manufacturers, the launching of the letter V as a worldwide symbol of luxury and not-so-discreet glamour. It was also Giammetti who decided Valentino must have a resplendent study on the first floor of the palazzo and is masterminding the total restoration of the building.

'I put a frame around Valentino. That is my work. I deliberately wanted his room to be different from mine. One has to know one has arrived in Valentino's study.'

Tomaso Ziffer and Massimo Zompa were the architects of the two key rooms, but many of the treasures came out of the houses of Valentino and Giammetti: an eclectic mixture of pieces from China, Japan, Africa, France and India.

'The function? To impress! No, I am joking.' He laughs, but his eyes are suspicious. 'All this, it is not just homage to Valentino. It's to sell clothes.'

Giammetti is in the middle of furnishing his own Tuscan villa in a landscaped park. Both men have come a long way from the furnished rooms of their student days. Valentino's first room 'with ambience' was the *chambre de bonne* he took in the Rue de Rennes while serving his apprenticeship to the Paris couturier Jean Dessès. With pocket money from his parents he had it papered in toile and put in a sofa and a Boulle table from the flea market.

At about that time at the button makers and photographic sessions he met two other young assistants from Dior and Balmain. They fell into the habit of going for a drink to the Café de Rond-Point on the Champs-Élysées, where the three apprentices would swap notes and speculate on one another's futures.

Would the moodiness of Yves stand in his way, make him unstable?

Would Karl's irony and sense of parody complicate his progress?

For Valentino there was never a doubt, for there was nothing to hold him back. The perfectionist who once said, 'I would rather not eat than eat from an ugly plate,' was already fully formed.

American *House and Garden*, July 1988

Vivienne Westwood: The Schlock of the New

GENTLE, fervent, scruffy, Vivienne Westwood is the image of an English missionary with a devil-sent vocation – to dress the civilized world in primitive warpaint.

Turning ideas on their heads is her stock in trade. Her aim is 'to make the poor look rich and the rich look poor'. She is, she says, an anarchist and an artist. 'It is an artist's job to wreak violence on a culture to give it new life. In taking from other civilizations I'm just doing what Picasso did when he used Negro sculpture imagery in his painting *Demoiselles d'Avignon*. He decided that the tradition of the human figure had finally lost its power and that he had to look to emblems of savagery to give it a future.'

If Westwood thinks and talks more like a painter than a fashion designer and sees herself as doing to fashion what artists did to art in the early part of this century, the justification must be the clothes themselves. Are they revolutionary? Do they dress the body in a way different from what we traditionally expect? Do they provoke shock and scorn, followed by acceptance and respect translated into hard cash? Will they enter the vocabulary of fashion and change it forever?

It is appropriate to look at her contribution this year, her twelfth in the business and her fourth in the international arena, as she has just taken a major step in the commercial game by moving her production to Italy. After a decade of *épater la bourgeoisie* in the King's Road, she opened the 1980s with the Pirates collection (as worn by Adam and the Ants) which had a tidal effect on the fashion world and sold right across the age barriers. She went from dressing a street to dressing the world in a single move. She announced: 'I wish to declare myself an international and not a provincial designer', gave up showing in London and took her next collection to Paris. 'You had to miss Givenchy to see Westwood,' a fashion editor told me. 'It was worth it.' With now two shops in

London and showrooms in Paris, Milan and Rome, she has been showing in Paris for three seasons, and her last collection, Witches, provoked £250,000 worth of orders from Italy alone.

'We've always been self-financed,' said Vivienne of her partnership with Malcolm McLaren. 'Suddenly our resources were not sufficient to fulfil the kind of orders I was getting. This country takes no account of talent – the banks won't give you the kind of financial backing you need to make your business international. Italy's different. Here all my bank manager wanted to know was whether I had a house I could mortgage. There they back talent with money and give you everything you need to make a million garments instead of two hundred.' She will also be doing consultancies and franchises, but has no fear that that might thin down her own collection. 'I'm overprogrammed with ideas anyway.'

While the Westwood/McLaren shop at 430 King's Road turned from Let It Rock to Too Fast to Live, Too Young to Die, to Sex and Seditionaries and currently to World's End, Westwood turned out a stream of clothes and looks unlike anything the fashion world had seen. She picked through time and space and the 'untouchable' areas of big city life to give us rubberwear, bondage trousers, 'muscle' T-shirts from gay gyms, the ripped T-shirt (do it yourself), the triple-tongued sneaker ('something steady to rock on'), the Chico hat, the Smurf hat, pirate swagger, graffiti prints in baked ink, duster shoes, bras worn over dresses, rags in braided hair, shorts with big hanging pockets . . . a cornucopia of images both palatable and unspeakable (the Cambridge rapist T-shirt, the court case gay cowboys print) all subversive, classless and undermining the status system of fashion which conventionally 'places' the wearer in a social hierarchy.

Her shop was where the Saturday parade down the King's Road stopped and she worked so close to the ground it was impossible to say which was the chicken, which the egg – did the styles spring from the street or the shop? Did it matter? Her clothes became a badge for the boy who left school early to live in a London squat and for the heiress determined to stand out. In the trade there was shock, there was horror, and there was an overwhelming interest. Joseph Ettedgui of the prospering Joseph shops (who stocked the Pirates collection) found himself constantly playing host to designers and buyers from America, 'and all they ever wanted to do was to be taken straight to Vivienne's shop to see what was cooking'.

Vivienne Westwood owes an enormous debt to Malcolm

McLaren for getting the world to listen. If she is the artist, he is the critic and salesman, manager, promoter and exploiter of her talent. 'He taught me everything. When I met him I had hardly read a book and never seen a play.' She is the daughter of a cotton mill worker from Tintwistle, Manchester, he the son of a cat burglar from the East End: Clean Slate meets Streetsmart. McLaren, the father of one of Westwood's two sons, soon had her making him Teddy boy jackets. 'Taking a drape suit or a Ted jacket apart stitch by stitch, studying the linings and interlinings, and making an exact copy was my only formal training. It's the best. Leonardo da Vinci said: "He who can spy can create".'

Manager and inventor of the Sex Pistols, Adam and the Ants, Bow Wow Wow and Boy George of Culture Club, McLaren released his own LP, Duck Rock, three months ago. 'For the young music *is* the medium,' he told me. 'The clothes needed the groups. Now she doesn't necessarily need the music, if her story's powerful enough. When I went into the music business no one wanted to know about the fashion connection. Now it's the biggest plus you can have. When a pop group signs up with a recording company today there'll be a clause written into the contract that the group will have £1000 a week to spend on clothes. The Sex Pistols got that ball rolling. As long as the group has the right look today, the music doesn't matter too much.'

Although they live apart, their partnership is close. 'I always thought all the ideas came from him,' says Westwood today, 'but I soon realized that getting the job done *was* the job. That's not to say he's not essential to me. He edits my work, gets all my ideas down on a board, sorts out the story, gives me an avenue of approach. He unscrambles my programming.'

When she talks about her clothes, Vivienne Westwood uses words like 'grand', 'strong' and 'free' instead of 'beautiful'. She cuts in the flat rather than the round, like someone doing origami, but in this she is not unique: it's a technique used by Rei Kawakubo of Comme des Garçons, La Maison Bleu and Kenzo.

For the last two months up to a collection, Westwood moves out of her sparsely furnished flat in Clapham and into the workroom behind Regent Street. She starts each garment from scratch, pulling cloth around her body and chopping at it from there. She uses an experienced pattern cutter, Mark Tabbard, to show her what is generally done before she works out her own approach.

'What I'm not trying to do with my clothes is to make a kind of shell that stays in place half an inch away from the body. My clothes are dynamic. They pull and they push and they slightly fall off. There's more to clothes than just comfort. Even if they're not quite comfortable and slip and have to be readjusted now and again I don't mind, because that's some sort of display and gesture that belongs with the clothes.'

A Westwood design fits in an unexpected way. When you wear her clothes you are reminded of your body all the time. It's a difficult fit for factories to get used to, which may explain why her clothes, though very well cut, are not always put together properly. Once the clothes are being produced in Italy, she says, her ambition is to hear customers say how well they are made.

McLaren sees the move to Italy as inevitable. 'This island is a third world banana republic with no bananas. It is hard to do well here,' he says, 'because we are a country of eccentric craftsmen and cottage industries. The British consider themselves above fashion. If you want to design interesting clothes you must make them in a bedsit and sell them from a market stall or go and work in a back-room at Dorothee Bis. Neither are Westwood clothes likely to sell in enormous quantities in the United States because there the rich like to look rich.

'In both countries the people who buy our clothes are the dispossessed, the disillusioned, the graphic artists and the liberated mothers.' The biggest orders come from Japan and Italy, which he finds appropriate. 'Japan was for so long an isolated island that it has never got over its hunger for the status of ideas. Italy is the country of Fellini and the grand gesture. They like to mess around.'

At the end of the year Vivienne Westwood will receive one of the fashion industry's highest accolades when, like Jean Muir and Zandra Rhodes before her, she will represent Britain in the *Women's Wear Daily* Biannual Best of Five event in Tokyo, alongside such names as Calvin Klein of the USA, Claude Montana of France and Gianfranco Ferre of Italy.

It seems that she has made a niche in the fashion establishment, and perhaps changed its point of view a little. Will she be able to keep one foot in the street and one in high fashion? If she is still getting her clothes talked about in five years' time, she'll have achieved something unique. As anthropologist Ted Polhemus, co-author of *Fashion and Anti-Fashion*, put it: 'High fashion has undoubtedly gained by admitting Vivienne to their fold. Has street style lost its greatest champion?'

Times, August 1983

Postscript

Still the world's most subversive and maverick designer, Vivienne Westwood took her clothes to the Paris catwalks in 1985, and in 1989 was voted by *Women's Wear Daily* 'one of the six most influential designers in the world'.

She says, 'I'm the only fashion designer who justifies what they do in broad cultural terms.' Her clothes are included in the permanent collection of the Victoria and Albert Museum. She remains the only really creative dress designer who is not a multimillionaire.

The Roster of Oscar

HERE's Oscar de la Renta in his usual red banquette at La Grenouille. The severity of his pinstripe suit just cannot keep that Latin flamboyance buttoned down. He has vivid, patrician looks and a taut figure, as straight-backed as a flamenco dancer's. His suntan is intensified by a blue tie and bluer shirt. Seemingly from the top of his head, as if he were Carmen Miranda, rises a ten-foot cornucopia of the restaurant's famous flowers – cherry blossoms, pink and yellow multiflora lilies and cabbage-size peonies. He flashes a glittering smile at Spiros Niarchos across the room and gets down to the serious business of lunch.

'You see that sexy blonde lady over there? She's married to a rich Brazilian and she has the most beautiful jewels. I was near her one evening at dinner when a friend brought her husband across to introduce him. The blonde was wearing the lowest neckline I ever saw, with one enormous emerald. "Look!" said my friend to her husband. "Isn't that the most incredible thing you've ever seen?" He had a good look and said, "It's the pearls that I adore."'

A young woman makes a big entrance into the restaurant, pulling off a straw hat with a blue bow, and is much appreciated by Oscar de la Renta.

'She's right, in this sun! You know what Zsa Zsa Gabor told me? She said "I always carry a hat to wear in the elevator." I said, "Why in the elevator?" And she said, "Are you kidding? Have you seen the *lights* in those elevators?"'

Easy to see why Oscar de la Renta, an unbelievable fifty-seven, is the darling of the matriarchs at the quick of New York high society. His company is light as champagne, his conversation laced like a leisurely woman's with gossip, *histoires* and discussion of clothes. A few hours of the treatment and 1989 gives way to another world, European in flavour, gently revolving around the creed of majestic houses, immaculate appearance and the pleasurable consumption of unoccupied time. It is partly his ability to conjure up this frame of mind that inspires his many, many friends to call him 'the most attractive and generous grand seigneur in New York'.

He is, of course, a shrewd, industrious fashion designer at the peak of his trade who sells over $500 million worth of products all over the world and whose promotional tours set a breakneck pace, covering a city a day. He has forty-five licencees and three perfumes. There are 110 shows of the Oscar de la Renta line (average price $2,000) and thirty of Miss O (average price $400) a year at department and speciality stores across America. But these facts are not permitted to intrude on lunch. 'He works very hard, but he does it with grace,' says a friend. 'He's the embodiment of the noble amateur. He never complains of tiredness or shows signs of strain.'

'I could work harder and have a bigger business,' says Oscar de la Renta. 'But there's so much more to life! This fish is not bad, not bad at all.'

Oscar Ortiz de la Renta, son of an insurance salesman, was seventeen when he left the Dominican Republic for Madrid, where he worked briefly at Aisa, the Spanish house of Cristobal Balenciaga. He went to Paris in 1961 to work at Lanvin for Antonio Castillo, and three years later was winning accolades in New York City for the elegant exuberance of his collections for Elizabeth Arden. In 1967 he formed his own company and married. Françoise de Langlade, a former editor of French *Vogue*, was the great formative influence of his life and, since her death in 1983, has become a legend among their friends. The Duke of Windsor called her 'my vitamin A'. Her sense of style, her pronouncements, her talent for decorating and entertaining loom large and still tend to overshadow any conversation about Oscar. If, as one friend insisted, he has achieved in twenty years what it took the Rothschilds two generations to accomplish, much of the credit is hers.

'One can learn a hell of a lot from the *demi-mondaine*,' she would say, or quote Chanel as she supervised dinner for twenty-eight: 'You have to see the people you're catering to!'

Her husband appears to have taken this maxim to heart.

'There's no fantasy about it!' says Boaz Mazor, de la Renta's lieutenant on Seventh Avenue. 'He dresses the people he dines with, who come over for the weekend. With Oscar you can actually name the clients: Brooke Astor, Nancy Reagan, Marietta Tree, Evangeline Bruce, Mercedes Bass, Anne Getty, Carol

Sulzberger, Grace Dudley, Pat Buckley, Marie-Hélène Rothschild, Mica Ertegun – would you like me to continue?'

He doesn't make sportswear like Calvin Klein, minimialize like Armani or push forward the frontiers of clothing like Issey Miyake. But he dresses some of the most socially prominent women in America for the main events in their lives: charity benefits, lunch, dinner and gala evenings. His clothes are digni-fied, body-conscious, feminine and head-turning, with Caribbean combinations of colour. He knows exactly what his customers want and exactly where they will wear the clothes.

'I never liked tough girls,' laughs the designer who lost money in the androgynous mid-seventies but regained ground in the eighties. 'If a woman's in a tux with shoulder pads, she'd better be ash-blonde with her tits hanging out!'

A woman blows him a kiss, and he telegraphs back a flash of snowy teeth. Another *histoire* is on its way.

'She's from Venezuela. Take a good look. She was once the most beautiful woman I ever saw. Then at nineteen she had a car accident. It was no big deal, but she had to have some stitches, and she fell in love with her plastic surgeon. Every month she found something for him to do. She improved her hairline, her jaw, her eyes, her cheekbones, her nose, her lips – and now she has a totally forgettable, shapeless face, no face at all!'

One of his best friends compares him to Fabrice, the Duc de Sauveterre, in Nancy Mitford's *The Pursuit of Love*. Fabrice won the undying love of Linda Radlett, the daughter of a *'très important lord anglais'*, by taking an intense interest in her clothes, making her laugh, and never boring her with his work. So has the cultivated and flamboyant Oscar de la Renta won the clever, reserved Annette Reed. Distinguished daughter of Jane and Charles Engelhard of Far Hills, New Jersey, reluctant social star and enthusiastic gardener, scholarly benefactress of the Metro-politan Museum of Art and the New York Public Library, she's popularly assumed to be heir to the prime role in New York society currently held by Brooke Astor. She has three grown children and one grandchild. And after a long drawn-out divorce from Samuel P. Reed, former president of American Heritage Publishing, it is expected she and Oscar de la Renta will marry.

Vulnerable and sharply critical, Annette Reed evokes the world of Henry James and wears an air of faint surprise at her capitulation to such a famously indulgent and silky charmer. As their friend Marietta Tree points out, 'Their tastes are not always the same. They pace each other.'

'Oscar adores people,' says Annette Reed. 'I don't, in the same way. He's open, generous and loving. I'm private, internal, dread going out, hate dressing up. I would rather weed. And I'm not stylish! My house is totally Yankee Victorian. And I'm not going to change *one single thing!*'

Annette Reed's style of decoration is masculine. Her Federal house in Katonah, New York, has been called the best house in America, with its serious entrance, profusion of needlepoint and Aubusson, fine porcelain and patina of age, English country-house furniture and flavour of a real family estate. The garden is a series of green enclosures as different as possible from the sun, sea and wide open fields that roll back from Oscar de la Renta's houses in Connecticut and Santo Domingo.

'His houses are all about views and looking out,' says Annette Reed. She is wearing jeans and no make-up and is weeding by flashlight. Her face is hard to see: narrow features, wide smile, thick dark hair.

'I don't know what he'd do with a herbaceous border! We have dreadful gardening wars. He asks what I think, and I say nothing. Pointedly!'

Already, under her influence, his New York apartment is slightly simpler. Although she says 'It's all Oscar,' the red velvet and green *faux-marbre* are gone, and there are no more Biedermeier tables or orientalist pictures alternating with heavily swagged windows. In the magnificently big library with a dining table at one end, Tudor portraits and a William Kent fireplace, there are three things unmistakably hers: two Cairn terriers and a length of Victorian chintz. 'And,' says a friend, 'Annette's learning to wear gardening gloves and go for a manicure.'

In the department of sensuous housekeeping, he has nothing to learn. 'Oscar is an even greater nest builder than Françoise or Annette,' says a Connecticut neighbour. 'He creates an environment that's lavish, sybaritic, full of tapestries, ornament, cosy comfort and a profusion of detail.'

His two houses in the Dominican Republic stand open to the breezes, squared by wide verandas. The new farm, each room a different colour in the local way, is a business venture and rises from twenty-five hundred acres of orange groves and a passion fruit plantation. 'I've spent a week in the house by the sea, and there is no more attractive house in the *world*,' says Kenneth Jay Lane. 'Breezes sift through the frangipani trees so the whole place is scented.'

Hailed as the greatest *maître de maison* in America, Oscar de la Renta acknowledges a superior, the late Duchess of Windsor. The Windsors have played a key, if obscure, role in the love life of Oscar de la Renta. It was at a dinner given by the Windsors for C.Z. and Winston Guest at Maxim's that he decided he would ask his first wife to marry him, and it was over a weekend given by Jane Engelhard for the Windsors that he met Annette Reed. They had enjoyably clandestine rendezvous in the larder with a chocolate cake neither had felt brave enough to tackle under the Windors' scrutiny.

Scenario: a group of people having a pre-lunch drink in de la Renta's Connecticut drawing room. Present are Dr Henry Kissinger, the Countess of Dudley, Diane von Furstenberg, Kim d'Estainville, Robert Silvers, Isaac Stern and Annette Reed. Suddenly the door is flung open, and five-year-old Moises, screaming with laughter, tears through the room and out into the garden followed by Oscar de la Renta, laughing and shouting, and more slowly by the nanny, with a face like thunder. Hands go out to steady tables. Conversation staggers, then slowly returns to normal.

For in addition to Oscar the socialite and Oscar the designer and nest builder, there is Oscar the Catholic benefactor who has founded and funded an orphanage for 350, the only institution of its kind in Santo Domingo. Twenty-two are actually orphans, the rest 'children in-between', the Dominican expression for those who go home at night after spending the day begging. At the orphanage they are given medical services, a good lunch and an educational game or two before spending the afternoon on the streets. Moises was an abandoned baby and weighed two pounds when found in 1984. Oscar de la Renta grew up the sixth child in an enormous, rambling family. His grandmother had eighteen children – eight inherited – by the time she was thirty-eight. Oscar, the widower, decided to take Moises home.

'After weeks in intensive care, Moises was still very delicate. The doctors thought he would have a better chance with me than at the orphange, where he might pick up infections. So I had a crib put in my room and brought him back. I have fourteen servants but I fed him, washed him and changed his nappies myself. And I decided he must stay.'

Having invented his ideal life, Oscar de la Renta now delights in sharing it. Friends are drawn ever deeper into his charmed circle of indulgence. Few can resist, certainly not Pat Buckley: after she complained to him in Paris that she had to spend days on trains, he presented her with a Lear jet to take her to John Fairchild in Provence and then on to the Erteguns in Bodrum. And Brooke Astor was overwhelmed when, on a visit to Dominica, he flew her to the town where she had lived when her father was a marine general, and had a marine band play all her favourite tunes.

There is an edge to this charm, and an effectiveness that makes it all the more seductive. Possibly the best president of the Council of Fashion Designers of America, de la Renta raised the profile of the fashion industry with gala events at New York's Metropolitan Museum of Art to celebrate the CFDA's Lifetime Achievement Awards, with presenters such as Barbara Walters. He helped develop Casa de Campo, the holiday enclave for the rich that brings much needed cash to Dominica. 'Today the only problem is the scream of private jets as they come in to land.' says a friend.

Entertaining the president and the local dignitaries in Dominica, or negotiating with Gulf & Western, he can't help revealing a greater range of talents than he needs for the life he has chosen. Henry Kissinger speaks of the breadth of his knowledge and information on Caribbean politics and says, 'It breaks my heart to admit it, but when we walk through the Dominican capital together and all heads turn, it's Oscar they are recognizing, not me!'

Back at La Grenouille, it's nearly four and the restaurant is virtually empty. A Texan lady on the far side of the banquette, who has been listening closely for at least an hour, extends a plump, bejewelled hand around the base of the flowers and taps him on the shoulder. 'I've been simply fascinated, Mr de la Renta,' she says. 'You must tell me, because we've got to go – when are you getting married?'

He does not enjoy this but suppresses all but the faintest flicker of rejection. Outside, the car door held open by his chauffeur Tomás, he answers the New York air.

'By the time this interview appears, madam, I hope I shall be married.'

American *Vogue*, September 1989

Michael Roberts: Seriously Dreadful

*I*MPOSSIBLY grand in the last vestiges of a torn black overcoat, isolated against a frieze of noble nudes, The World's Greatest Fashion Editor assumes an aura of pain appropriate to the martyrdom of Saint Sebastian, tapering fingers at his throat. A mixture of Velasquez majestic and El Greco mystical, Snowdon's picture transcends Michael Roberts's media legend as a cross between Michelangelo and someone rather more talented.

While the film is changed the models straighten up, scratch their blond heads and yawn. Agony drops from Michael Roberts's shoulders. He fishes three squashed Dunhill Menthol cigarette packs out of his tattered pockets and throws a warm, appreciative glance over one shoulder at the flexing beefcake. 'Just another quiet little evening *chez moi*,' he says in his dryest, most indolent voice. When he laughs, his head goes back like the lid of a box and out jump the hilarious, filed-off, horizontal teeth.

Roberts is to fashion what Tynan was to the theatre, aided and abetted by the fashion world's inordinate respect for those who have read more than they have. He specializes in the debunking one-liner and the Wildean epigram that can close shows. Fashion people are not used to this. They tend to remember what he writes.

Some still quote the write-up Roberts gave to Bill Gibb's show in '74 which, in the wake of Gibb's recent death, many recall as the beginning of his decline.

Buyers hurried to the phone to cancel orders as, over their Sunday morning coffee, they read, 'Mr Gibb is the Cecil B. de Mille of embroidery' and 'Over-theatrical? Alas, yes, but which? The theatre of the absurd or the theare of cruelty? With the appearance of his evening wear we realised that it wasn't theatre at all. It was pantomime.'

He skirts the hyperbole and whisks the rug out from underneath. At some stage he has read Dorothy Parker – '*The House Beautiful* is the play lousy' – and Walter Kerr, who wrote the only three-word review of *I Am a Camera*: 'Me no Leica.'

Great and small, friend and foe fall under the stiletto of his disdain. 'St Laurent calls his narrow look the Tube,' he wrote in spring '75; 'Karl Lagerfeld calls his the Tunnel; I can see no light at the end of it.' Adrian Cartmell still bites his lip over the occasion when he volunteered that his collection was based on 'throw away chic', whereupon Roberts taxied to his office to pen: 'Some of it is indeed chic; much should be thrown away.'

'I am very good at editing my writing,' says Michael Roberts. 'I'll run a pen through it quicker than any editor – that's boring, yawn, yawn, *don't* want to know that. They always want five hundred words and I give them one hundred and fifty. But they are the right one hundred and fifty words.'

Some would say that Michael Roberts the photographer needs tighter editing than he is given by Michael Roberts the art director. Ever since he was a soubrette in a candy pink St Laurent satin jacket reporting men's fashion for the *Sunday Times* his propensity for naked blond public school boys has been a difficult element for editors to deal with. His last year's cuttings book for *Tatler*, where he is fashion director, yields 104 naked blond boys in comparison to 64 well-dressed girls and a dozen old ladies.

For Michael Roberts as for Tom Wolfe, Truman Capote and Marcel Proust – have I got that? – fashion has become a point of departure. Sometimes literally.

'He's keen on chaps, and he frequently goes too far,' says editor-in-chief of *Vogue* and *Tatler*, Mark Boxer. 'I give him latitude, he takes it. I have on occasions said no. The last time I did that he got on a plane and went to America for a year.'

At forty he is uncontrollable; he obeys no laws and is unaccountable. There is no guarantee he will cash his salary cheques or collect his expenses. He perches in grand hotels or borrowed flats and sometimes sleeps in the office. Once, long ago, he had a flat in Finborough Road, south-west London. When he moved on he put his art déco furniture into store, but never paid the bills. He is deeply subversive, and authority regards him with due mistrust.

'All I require of an editor is that he leaves me alone,' he reflects. 'Actually, he doesn't even have to do that. A good editor recognizes talented people even if they have a viewpoint that comes way out of left field from where he stands.'

Editors take this sort of thing from him because his pages get noticed. Fans will remind themselves why at his first exhibition, where he adds painting and film-making to photography.

'He does *Tatler*'s fashion for his own pleasure, and we indulge him,' says Mark Boxer. 'It's worth it. His greatest asset as a fashion editor is his outstanding disloyalty which allows him to prick bubbles and be truly selective.'

Pastiche and parody are his forte. See his Bianca Jagger and die! But he resists becoming an entertainer.

'I'm not a performer,' says Roberts. 'I save that energy and spend it in my work. The lookalikes; the old ladies I photographed for *Staggering Beauties*; turning the focus on the fashion editors at the collections so readers could see who was telling them how to dress, these visual jokes are my version of after-dinner entertainment. A lot of these things I couldn't persuade anyone to let me do. I'd *pay* for it myself. I'd fork out, we'd get on a plane and go and do it anyway.

'Who's it for? Well, not me, oddly enough. It's for the public, for Mrs Smith. Why not? If she's a nice bright woman I've more time for her than I have for many in the fashion world.' He shrugs off their admiration. 'There's not much intellectual depth in most of the people you meet in fashion. Shallow is a polite way of putting it. They have a dreadful capacity for deluding themselves. I spend an inordinate amount of time acting interested when I want to be doing something else. So I certainly don't do it for them. They're an unappreciative lot.'

Notably they fail to appreciate the personal sting that his pieces tend to leave behind. Twenty years of a maverick personal life which has led him to take up temporary residence with several prime fashion names, David Bailey, Joseph, ex-*Vogue* editor Anna Wintour among others, has only sharpened his cutting edge. Some see this as integrity, others as biting the hand that has so frequently fed him. Zandra Rhodes, who taught him at High Wycombe art school, has not forgiven Roberts for planning to photograph her dresses on the professional model who looks like a drag version of the Queen. She has banned him from her shows forever. Grace Jones was a friend until she read that she 'has the body of a light-heavyweight boxer, the finely sculptured head of an African carving, and the table manners of a pig'. Jasper Conran says, 'It's very funny, as long as it's not you. Michael is thick-skinned, totally charming and doesn't give a toss.' He has forgiven Roberts for previewing his collection – along with those of other London designers – in the *Sunday Times*, when they assumed he was planning a later issue for a magazine.

'He is a little shit,' says Molly Parkin, who took him on as assistant when she was fashion editor for the *Sunday Times*. 'I say that with *deep* affection.' In the same vein, David Bailey calls him 'one of my good friends I don't like'.

The origins of the glorious entertainer and the fugitive vagabond lie under the surface of his self-made life, in the childhood he has never mentioned or admitted to any friend. Even to those who know him best, to Tina Chow, Nadia La Valle, Joseph, Molly Parkin, his background has always been a locked door.

'There is a story to be written there, but I'd rather not. If you don't mind. It was unfortunate, and I don't want to appear to be trading on it.'

Another day: 'Allied to fashion, it trivialises it. It's certainly a story. I could be quite dispassionate about it, now. Maybe I'll do it, but not now.'

Another day: 'Well, it has already been said my mother's English, my father was West Indian, a GI and an engineer. He's dead. I don't have any actual brothers and sisters. Half-brothers and half-sisters. My mother married again, when I was eight or nine. He was a very violent man. I don't really want to go any further. I'll have to think about it.'

Another day: 'I'll tell you a little bit. Well . . . it was seriously dreadful.' He gives a light laugh. 'I went to a children's home. My mother was on her own at the time and . . . uh . . . I got into trouble at school and I was sent away. In the first place, I just didn't bother to go to school. I mean, there was a lot of prejudice when I was young. It doesn't make you want to stay. It's the baiting you get, through no fault of your own. Children can be very cruel, and particularly to minorities. I went from school to school and the thing is, I would just run away. Then I went to places like remand homes and I still ran away. One of them was in Redhill, in Surrey. So *eventually* the courts decided I was beyond parental control and I was put into a place where I wasn't allowed to run away any more. You know . . . wardens.'

His right hand is tightly clenched around a large grey crystal, a present from Tina Chow who markets them in her jewellery. Their purpose, she says, is to balance energies, stimulate vibrations and clear the electro-magnetic field.

'Remand's temporary, Approved is longer-term. I was there for about four years. It was in Cambridge. It was one of the freer ones, but there was a hierarchy of bullying. You began at the bottom of the heap and you ended up on top. I just kept quiet a lot. I mean, you had to survive. You had to keep very, very quiet. One of the boys there hanged himself. Another set fire to himself in a barn. It was a very, very nasty place.' He laughs lightly once more. 'I got quite insular. See my mother? Very, very occasionally. Too many painful memories.'

This is the key to Michael Roberts's attitude to authority, to his waywardness and his rule of thumb when there's confrontation in the air: get on a plane. Most people wear their prejudices up front. He survives by absenting himself.

In Paris to cover the couture collections for French *Vogue*, Michael Roberts has been running from show to show all day with editors Irene Silvagni and Colombe Pringle. The cocktail hour finds him back at the gilded and flowery Lancaster Hotel, auditioning male models, while talking to Inès de la Fressange, Chanel's muse and chief model, and Nicole Wisniak, editor of *l'Egoiste.* For dinner he's at the Crillon, where André Leon Talley, fashion editor of American *House and Garden,* and fashion artist Joe Eula greet him with hoots of delight and settle down to tear the day's shows apart.

Joe: 'Did you notice John Fairchild's red fichu? He looked like an old turkey!'

Michael: 'To me, the telling thing was seeing him orchestrating the applause. Did you see him nudge his sidekick? She wasn't clapping hard enough!'

Joe: 'All those flowers! Stick a rose in front, darling, or they don't know it's a frock.'

André: 'What are you going to photograph? You can rip off the rose and put it between the boy's teeth! You can have him carrying one of those dinky baskets!'

Michael seizes a doily and does the drawing. André cackles and folds up in his chair. 'I think it could be major!'

At this point two girls shimmer across the plushy red room to the table. The lead is taken by a perambulating black hat of singed vulture feathers which straggle over the white face and stick to the red lips. This is Isabella Broughton, assistant features editor of *Tatler* and granddaughter of 'Jock' Delves Broughton who was cleared of Lord Erroll's murder. She goes down big in Vogue House, where she was recently overheard asking: 'What shall I do today to earn my crust?' and being answered: 'Oh, darling Izzie, just come into my office and BE'.

Trailing behind her is Lucy Ferry, a colourless, tired person who is experiencing the symptoms of all who attempt to accompany Isabella Broughton for two entire days.

Isabella: 'So this is where the naughties are hiding!'

Lucy Ferry murmurs something about getting back to the nanny in London tomorrow, and Bryan's record doing well in the States. She must get to bed. André signs the bill and the party drifts to the reception desk where he pauses for messages. 'No,' says Isabella Broughton. 'Not a single, single one.'

The group disperses into the rain. Everyone is going to bed but Michael. He is going to the studio, to photograph dresses all night for *Vogue*.

'I'm going to do it like Jean Genet. It's going to be called *Notre Dame des Fleurs*. First I've got to photograph all these girls in flowery dresses, then I'm going to stick the pictures on a dressing table with madonnas and flowers, like they do in cheap Catholic homes. Then I'm going to get a prison bed, and I'm going to have this boy lying back across it. . . .'

Five days later he's back in London, finishing the filming for his *Midsummer Night's Dream*, the 16mm twenty-eight-minute movie for the exhibition. It's a blurry frolic of painted boys in antlers and sunglasses to music by Elgar and Mendelssohn, with magical moments by Michael Roberts.

> If we shadows have offended,
> Think but this, and all is mended,
> That you have but slumber'd here
> While these visions did appear.
> And this weak and idle theme,
> No more yielding but a dream.

Sunday Times Magazine, March 1988

Issey: The World's Greatest Clothes Designer?

WHEN the outside of clothes is the whole point, what you have is merchandise. When the inside is as pleasing as the outside, what you have is couture. But when the inside is more important than that, what you have is Issey Miyake.

Acrobats who wear his clothes talk about freedom of movement, jazz musicians of self-expression, artists of the way his clothes don't date. People say the clothes make them 'feel better'. More precisely, Miyake has a sensitivity to the comfort of the body that goes beyond the normal and which makes his clothes different from everyone else's. The reason lies in a special vulnerability, the legacy of an event written so large in human history that it will never be forgotten. Miyake himself decided, 'I'd better forget.' He doesn't talk of it, and the fashion press are only too glad to leave it at that.

On 6 August 1945, an American B29 bomber dropped the atom bomb on Hiroshima, destroying two-thirds of the city, killing two hundred thousand and burning shadows to the ground. One of the small children within four kilometres of the epicentre was the six-year-old Issey Miyake, with his bicycle, on his way to school.

Most of his family were killed, and his mother was horribly burned. There were no drugs. Her family treated her with raw eggs. She survived for four more years, continuing to teach.

At ten years old Miyake developed osteomyelitis, a disease of the bone marrow. He is often in pain, although you would never know it, and he has a nagging limp. End, as Miyake would say, of tragic story.

At fifty, Miyake is movie-star handsome. When he comes into the crowded restaurant it is as though a spotlight has fallen on him. A lecherous buccaneer moustache doubles the wattage of the brilliant white smile. His black eyes sparkle and snap in his pleasant brown face, his curly hair is lightly oiled. It is as if Errol Flynn or Douglas Fairbanks Senior had whipped the cutlass out of his teeth and sat down at your table.

He loves England as foreigners do and now, for breakfast, he orders kippers and Earl Grey tea. Outside, a black taxi, the one he always hires for the duration of his London visits, ticks over at the kerb. Lying on the back seat are the sketch-pad, coloured pencils and pens he takes with him everywhere.

At twenty-six he left Tama Art University, Tokyo, with a degree in graphic design, then trained in Paris with Guy Laroche and Givenchy and learned merchandising in New York before setting up his design studio in Tokyo in 1970. He had decided in the zeal of the French student revolution that the couture was not for him: 'So beautiful, so static. Stuck, the society also.' All the people he cared about were wearing blue jeans with shades, shawls, flowers, hats and flowing hair. Looking for an eastern equivalent to denim he fixed on *sashiko*, the featherlight quilted cotton worn by peasants all over Japan, and garments that were frozen in time like the kimono and the fisherman's traditional smock. He had already stepped outside the limits of fashion, and wanted to make clothes that people would wear all their lives. But any idea that he was inspired by the flat cut and wide, stylized sleeves of the kimono is wrong, for that would have been the conventional, outside approach to clothing. For Miyake the point was the feeling of being inside a kimono, the comfort the body derives from the volume of air around the arms and shoulders, the lightness of the fabric and its sympathetic touch, the 'held' feeling at the hips.

To put on his clothes is to feel a sense of relief. Miyake, testing out each garment he designs, whirls his arms up and back in a characteristic gesture. If the fit body delights in his cut, the fragile or elderly body takes comfort in the gauze-backed double cottons, the soft, thick weaves and the wrap and drape of airy wools. In the end the clothes are addictive because they make most other garments seem scratchy and over-constructed.

The latest exhibition, at the Musée des Arts Décoratifs in Paris from 4 October until 21 December, is called *A Ūn*. The name is not the French '*à un*', but the unspoken Sanskrit communication between the two figures at the entrance of a Buddhist shrine, usually muscle-men or lions. 'It came to me during the spring pilgrimage to the temple at Shinkansen, just before the women's collection,' says Miyake, inhaling the steam from the teapot. 'One lion at the gate say "A", the other responds with "Ūn", like breathing in and breathing out.'

The idea is a model for Miyake's relationship with those who wear his clothes, and he is explaining his philosophy, by which a garment isn't complete until the wearer has changed it by making it her own. He doesn't want to dictate a look, and nothing delights him more than to see someone wearing his clothes in a way he didn't expect.

Because his clothes are not in fashion, and not out of fashion, he tries to sweep away all received ideas. He searches out fashion magazines in his workrooms and shops, and hides them away: 'I make clothes, not package ideas. They can wear all they want. I leave some space for them.' One of his lines, Permanente, sells clothes from his archives. They may have been designed ten or twenty years ago but, whatever other designers may be doing, these clothes don't change.

A new book *Issey Miyake: Photographs by Irving Penn*, edited by Nicholas Calloway, published to coincide with the exhibition, is the remarkable product of an *A Ūn* relationship between a Japanese designer and an American photographer. When Irving Penn, who has been producing some of the world's most unforgettable pictures for forty-five years, decided to take the photographs, Issey Miyake simply sent three hundred garments and his favourite model to New York with the message: 'Please now forget me. My work is already finish.' In London, Snowdon takes the Miyake photographs and the people who wear the clothes may not be fashionable, famous or particularly beautiful, but the result is stunningly original. 'The only thing I ask Snowdon,' says Miyake, 'is I don't want pictures that look like the photographs in fashion magazines.'

When Penn's pictures were shown to Miyake he was 'so happy'. The only request he made was that one or two be omitted for being 'too Japanese'.

Miyake's clothes go far beyond the limits of national fashion, and the one thing that always enrages him is the assumption that his place is within the Japanese school. Someone who understands him well, Jay Cocks, the writer and *Time* magazine contributor, says: 'Miyake likes being on his own. He is an adamant modernist, a determined internationalist, and doesn't much care for being swept up with a movement for which he pointed the way.'

Our ignorance of this can drive him to despair. Once, in a story I was told and then forbidden to repeat, he shouted at an obtuse journalist: 'My ass may be Japanese, but my brain is international!' In fact, it is nearly cosmic. If an alien were to land on earth with the somewhat limited ambition of revolutionizing the way we dress, the clothes would probably look as archetypal, statuesque and dramatic as Miyake's.

He is a famous showman. All Miyake shows are alarmingly, excitingly different. His first exhibition in Toyko had a half-hour fashion show with no music, but a souped-up sound system. 'The girl came out in many layers of clothing. She takes off shoes, throw them down. BANG! BANG! She take off garment. SSH. She drop it on floor. CRASH! She take off everything. She has no clothes. End of show. It become big Tokyo scandal. Sponsorship company beg me to stop.'

For *Bodyworks*, Miyake's round-the-world exhibition that marked the height of his love affair with mass production, mannequins were suspended from the roof above a black desert with glutinous pools of black water. Moulded plastic female torsos zipped over the clothes like corsets worn on the outside. At *Fashion Aid* at the Albert Hall, Miyake's team of acrobats and performance artists descended on ropes from the dome, slid down chutes of water, swung and tumbled. At one o'clock during the chaotic all-day rehearsals, with thousands thronging the catacombs beneath the seats, Jasper Conran looked up for a minute to see an island of cool organization – a table being beautifully laid with flowers and *sushi* for the Miyake team.

At the exhibition in Paris visitors will encounter mannequins that are insubstantial tangles of wire, but who will speak to them through microphones in the mouth area. 'When I did *Bodyworks* I wanted to show body,' says Miyake. 'This time is to show clothes. I make body to disappear.'

He is well aware of the glamour of mystique. From his side of the language barrier he is precise and pragmatic but, in a world where selling clothes is synonymous with hype, his clothes attract a cloud of high-flown language. In the exhibition literature ideas turn into 'concepts': now becomes 'this air we call the present', and the show is described as 'a creation, a space sculpture which is found in a casket of an edifice'. The rhetoric of publicity goes down better in France and in California than it does with the British, who tend to see fashion philosophizing as pretentious point-scoring. And, for those who don't like the clothes and who criticize them from the outside, they can seem too cerebral and arty. His clothes aren't pretty, although they might be beautiful or sensational. They can look frightening. That's okay, says Miyake. 'In frightening is also beauty. Some clothing too bland, too kind. I hope when I create something there is a little poison. I want break Paris mood, have energy instead!'

His work developed during the feminist impact of the late sixties and early seventies and became identified with 'the Japanese look' – the category of dark, shapeless, comfortable clothes in which sandalled women with cropped hair and scrubbed faces found their identity in *not* dressing for men. The couturier Karl Lagerfeld summarized the work of Miyake and other Japanese designers recently on film as 'intellectual, most unbecoming, no make-up, hair any way' but concluded: 'The idea of what was beautiful had to be reconsidered.'

The clothes are futuristic, but romancing about the future is a preoccupation of the past, and of the late sixties in particular. Only those who are not caught up in fashion can really appreciate clothes that aren't meant to die with fashion trends.

Yet the Miyake company is hugely commercial. The fact that he strikes a chord with many who spend large sums on clothes, but are weary of fashion, is proved by the figures. Miyake's clothes aren't cheap, averaging around £350 for a raincoat, and they are all collectors' items. The men's and women's collections, with Plantation, Permanente and a couple of lines sold in Japan, together with royalties from fourteen licencees, pull in around $70 million yearly. Of course Valentino pulls in $350 million, but then Valentino is the stratocruiser of the mainstream, playing Frank Sinatra to Miyake's Miles Davis – who, incidentally, is one of Issey's greatest fans and wears his clothes constantly.

Miyake eats a square two inches of kipper and lays down his knife and fork. He touches a pink peony on the table.

'Aren't you going to finish that?'

'No. Is enough. I just taste. Delicious.'

He has just arrived and is just leaving. It is hard to keep him anywhere longer than two or three days. He likes to live on the edge, keeping on the move, never letting himself become 'static'.

He hates social life. American hostesses, dazzled by his charm and looks, attempted to adopt him like an Oscar de la Renta or Bill Blass. On a recent trip to L.A. he was inundated with dinner invitations; to the chagrin of one lady, he cancelled at six hours' notice to drive out to Berkeley to meet the students and watch a group of young performance artists. These, Momix, he swept off to Tokyo: they were the acrobats who performed for him at the Albert Hall. He is quite clear about what's important. 'No problem. I don't want go, I don't go.'

Marooned in London in a grand hotel room with festooned curtains, chintz-covered tables and a gilded Indian bed, he is at a loss: 'I don't know what to do. It take me twice time to get ready, I can't find anything, I don't know what I have. I hide bedcover and all cushions in cupboard.' Struck by the pathetic picture he has painted, he roars with laughter.

In Tokyo he is the centre of an adopted family, the staff of the Miyake Design Studio, and also supports a whole community of performance dancers, artists and musicians. His best friends are the woman with whom he has worked and lived for more than a decade, a Kabuki actor, a gallery owner, an architect.

He runs the studio like a film director, courting opinions and contributions, taking groups out to lunch or supper in a student restaurant nearby. His one-room apartment, big by Tokyo standards, is almost empty but for a few pots, and commands a dramatic view over the Nagatacho quarter, Tokyo Railway Station and the government offices. At night the area is deserted but for the geisha restaurant below.

His staff is an unexpected mix. One was a lorry driver on the Manchester run until a chance meeting with Miyake a few years ago, another an anthropologist from Trinity College, Dublin. Customers are drawn into his magnetic orbit, too: one a Buddhist nun who wears his clothes while sitting motionless for hours in meditation; another one of the Sony workforce who wear Miyake on the factory floor. A colleague who worked in his studio for a time accompanied him one day to visit a musician who lived in a cave, the next week to a temple celebration attended by two hundred people wearing Miyake paper jackets.

To see him work, she says, is to watch *A Ūn* in action. His Permanente textile designer Makiko Tamura explains. 'He will say to me words like "light" or "pure" or "abstract", and I respond with fabric. We play catchball like this. He wants to see how I will interpret.' It wasn't always like that. Many years ago Miyake was so exacting that his staff grew rebellious. Today the balance is congenial and productive. When he reached his fiftieth birthday the workroom, having discovered he was born the day of the first Superman comic strip, made him a Superman T-shirt with the 'S' the central letter of his name.

Even if you ignore the showmanship and think, 'It's just clothes,' there is still something that makes Miyake fascinating and curious. People who know him well swap stories about odd things that happen around him. He attracts coincidences and memorable events. A couple of days before I met him in London he had been to tea with the distinguished potter Lucie Rie, now in her seventies. While she was upstairs making tea and setting out Miyake's favourite chocolate cake and tiny sandwiches of salmon and caviar, he was free to wander about her workroom among some three hundred pots. Accompanying him was Maureen Docherty, ex-managing director of Miyake London.

'Issey took one pot very carefully from the shelf and turned it around in his hands, admiring it. Then he put it back in its place. When we had eaten tea and were ready to go, Lucie Rie decided to give him a present. She went without hesitation to the same pot, and wrapped it up for him.'

I asked him about the occasion. It sent him into peals of laughter. 'The pot is shiny, completely white. It look exactly like her,' he told me, bafflingly.

Issey Miyake may not be Superman, but there is an element of the unexpected about him – the enigmatic *A Ūn* factor.

Sunday Times Magazine, October 1988

Couture Behind the Veil

CONTINUALLY on the move between the family houses in Beverly Hills, Paris and Geneva, the apartment in New York, the country estate in Britain and the hotel suite in Gstaad, the wealthy Arab wife spends perhaps less than three months a year at home in Dubai or Kuwait. Beneath her black *chador*, signifying a closed-circuit family life, she is one of the most pampered creatures on earth, wielding the spending power of Elizabeth Taylor without having to lift a finger. Her life, like that of a *Dallas* heroine, necessitates no fewer than four changes of clothes a day.

The first, from bedtime satin and lace to Jane Fonda workout wear, introduces a not-too-early hour of video-directed aerobics in her private gym. In the eighties, Arab women place a high premium on keeping their figures trim. Later in the morning she will emerge into the nylon-curtained Oldsmobile or Mercedes-Benz accompanied by a female cousin, an aunt and a paid companion to be driven to visit a married sister, the chauffeur doubling as armed bodyguard. Under her *chador* she wears a Paris boutique buy, a suit by Gianni Versace or Claude Montana. Back at home for the third change of clothes she puts on her first couture outfit of the day, an embroidered silk jacket and skirt by Jean-Louis Scherrer with the biggest shoulder pads and shortest hem in her wardrobe, for a twelve till four video tea with girl-friends. She has to be back for the three-hour preparation of face, hair and nails for an evening at home.

Tonight her husband's guests are closely related male members of the family by whom the Koran specifies she may be seen unveiled, and so she chooses Yves Saint Laurent's modestly cut lavender and gold ruffled evening dress, and adds the matching shoes and accessories sent in the same white and black corded box from Paris. At around £28,000, she hopes to wear this outfit at least five times before abandoning it at the dry cleaner's – for by then it will be last season's dress, as all her friends will know.

Arab extravagance is a legend in the couture. One Saudi princess has ordered the entire Nina Ricci collection, another has paid $100,000 for a mink-trimmed wedding dress. The wife of a certain Gulf state minister has asked Balmain to copy her new evening dresses in miniature for her baby daughter. A certain merchant's wife from Kuwait has specified that the beading on her new ballgown should be executed in real jewels. No wonder the salons rejoice to see *chador*-clad women elbow-to-elbow around the grey velvet banquettes, while bodyguards throng the pavement outside.

Yet, asked by the press to name their best customers, the couturier develops total amnesia where the Middle East is concerned, as Nicholas Coleridge discovered when researching his book *The Fashion Conspiracy*. 'The designers are happy to talk about their loyal following in New York, Paris, Milan, London and Tokyo, but forget to mention Kuwait, Dubai, Riyadh, Jedda, Abu Dhabi, Bahrain, Sharjah and Ajman.'

Coleridge estimates that the Middle East forms at least 11 per cent of the fashion industry's world market, but the figure is probably far higher. It is a difficult sum to assess because wealthy Arab women buy so many of their clothes on their travels abroad, making Gulf imports no indication of quantity.

For a decade and a half the couture has been responding to the influx of Middle Eastern money by targeting specifically at the Arab love of colour, glitter and intricate workmanship. They have kept quiet about it in case their French, British and American customers should confuse market tactics with true house style. At the same time, Paris designers regularly incorporated a section of elaborately beaded or embroidered dresses in brilliant red or orange, with necklines never lower than the collar bone and skirts never shorter than the knee.

At the Frankfurt fabric fair a couple of years ago, one well-known British fashion designer discovered just how deliberate was the play for the Arab market when he stepped into a reputable Swiss manufacturer's booth to find it awash with lime green gonk fur sparkled with gems, multi-colour lamés and orange and purple beaded lacework. As he backed out the embarrassed salesman hurried after him to explain he was just about to receive a contingent of dress manufacturers from the Gulf states.

Today, according to Fady El Khoury, the Lebanese fashion editor of *Al Mostakbal*, a news magazine which sells in seventeen Arab-speaking countries, this would not happen. 'Arab women have been travelling and educating themselves since the early seventies. Today they understand the Western approach and appreciate the "less is more" way of thinking.'

However optimistic this fashion editor may be, the fact remains that most Arab women dress to impress other women with their wealth, fashion knowledge and bargaining power. The price of outfits, and whether you can beat them down, is one well-aired topic at fashion video afternoons.

If a change is in the air, says London designer Bruce Oldfield, it is because Arab women are well aware of their reputation as the Marie Antoinettes of the twentieth century.

'The result is that they are convinced you are charging them more for a dress than you would an English customer. On several occasions an Arab client has tried to underpay by pressing cash into my hand. It's a nightmare, having to count it before they leave the shop and then pointing out it's £300 short.'

Many ready-to-wear designers believe that couture houses resort to the techniques of the souk themselves, adding a supplement for an Arab customer and then letting her beat down the price to its normal level so she can feel she has a bargain.

Arab women who order their clothes from the collections vary from Kuwaiti merchant families, heavily influenced by fundamentalist ideals, to ex-Iranians with their famously lavish dinner parties, rival clans of Saudi princesses continually competing and vying with each other, and the Gulf Arabs in Europe, who have a separatist culture even at ambassador level.

The common factor, says Erik Mortensen, the Danish name behind Balmain, is a desire for a dress that will turn heads. He specializes in Middle Eastern royal weddings, for which he may make dresses for the bride, the bride's mother, the mother-in-law, sister and four or six bridesmaids. 'A big wedding may be attended by two or three thousand people, with a succession of receptions and parties. But whether it's that or half a dozen evening dresses, what is wanted is an *outstanding* design, something that will be a talking point among the women for weeks. The taste may be very refined. They don't want a revolutionary dress, but they want a new touch.'

After all, the day revolves around appearing in one outfit or another and this results in one of the curious effects of the Middle Eastern wardrobe. The lack of any work-based schedule means that all clothes are dressing-up clothes. There is no notion of functional clothes, and the knockout cocktail outfits are for the other girls to admire over tea. Whereas the Western woman with a job dresses for the office, and will usually wear the same clothes to go out to dinner afterwards, the wealthy Arab wife spends most of the day dressing up to the nines. 'It was odd', says Nicholas

Coleridge, 'to see a roomful of Dubai charity organisers in couture overkill accompanied by their husbands in creased dishdashas or pinstriped suits.'

Label snobbery is strong, and women tend to dress from head to toe from one designer, as shown in fashion photographs from magazines such as the Arab editions of *L'Officiel* and *Marie-Claire*. English-edition magazines, including *Vogue* and *Harpers and Queen*, go on sale in Riyadh with censored pages ripped out by the clerks of the Committee for the Propagation of Virtue and the Suppression of Vice. Home-grown magazines such as *Sayidaty* or *Achabaka* mix a few unsophisticated fashion pages with romantic moral stories, home and family features, and the familiar advertisements for Chanel and Calvin Klein scents. The ever-popular Scherrer sells his perfume with a special photograph showing the designer surrounded by glamorous Middle Eastern models, found presumably in Paris.

The Middle Eastern customer, say designers, still loves brilliant colours and intricate workmanship but she wants to be novel instead of over-the-top. The great appeal of buying couture is that the customer will never see it on anyone else. 'If a woman should run into another guest in the same couture dress in Jedda or Kuwait it assumes the proportions of a diplimatic error,' says Fady El Khoury. 'International telexes fly, orders are cancelled. The fashion house team has to keep precise records country by country.'

The personal endorsement – the voice of the souk – brings the majority of customers to particular couture houses, and each new client will introduce sisters, cousins and friends before moving on. Some salons send teams to the Gulf to set up a series of appointments in the homes of leading families, to show videos and fabric samples and take measurements, returning, perhaps twice, to take fittings. Family retinues visiting Paris may request a modified fashion show in their hotel suite, or a princess will visit a showroom which has been cleared of other customers for the afternoon. Some, the most Westernized, sit in the front row at Chanel or Yves Saint Laurent, the less acclimatized holding their programmes over their faces like yashmaks.

Videos have been the greatest asset to Arab women, says Fady El Khoury, 'not just because they enable the customer to see the latest collections, but because they are such an effective teaching aid. Jeddah, for instance, has wall-to-wall video stores doing a roaring trade in all aspects of do-it-yourself beauty – how to keep fit, what to eat, how to do a professional make-up, most of all how to manage your hair.' One of the hardest details of life for Arab women is that they have no hairdressers. No women may work, and no male outsider may see a woman without her *chador*: ergo, women must learn to be their own beauty expert. The rules are often dropped when the family go abroad. Then, Arab clients spend day after day at the hairdresser and beauty salon. Sometimes, for a big event such as a wedding, a matriarch will fly out a top hairdresser to treat friends and female relations to a hairdo.

The buying pattern has changed since the Lebanese war sent the wealthy Arabs west of Beirut thirteen years ago, to London, Paris and the Mediterranean playgrounds from Marbella and Monte Carlo to the Greek islands. Wherever they stopped, expensive boutiques sprang up to sell ready-to-wear specifically aimed at Arab taste. When they moved on to New York and LA, Gstaad and Geneva, the boutiques closed.

Paris couture has remained the Middle Eastern ideal, although particular salons wax and wane in Arab favour. Most popular at the moment, says one Paris-based fashion consultant for a famous Saudi store, are Jean-Louis Scherrer, Balmain for prestige, Lanvin, Chanel, Yves Saint Laurent for the most sophisticated, Nina Ricci, Ungaro, Dior and Per Spook, with Valentino for ultimate Italian chic. 'Lacroix will be very popular with the eighteen to twenty-five year-olds,' says the consultant. 'He is perhaps a little eccentric at the moment, and the skirts are way too short, but the *de luxe* will do enormously well.'

From fashion victims to fashion dictators in a generation, Arab women's fashion power has recently reached a further phase in Paris – perhaps the beginning of a new era altogether. An ex-Iranian Princess from Tehran, Parvine Farmanfarmaian, who came to Paris after the revolution, has opened a couture salon at 14 Rue Royale. She alrady has 1350 international customers, a thousand of them Frenchwomen. She manages to give the French the elegant simplicity they crave, while supplying her Arab customers with head-turning colour and detailing, at around £500 a dress. Just one thing. Don't try to strike a bargain.

Sunday Times Magazine, April 1988

Catwalk Crucifixion: Yves Saint Laurent

Y VES is a recluse,' a member of his staff told me. 'He lives *tout seul* in the Rue de Babylone with his staff and his dog. He sees maybe five people, one by one. The only place you ever see Saint Laurent outside his studio is backstage at the show. And no one who doesn't work with him is allowed in the studio or backstage.'

But backstage in the tented courtyard of the Louvre, with the summer collection about to begin, the genius is absent. His beloved models, half prepared for their first numbers, sprawl around on the floor like a dark-skinned *corps de ballet* from a Degas painting. Above their sculptured heads anxiety and speculations spread like a virus between knots of speculating staff. There is a sudden vacuum. The noise level drops. Television cameramen hesitate and come to a standstill.

'You see, it's quite possible he may not come, after all,' whispers Joy Henderiks, angelic blonde press *directrice* of the house of Yves Saint Laurent.

A small man in a suit rushes to a telephone on the wall of the hairdressing unit and makes a monosyllabic call. He bangs down the phone, bellows: *'La collection commence tout de suite!'* and darts feverishly around the *cabine*, hustling out the press.

The models, now trimly suited in navy and white, have sailor berets tipped on to their sleek heads. The Saint Laurent muse, Loulou de la Falaise, rake-thin, surveys the familiar scene of barely-controlled hysteria with scornful green eyes. The minutes pass.

And suddenly, there he is!

Head and shoulders above the crowd, the sombre, sensitive features with their tortoiseshell glasses are familiar from a million photographs. Here is the one and only, the single greatest fashion designer of our lifetime, the fifty-two-year-old supremo who has for three decades set an absolute standard for world fashion. Even for his staff, it's a rare sighting. People hurry towards him from every corner. He moves before the hedgerow of smiling faces. His devoted staff reach out to him. He lifts a hand, smiles fleetingly. It is a royal progress. But something is wrong.

His face is a mask from a Greek tragedy. His step is clumsy, his once willowy figure heavy inside the lilac striped shirt and the sharp green linen suit. As the opening announcement is made and the music begins, he feels his way through a flurry of embraces and stumbles over the first step up to the catwalk. Steadying himself against the wall with both hands, he climbs the five steps. Now, scarcely looking at the faces of the six models poised in the wings, he at once moves with complete authority to rearrange a flower in a buttonhole, tweak a shoulder pad, tug the hem of a jacket-back.

To a burst of Stravinsky the first model is launched out into the lights. Pouting, Saint Laurent twists a collar, shakes a bow violently undone and coaxes it into a fat knot like a cabbage rose. Isolated against the white partitions, his involuntary movements are cruelly highlighted. His right hand clenches and unclenches. He continually purses his lips. He descends the steps, braces himself against the edge of a table loaded with hats, and drops his head on to his chest, the picture of despair. Then he's at work again, dropping stiffly on to one knee to waft air inside a leopard print chiffon skirt. 'La Vie en Rose' billows through the sound-waves, signalling the entrance of the formal evening dresses. As the audience gasps and applauds the company of goddess-like white sheaths, their creator slouches against the partition, head lolling, sucking his lips.

As the final model shimmers out into the lights, the man in the suit swings one hand, conducting the closing crescendo, grips Saint Laurent's arm tightly with the other and pushes him violently out on to the stage. Tumultuous applause culminates in the only standing ovation of the season's collections.

Saint Laurent treads uncertainly down to the end of the runway, smiles shyly, revels in the applause – and just stands there. The models, still clapping, wait for him to lead them back into the wings, but instead he half turns and begins to readjust a cape, turning it back to show the dress beneath. Confused, the models glance at each other. Two of them take him gently by each arm and coax him back along the catwalk.

Backstage, press and buyers surge into the *cabine*, and all at once Saint Laurent is the nucleus of a mob of excited people. He smiles, kisses, responds. And suddenly, he's not there any more.

Already blanket-wrapped in the burgundy Renault with the tinted windows, he sits with his dog Moujik behind the uniformed chauffeur and bodyguard. In less than 20 minutes he will be back in the Rue de Babylone. The black-jacketed butler will close the door softly behind him and he will pull himself up the stairs, holding tightly to the handrail. He will enter a resplendent panelled room – Matisse painting, cream and lilac orchids in a Lalique vase – and close a second door on the world. Out there, people will still be searching for him. Bottles of champagne will pop, faxes will whirr, fantastic bouquets will be ordered.

In here he will sit in the velvety silence, head sunk on his chest, confronting himself. Once more the wrenching effort has been demanded and made. All too soon it will be time to start again.

A small, middle-aged man in a quiet brown suit, Pierre Bergé sits in a low-key, overheated *bureau de luxe*. The tables are heaped with thumbed books. An unspectacular chandelier gives a sombre glitter beneath its roped-up red baize bag. Pleasant Frenchwomen come and go in little grey smock dresses belted on the hip.

The photographs on the mantelshelf are not to do with snobberies of class and title and instant fame, but with global influence or subversive talent: Mitterrand, Raisa Gorbachev, Cocteau, Aragon, Warhol, Nureyev.

The fifty-eight-year-old president of the Yves Saint Laurent group looks like a discreet and cultivated family doctor. Notwithstanding the fact that he heads a £438 million conglomerate with are old and he wears a librarian's spectacles. The tiny red thread in his buttonhole represents the Légion d'Honneur, the highest civilian honour in France, bestowed on him together with the Order of Merit. He is President of the Théâtres de l'Opéra de Paris, President of the Chambre Syndicale, of the Institut Français de la Mode, and of the exhibitions at the Musée des Arts de la Mode. His personal net worth is estimated at £94 million, although he gives away a large part of his annual income. A faceless businessman, an unrecognized public figure until he recently took over the opera, he has been the hidden hand of Yves Saint Laurent for thirty years.

Bergé is the other half, the bully, the financial brain, the astute politician. He is Pierre *la Panthère*, possessor of a rather famous temper, the man who screams at his fax machine for printing so slowly, who kicks the camera out of the hands of persistent photographers, who recently fired the eminent Daniel Barenhoim from the post of musical and artistic director of the Bastille Opéra with the maximum of unpleasant drama and publicity. Yet the Saint Laurent staff say everything he does for the company is done for Yves alone.

'If Pierre shouts, it is because Yves whispers.'

Saint Laurent and Bergé together form one of the most successful business relationships of the century. It is the envy of every creative talent. The fashion world is full of makeshift parallels, none so durable or effective. For while Saint Laurent shines brighter than any other designer, casting his influence so wide that no baby doll, flower child, free spirit or power dresser has ever moved beyond his influence, Bergé outwits the financial wizards of the luxury goods market time and again. In his latest coup, Pierre Bergé masterminded the 1986 strategy that called in the extra financial muscle of Italian financier Carlo de Benedetti to outbid Revlon and Avon for the Charles of the Ritz group. In one move Bergé had taken the company's operating income from £9.5 million to £44 million, and made Yves Saint Laurent the only living courturier with his own perfume house.

'I hate business,' says Bergé, with a very thin smile. 'I am obliged to be a businessman because I took that decision beside Yves's hospital bed in 1960. And when I decide to do a thing, I do it.'

Bergé and Saint Laurent met in 1957, when the death of Christian Dior saw the boy apprentice prematurely projected to the head of the great Paris fashion house. Bergé, a good friend of Dior, attended Saint Laurent's first collection and met him later that eventful week at the dinner table of Marie-Louise Bousquet, catalytic Paris editor of *Harpers Bazaar*.

It was love at first sight which became a life's companionship. Remembering that first encounter with the slim, bespectacled prodigy, Bergé's habitually vigilant expression softens. 'He was so shy. So young. So talented. We talked of everything *but* fashion. We discussed theatre, movies and painting, we talked of food!'

The hypersensitive Yves found himself in an unbearably precarious position. Traumatized by school, he had only been happy at home, the spoiled only son of wealthy sociable parents living in some luxury in Oran, North Africa. At seventeen, he won first prize in a French competition to design a black cocktail dress. Through the auspices of the then editor of French *Vogue* he was introduced to Christian Dior, and went to work for him after just a few weeks of a pattern-cutting course. In just under one year he had already become the natural and obvious successor to the greatest name in fashion.

When Dior died, he found himself at a needlepoint of pressure.

The people he worked with were terrified to find themselves led by an insecure boy with no experience. Yet his first collection was a triumph. In 1958 'trapeze' was not too different from Dior's A-line, but just different enough. In scenes scarcely believable today, his first show ended with people in the audience being trampled underfoot in the rush to congratulate him, while newspapers went to press with the headline, 'Saint Laurent has saved France!' He had reassured the world that Paris was still the centre of high fashion.

But Saint Laurent began immediately to exhibit the unpredictable fireworks and innovations of a virtuoso performer. His next collection dropped hems by a full three inches, then bared the knees. He put knitted sleeves on fur coats; he visited the King's Road and followed up with thigh-high boots and motorcycle jackets in alligator. As the boy designer predicted the entire sixties, talking of street chic and the dangers of confusing elegance with snobbery, buyers and press lost confidence. At this most difficult point in his career, the army draft, three times deferred, wrenched the designer from Dior.

A *Vogue* editor recalls a last weekend spent on the beach with Bergé and Saint Laurent before he left for training camp. 'Pierre and Yves talked of nothing else, obsessively. And under the burning mid-day sun, Yves was shivering with fear.'

It took less than two months for him to suffer a massive mental and physical breakdown. During his extended recuperation, his erstwhile assistant, Marc Bohan, was quietly instated as Dior's new chief designer. When Bergé discovered Saint Laurent was isolated in a seventeenth-century military hospital outside Paris, and that not even his mother was permitted to see him, his rescue became a personal mission. Working through his already powerful web of contacts, Bergé went to see the hospital commander.

'I told him that in his hospital he had a living genius. I told him that Yves was very, very delicate and I said it was the general's responsibility to answer for his safe keeping.' So alarmed was the general at the prospect of having to answer to posterity for the prodigy's well-being that he immediately issued Bergé with a twenty-four-hour pass to the invalid's bedside. And so Pierre Bergé wore a path to Val de Grasse three times a day, bearing fruit, flowers, and such paintings and objets d'art as are allowed by a military régime.

As Yves recovered, Bergé outlined his strategy. And now, just when Saint Laurent's meteoric career seemed to have ended, he executed a miraculous recovery. Pale, but composed, he sued for

£48,000 damages, won, opened his own salon in 1962 with the proceeds, stole the cream of Dior's staff – and the rest is history. It was just the first act of Bergé's devotion, the dramatic overture to a lifetime of service.

Yves Saint Laurent is as near to genius as a designer may be. He is also a hypersensitive, reclusive neurotic who has written of his mental sufferings and of 'the anguish of not being up to the expectations of the critics, and more important, not being equal to the task itself, waiting for three weeks out of four for the click that sets my fantasies in motion towards their appointment with the physical world.'

Without Bergé, we might have had no Saint Laurent. For Bergé is still his prop and protector, the lover who has found a way for the flayed-alive couturier to work and who has never let him fall from grace. For as the fragile figure of Yves Saint Laurent painfully performs high over the heads of his would-be rivals, fighting for balance between his nervous breakdowns, his uppers, downers and his drinking, it is Bergé who operates the ropes beneath, holding his breath, lavishing on him anything that makes his life more bearable, forever taking the strain and playing alternate roles of ogre, doctor and nanny. However delicate the equilibrium at the centre, the unstable fashion genius and the reluctant business-man together make a unit that appears to be artistically and economically unassailable.

'The relationship's still so passionate, so volatile!' says one of Bergé's familiars. 'One week they're so close, the next they're not talking. Pierre is slamming doors, Yves is slumped tragically across a sofa, throwing burning looks after him.

'Pierre would slit your throat if you criticized Yves. Yves wouldn't do the same for Pierre. He's got the selfishness of genius. It's me! me! me! with Yves. He's like Andy Warhol, a spoiled child!'

Recently Saint Laurent's worsening state of health was so widely noted in the American press that Bergé issued a statement denying cancer or AIDS, but admitting to Saint Laurent's reckless mixing of tranquillizers and alcohol. In the Avenue Marceau, Saint Laurent's absences only increase his mystique. He recently complained that new members of staff failed to wish him good morning. An aide explained they were terrified.

'Yves is brilliant, but he's nuts,' says another acquaintance. 'He'll always be Pierre's number one concern, but eventually who can take the strain of playing mother twenty-four hours a day?'

Ten years ago, Bergé left the house they shared in Paris, and has since lived in a hotel apartment, as he does when he visits New York. But lunch together is a sacred ritual, and Bergé's friends know to their cost that Yves always comes first. Holidays are spent together in one of the three houses they share in Deauville, Marakech and outside Paris, where they have bought a wooden dacha together with the Minister for Culture, Jack Lang. At the Château Gabriel, near Deauville, they arrive by helicopter, then drive about the estate in pony and trap. The friends who visit them there miss the exuberance of the younger Saint Laurent who, after dinner, would clap a straw hat on his head and a cigarette holder between his teeth and transform himself into the heart and soul of Coco Chanel.

After a lifetime of playing second man while Yves stars, however remotely, centre stage, Pierre Bergé appears to be emerging at last from the shadows. Transcending the role of president, Bergé revitalized the couturier's career in 1983 by engineering, together with Diana Vreeland, the Metropolitan Museum's first ever retrospective for a living fashion designer, then took the show on to Moscow where they were invited to lunch by Raisa Gorbachev. When Bergé and Saint Laurent were named consultants to the Chinese Ministry of Light Industry after talks with the seventh-ranking member of the ruling state council in Beijing, it began to seem that the company president was becoming a national statesman.

These days, while Yves chooses luxurious isolation, Berge's social life is a carnival centred around some fifty friends including the Pompidous, the Mitterands, Jack Lang, Jessye Norman, Jacqueline de Ribes, Françoise Sagan, Marie-Helene Rothschild and a younger circle of talent with whom he is frequently spotted in his opera box – international painters, musicians, political idealists and salon groupies such as the American landscape gardener, Madison Cox.

However devoted he is to the consuming needs of Saint Laurent, it has been clear for some time that he has talents to spare. Shortly after producing *Equus* in France in 1977, he bought the Théâtre de l'Athénée as a showcase for experimental drama, but his real passion has been for music. At the Athénée he established musical Mondays with performances by singers of the calibre of Montserrat Caballe, Placido Domingo, Kiri Te Kanawa and Joan Sutherland. He produces a free-ranging monthly column for the avant garde magazine *Globe*. He owns a restaurant, Le Doyen, on the Champs Elysées. And it is not long since he turned down an important political post.

As if to compensate himself for forgoing public office, Bergé has recently taken on his biggest independent project so far. His prestigious appointment as president of the three Paris Théâtres de l'Opéra places him at the head of the august Palais Garnier and the Opéra-Comique as well as the political punchbag of the Bastille Opéra. A pet project of President Mitterand, the brand new £70 million opera had been intended for the showpiece of the bicentenary of the French Revolution, but was soon bogged down in conflict. Bergé inherited Daniel Barenboim as artistic director, but Bergé's lawyers questioned the legality of the contract by which Barenboim was to earn almost 7 million French francs annually (£650,000) for a four-month working year. Bergé may well have felt that was an unreasonable salary, but more fundamental appears to have been the initial stumbling block over the interpretation of Mitterand's demand for a 'modern and popular' opera. Bergé has recently announced the appointment of the new musical director, the thirty-five-year-old Korean conductor Myung Whun Chung who does not yet speak French. The opera programming will begin with forty presentations a year and climb to 250: all portents suggest that President Mitterand will get his 'truly modern' opera.

This has not by any means been the only headache of the year for Bergé. Back at the Avenue Marceau he took a decision crucial to the future of the company. He determined that the master holding company would go public on 28 June, with an epoch-making 'roadshow' held within I.M. Pei's glass pyramid at the Louvre.

Over the last three months Bergé has been restructuring the organization and transforming its status to that of a '*commandite*' or mixed liability company. The four principal shareholders are now Saint Laurent, Bergé and Jean-François Bretelle, their finance director, together with Alain Minc, the well-known economist and head of Benedetti's company, Cerus. Such an arrangement effectively ensures that there can be no take-over unless the organization starts losing money – an unlikely eventuality for a company whose net sales last year amounted to £245 million, with net profits of £12 million. With its two hundred licensed agreements and 85 per cent of the turnover coming from the newly acquired Yves Saint Laurent perfumes and makeup, it would seem that the future looks rosy. So why make this move now?

'With the encroachment into the luxury goods market of the big financiers such as Arnault it's a good moment for safeguards,' said *Women's Wear Daily*'s financial expert in Paris, Godfrey Deeny. 'And Bergé has tried to go public before. That time they were blocked by the Wall Street crash.'

Joy Hendericks of Yves Saint Laurent found another reason. 'Carlo de Benedetti tied up a lot of his capital with us,' she says. 'Now he wants to realize some of that. And Pierre Bergé would like to do the same thing, to pay back the banks who raised part of the £394 million with which he bought Charles of the Ritz.' Net debts of the company at the end of 1988 amounted to £179 million.

The salon itself has not been a particularly happy house of late. Saint Laurent's shaky health has worried his staff, both because they adore him and also because they are worried about their future. Some of the longest-serving members have even been asking for their first official contracts, since seeing Marc Bohan so brusquely ejected from Arnault's commercially streamlined new Christian Dior. They are also asking 'What if Pierre Bergé goes to the Opéra?' Implicit is the further question: 'What if Yves's health worsens? What if he collapses?'

Stock may tend to move sluggishly while press reports on Yves Saint Laurent's chemical dependence proliferate. But if the worst happened and Saint Laurent were unable to continue, wouldn't stock be even harder to sell? And isn't that the real reason why, after years of discussion, the company decided to go public this summer?

The Saint Laurent contact I spoke to fell silent at this point in the conversation. Then he admitted: 'I've heard Bergé say "Look at Dior! Christian has been dead thirty years and they sell more make-up than we do! Chanel are still making a fortune with her perfume."

'As long as Yves is with us, he is the embodiment of everything the couture has to offer . . . and even if he is not with us the company will still go on.'

The future would look better to outsiders if Saint Laurent had an understudy but nobody dares suggest such heresy, and even if they did, the couturier would dismiss him out of hand.

'Where would we find anyone capable?' says Joy Henderiks, with a shrug of her grey cashmere shoulders. 'All those brilliant young designers – you only have to mention Yves's name and their talent drains out of their boots. They can no longer make a simple sketch. *Rien ne pousse dans l'ombre des grands arbres!'*

While Saint Laurent retreates even further from the world, Pierre Bergé appears to be increasingly uncomfortable with his middle-aged image of discreet anonymity and privilege. Behind the mask of élitist power and wealth, Bergé is unexpectedly subversive and anti-establishment. You suspect he had always had to tread a careful line in the world in which he operates. The idea of a people's opera to be built on the very site where the Revolution began has a special significance for him.

'When you grow up you forget your youth, your outrage. You forget real life. Well, I still feel outrage!' He leans forward in his chair, positively excited, looking ten years younger.

'When I came to Paris at seventeen, I joined the World Citizen movement and became an anarchist. I'm still an anarchist. I wanted to blow everything up! The government, everything. So now I can understand it if someone wants to blow me up!'

If a new note of frankness has crept into Bergé's comments on the well-being of his friend, it may be that he, too, wonders just how long Yves Saint Laurent can continue along his present path.

'Yves is very delicate. Some days are better than others. All I can do is reassure him, tell him that after thirty years he had nothing to prove.'

He rises and crosses to the window looking down at the famous entrance where Yves Saint Laurent might arrive, or might not, depending on whether today is better than yesterday.

'What can I do?' he says, loudly, and he shrugs.

'Finally, it's his problem, not mine.'

Sunday Times Magazine, July 1989

Postscript

On 17 March 1990, three days before the gala opening of Pierre Bergé's Bastille Opera, Yves Saint Laurent was rushed to hospital in a state of nervous collapse, suffering from what the press communications termed 'intellectual exhaustion'.

Tina Brown: All Is Vanity, Nothing Is Fair

CARELESS of sensibilities, wide blue eyes behind drifting contact lenses firmly focused on the ultimate goal, Tina Brown is a dangerous companion to choose for an unburdening of the soul. It is all too easy to fall under her spell and suspend judgment as her poisoned arrows fall where they may, unerringly drawing blood. She can puncture self-esteem with a memorable phrase, commit the unguarded confidence to a headline and tell the tale so that life itself becomes a strip cartoon of scenes from her own quick perceptions. Twice blessed with disarming looks and a swiftly calculating brain, she is an inspired documentor of the social scene.

It has taken her thirty months to emerge as the editor with the highest profile in New York. If she falls out with friends, as she not infrequently does, it gets into the papers. When she walks into the Four Seasons restaurant, heads turn and draw closer together to ask, 'Who's she with?' 'What's she up to?' As editor-in-chief of *Vanity Fair* she has all the success she ever wanted. She has an expensive uptown apartment. The block is fronted with greenery and fountains, two uniformed doormen and a black marble foyer, but the apartment itself resembles a pleasant office with a pram incongruously pushed among the plants and pale sofas. It has the style-less masculine air of a home from which the owner is physically and mentally absent. She has a clapboard house in Long Island where husband, wife and baby rendezvous for weekends. She also has a 6 am to midnight New York day, a Filipino nanny, and a diary of wall-to-wall appointments for the three months. None of these things matters enormously to her because, for an Englishwoman, she has always been American in her tastes, and she is a workaholic who leaves other workaholics at the starting gate.

'I'm a driven person,' she says. 'I have a high creative energy and if I can't find an outlet for it I feel I'm a non-person. I once took up tapestry for serenity and I had to throw it away. It was supposed to take four years and I was beating the damn thing to death, trying to get it finished by four o'clock.'

She misses the London gossip – 'Those evenings in people's kitchens in north London, gassing. New Yorkers don't entertain at home because unless they are millionaires their apartments are too small. So you go to restaurants and you talk relentlessly about money until the waiter tells you to go because he needs your table. But it's a great place if you enjoy the antics of the rich. There's this hilarious new tycoon who has just bought a cosmetics company, and at dinner the other night his wife started to get delusions of grandeur. She turned to the hostess and said, "Ron's ready to eat now." It broke me up! And when I hear that someone I know bought the Kissingers a tractor for Christmas, I realize I'm in the right place.'

One of the brightest of a bright generation at Oxford, she wrote successful plays which were performed at Edinburgh and at the Bush Theatre in London, married the *Sunday Times* editor Harold Evans in 1981, and became the youngest magazine editor in London, turning the creaking antique that was *Tatler* into a sharp new vehicle for social satire. *Tatler* reinvented snobbery, which the sixties had turned into a joke, but with a spin of mockery to it that exalted and debunked simultaneously.

Readers learned to look out for her spine slogans, many of them witless puns but some that live on in the memory: 'The magazine that bites the hand that reads it', 'The magazine that *shall* go to the ball' and, one triumphant Christmas, 'Deeper, crisper and breaking even'.

The small, tense circle of *Tatler* readers seemed to be divided between the one half who were always threatening to cancel their subscriptions, and the other half who wrote in to revel in the high point of their week's reading. The editor set a frantic, headlong pace, exploding budgets and deadlines, throwing out features just as they were going to press and substituting ideas worked out at dawn. When disposed she was marvellous company and an unparalleled mimic, bouncing out of her office to regale the staff with both sides of a telephone drama or a row with a photographer over expenses. At other times, when features weren't progressing fast enough, she would prowl the office like a caged tigress.

Tatler succeeded where earlier attempts at similar publications had failed – notably *London Life*, edited by Mark Boxer, who currently edits *Tatler*. The magazine so prospered that it was bought by Condé Nast, who presented Tina Brown a few years later with the editorship of America's *Vanity Fair*, probably the most glamorous job in magazine journalism.

Condé Nast had tried to breathe new life into the grand old magazine title which went under with the Depression in 1936. It had a rapidly sinking circulation and two editors had already been hired and fired when Tina Brown was recruited for a third and final metamorphosis. The circulation stood at 259,344, mostly committed by launch subscriptions and, in any case, a negligible figure in US terms. Advertising pages had dropped from 150 in the first issue to fifteen.

The new editor-in-chief has steered *Vanity Fair* to a circulation of almost four hundred thousand, and recent figures released by the audit bureau show it to be one of the fastest growing consumer magazines across the USA, although not yet profitable. A racy mixture of current and flashback society glitz with up-market murder stories, sex, cultural icons, featurized fashion, glamour and insiderly gossip from hotspots such as Palm Beach and Washington, it is an Americanized *Tatler* on a wider, richer, more popular scale.

'Of course *Vanity Fair* was never meant to be like that,' says Michael Roberts, design director of British *Vogue*, who fell out with Tina Brown while fashion and style editor of her early issues in New York.

'It has become a glorified *People* magazine. All right, it's a success, but that's also due to her team, and they never get any credit for it. You've got to realize you are all working for the greater glory of Tina Brown.' She does not, he says, have the inspiring qualities that make a good editor. 'She's got chutzpah, she's good at hit-and-run features, but she uses up her contacts too fast. And she's jittery. She's the kind of editor who changes the pages every half hour.'

It would have been surprising if she had not been jittery for that first year and a half. She lived in fear that she might not turn *Vanity Fair* around quickly enough. She regularly rang Si Newhouse, chairman of Condé Nast, for reassurance that he was not going to fire her and fold the magazine. In her strategy for *Vanity Fair*'s revival she notched up the circulation with a succession of high profile, deliberately provocative features, a third of which she wrote herself.

With 'The Mouse that Roared', *Vanity Fair* impinged on British consciousness with a portrait of the Princess of Wales, depicting an alienated personality who 'spends hours cut off in her Sony Walkman, dancing on her own or studying her press clippings. Her panic attacks come when she is left alone and adulation free on wet days at Balmoral. His [the Prince's] come when his father tells him he must stop being such a wimp.'

Picking up the fact that forty members of Prince Charles's staff had resigned since his marriage, filling in with seductive strokes of scene-painting – 'all the royal houses are like second-rate hotels to live in, with the inmates complaining rustily that dinner was "bloody awful"' – she concluded that 'the debonair Prince is pussy-whipped from here to eternity'. This portrait of their marriage goaded the royal couple into an unprecedented response through a television interview with Alastair Burnet. The *Daily Mail* editor, David English, gutted the piece offered by Tina Brown's agent, Ed Victor, for second serial rights, and spotlighted it with lip-licking avidity as an abusive attack on our royal family.

Sitting in Tina Brown's fourth-floor Madison Avenue office, from which she commands a salary in the region of $150,000, I asked her what she thought about the furore that followed. From the far side of the desk she designed in the shape of an apostrophe, her curly-lashed eyes signalled wide blue astonishment. 'I was surprised by all the flak,' she said primly. 'Over here it was considered a very sympathetic piece. My job is not to set out to create a story that will please the subjects. As far as I was concerned it was wonderful. We sold a hundred thousand on the news stands and I got a couple of noughts added to my name.'

While I was mentally reviewing her probable contacts – from the *Daily Mail*'s own Nigel Dempster to 'Burghie', or Lord Burghersh, heir to the Earl of Westmorland, and Tory MP Nicholas 'Fatty' Soames – she admitted she was less happy with the way the *Daily Mail* had exploited the piece without paying for it.

Tina Brown's satire always has a particularly savage edge when she is writing about the upper crust. It is possible that she enjoys undermining the aristocracy more than other people she mocks – the new rich and the pretentious.

Her own family are united, supportive and festive, but not exactly typecast for the sophisticated and powerful woman she has become. She grew up in Little Marlow, near Henley, in a house frequented by the British movie establishment who had appeared in the comedies and Agatha Christie films directed by Tina's father in the forties and early fifties. 'She was an adored and angelic-looking girl, the only one of us to have a real fur coat,' says a friend. 'At parties you would find her sitting on the lap of the most important man in the room.'

George Brown had already been briefly married to the film actress Maureen O'Hara when he met Tina's mother Bettina at Pinewood, where she was PA to Laurence Olivier. In retirement they live at San Pedro de Alcantara in Spain, where Mrs Brown is the social columnist for the Costa del Sol expatriate magazine and provides an occasional escape route for Tina and her brother Christopher, producer of *Absolute Beginners* and *Mona Lisa*.

Most successful and strong-willed women have clashed with school authorities, but for Tina Brown expulsion became the inevitable conclusion of the many new beginnings in her education. The angelic-looking little girl was a catalyst within the system. 'I got other girls to run away, and I organized protests because we weren't allowed to change our underpants. At one school the headmistress poked about in my locker until she found my diary – which I have kept all my life and which always gets me into terrible trouble – and opened it where I had described her bosom as an unidentified flying object.'

Nevertheless, she arrived at Oxford University via Beech Lawn Tutorial College at the age of sixteen – or did she? Uncharitable souls suggest that a couple of years have been forgotten in a carpet bag and left in a station somewhere along the line. She is thirty-two, for her twenty-first birthday party was certainly in 1974, but friends from Oxford remember that she was eighteen when she arrived at St Anne's. Sally Emerson, an editor of the university magazine *Isis* and occupant of the room above, is quite sure of the fact. I put the point to Tina Brown, who conceded, 'Well . . . I might have been just seventeen.'

She worked hard, went to all the 'right' parties and none of the wrong ones, and was idyllically happy at last. She had always preferred grown-ups to boys of her own age, and now her boyfriends tended to be older men, established journalists and other mentors outside university, such as Martin Amis, as well as the more vivid undergraduates like 'mad' Lord Neidpath. Her peers thought her pretty and entertaining and rather too success-ful. She had a puritan side, says one boyfriend, which extended to sex: 'She always kept her eyes tightly closed.' She never took drugs, hardly ate anything and didn't smoke or drink.

She began writing for *Isis* and revealed a considerable talent for dialogue. 'She was so pretty,' says Sally Emerson, 'so funny, young and feminine that the men she got to talk never dreamed that she would remember what they said, let alone use it against them in print.' Although she intended at that time to be a playwright, Tina Brown had already begun to exploit writing as a way of meeting interesting people. She still says that access is the best thing about journalism: 'It's why faceless millionnaires buy publications, so they can ring up Norman Mailer and ask him to dinner.'

By her own efforts and the good offices of friends, such as the journalist Auberon Waugh, she was already part of the world of Fleet Street, going up to London for *Private Eye* lunches and writing essays for her tutor on the train back. Her finals gave her a good second 'which is just right. I've got a first-rate second-class brain.'

When Tina Brown was introduced to Harry Evans in 1974 he was immediately intrigued and arranged for her to write a series from the USA, somewhat to the surprise of the *Sunday Times* Look pages editor, then the award-winning writer Ian Jack, who was to find space for them. When the pieces arrived they were the fast and funny accounts of an English girl's sexy adventures abroad, one about being goosed on the Staten Island ferry, another about a Hollywood lunch with the writer Anita Loos. When she came back to her bed-sit in London, Tina Brown asked Ian Jack to a party she was giving. Rather amused to be asked by a girl ten years his junior he went along in the spirit of doing her a favour, and was taken aback to find himself in the company of Ken Tynan, Auberon Waugh, Kingsley and Martin Amis, Clive James, Tom Stoppard and other assorted stars.

More than a passing interest was taken by the *Sunday Times* editor, so much so that when she was writing a piece on David Bowie he managed to find time out from the Thalidomide and DC10 campaigns to pen a detailed memo on the minutiae of the *Space Oddity* lyrics. It is usually taken for granted that the experienced editor played Pygmalion to the young writer, but in fact she had a great and immediate effect on him. Married to a school teacher and magistrate with three children, the editor began to suffer a sea change. The staff noted with interest that the combed-back hair was cut and brushed forward. The glasses disappeared one day and were replaced by contact lenses. New names cropped up at the morning conference – Oxford names of then little-known writers and poets such as James Fenton and Craig Raine. At about the same time the editor took to turning up at the office astride a black BMW motorcycle. The names of Dame Harold and Tina Barg were already being regularly coupled in the pages of *Private Eye:* Harold Evans's marriage was dissolved in 1978.

Soon after becoming Harry Evans's live-in partner, Tina Brown stopped working for the *Sunday Times* and took on *Tatler*. The prospect of reviving a once-distinguished magazine was attractive, and it was not lost on her that if she could make a success of it she could capitalize on the publicity and turn it into a personal triumph. She wrote many of the features herself to eke out the tiny £6000-per-issue budget. When she exploited, hilariously, a week's tour of aristocratic highland hospitality, one of her luckless subjects – Patrick Rattray, of whom she had written 'the fact that he looks as if he's climbed out of a sock is no reflection on his pedigree' – wrote to call her piece 'the worst act of betrayal since the massacre of Glencoe'. As usual when insulted or cold-shouldered as a result of something she had written, she was surprised, displayed mystification, and was greatly entertained. 'Who cares?' said a close friend and member of her staff. 'Those families were only good for one story, anyway.'

'One's betrayals here have to be rather more subtle,' she told me in New York. 'One has to be a little more careful. Here it takes three years for a beer-can millionaire to become the equivalent of the Astors. It's something that would take four generations in England. That makes New Yorkers insecure. They've got very far very fast and they want to be told that what they have achieved is worth the sweat. They do not want to be mocked for it. I can't be nearly as iconoclastic as I was at home. Also the money here is very heavy. I wouldn't want to risk getting my kneecaps shot off.'

Author Sally Quinn, married to *Washington Post* editor Ben Bradlee, considered Mr and Mrs Evans close friends until recently. The Evanses, after all, were married at the Bradlee house on Long Island, and when Harry Evans came to Washington to take over the *US News and World Report* the Bradlees threw a party for him and gave him the garden key so that he could always use their pool. So Sally Quinn was somewhat surprised to be telephoned by a reporter to ask what she thought of *Vanity Fair's* review of her latest book, *Regrets Only*. Writer Christopher Buckley labelled the book 'cliterature': further, 'a one-pound beach cutting board and suntan-lotion absorber'.

'As an experienced journalist I accept that Buckley had every right to say whatever he thought about my book,' says Sally Quinn, 'although for a book with no explicit sex, "cliterature" seems a little strong. What does sting is that Tina Brown left me to find out about it. When I had a bad review for another book, and it appeared in the *Washington Post*, the literary editor at least had the courtesy to ring me and say "Sorry, Sal. I can't do anything about it but I wanted to tell you myself." Tina didn't do that, and it made me realise I didn't know her at all.'

Sally Quinn had already asked the Evanses to her husband's sixty-fifth birthday party. She cabled to say she would find it more 'appropriate' if they didn't show up. She concludes that 'Tina's young and desperate for success, and nothing matters to her except her magazine.' To Tina Brown it must be more proof that you cannot get away in American society with what you can in London.

Tina Brown had handed in her notice at *Tatler* and was already a contributing editor to *Vanity Fair* when, on the eve of a holiday in Barbados, she was summoned to lunch in New York by Si Newhouse, chairman, and Alexander Lieberman, editorial director of Condé Nast. Having tried out an intellectual and a figure-about-town as editors of *Vanity Fair*, they recognized in Tina Brown an editor who had already taken a no-hope magazine and made it a success. They offered her the editorship immediately.

She came to New York on 1 January 1984, in the middle of one of the worst winters in memory, with a cheesecloth dress and a bikini. As the unknown editor of a failing magazine she had a rough overture in a city where you not only have to succeed but be seen to succeed. An editorial budget of $100,000 an issue was of little help, for she couldn't get the writers interested enough to work for her. She had inherited a double set of enemies, first the intellectuals, the Renata Adlers and Francine du Plessix Grays who had been alienated when the original editor was fired, then the socialites, the friends and contributors of the second editor, Leo Lerman. 'At the beginning my wan face was seen at a few cocktail parties and people would come up and say, "I hear you're *right* down the toilet." I dreaded going out, and I dreaded going home to the tacky apartment I had rented, with disgusting leopard-skin sofas. I developed some strange fantasy virus like an emotional collapse.'

She soldiered on courageously and, as the magazine slowly found its voice, she decided on a personal change of policy. 'I realized one day that New York is a matriarchal society and the way to crack it is to win over a crucial circle of power women. I noted names like Brooke Astor, Pat Buckley, Nan Kempner, Jane Herman and Annette Reed, and I went to any event which had those names on the invitation.' She also fired a lot of people. The sixty or so editorial staff teetered on the masthead like boy sailors in the rigging, frequently toppling in the battle to turn the ship around. 'She's got through Lerman's leftovers, now she's starting on her own team,' said one who fell.

She came to the magazine carrying a banner for good writing, but she has ruthlessly exercised her prerogative to chop, amputating James Fenton's piece on the fall of Saigon and pushing a major profile of Brian de Palma by Martin Amis into the small Vanities section, aptly headed 'All is Vanity, nothing is Fair!' When the piece reappeared in his collection *The Moronic Inferno*, Amis referred to it as the only piece in the book that had been badly cut when it was originally printed.

Astute as ever, Tina Brown has ensured that the magazine's new popularity will be recognized as a personal triumph: she is the only Condé Nast editor on any magazine in any country who introduces each issue in person through the medium of an editor's letter complete with a winsome photograph. The editor's letter did not begin until the magazine's success was assured.

She has an undeniable instinct for what people will talk about. She also has a sense of timing thought by her staff to be 'sort of spooky'. The profile of Benazir Bhutto by her former colleague Ian Jack was commissioned many weeks earlier than its publication nineteen days after the surprise return to Pakistan to reclaim her father's turf. The intimate portrait of the Duchess of Windsor and her way of life by her best friend Aline, Countess of Ramonones, was already in the pipeline when the Duchess died and the world press was casting about for any fresh morsel of information on the woman who had been a senile recluse for a decade. When they met, Ramonones had just completed a book about her espionage activities during the war, but had never written any kind of magazine article or social reportage. Brown suggested she should write about the Duchess and followed up with a letter explaining just how to structure the piece. The result was a revelation, the account of 'a refugee from the pages of *Women's Wear Daily* in a society of *Horse and Hound*'.

She also nurtured Dominick Dunne, now *Vanity Fair*'s star writer, who was on the run from Hollywood and at a personal and professional low point when his lesser misfortunes were capped by the murder of his actress daughter Dominique. When he met Tina Brown, he was about to attend the murder trial. She suggested he keep a diary 'and said if I wanted her to read it, she would'. The resulting piece in the magazine was compulsive reportage on the most farcical aspects of the American judiciary system.

Part of her talent as an editor is her ability and willingness to win over the advertisers. She is, says the advertising director, the quintessential salesperson. She tells how Tina Brown wowed a prestigious watch manufacturer who had, up to then, only advertised in the snob publications *Town and Country* and *Connoisseur*. 'Tell me,' he asked her, 'what's the difference between *Vanity Fair* and *Town and Country?*' '*Vanity Fair* is for the thinking rich,' said Tina Brown instantly, 'and *Town and Country* is for the stinking rich.'

An important accolade came when the ponderous *New York Times* business section announced in August 1985 that the magazine under Tina Brown's editorship was a success. The perception battle was over. 'When the *New York Times* says your business is working,' said one New Yorker, 'it's working.'

Early this year, in an apparently uncharacteristic power move, Tina Brown had a son, George Frederick. She is a delighted and adoring mother, perhaps surprisingly, for she once told a contributing editor who turned up in her office with a shrieking baby, 'Get that goddam child out of here!'

'I adore being with George,' she said, when reminded of the incident. 'I wear my epaulette of sick with pride, but it isn't going to charm anyone else. I don't believe in bringing him into my office life. Nor would I whip out a tit and feed him in the middle of the Four Seasons. It's not my style.'

Like all working mothers, she worries that she doesn't give the baby enough time. She also would like him to have an English eduaction. 'I'd drone on about Mrs Tiggywinkle because I think an English childhood is more romantic. I hate whining American children, and I would like him to have an English accent.'

George Evans was christened in an endearingly simple ceremony in early July at Quogue on Long Island, the chic new overflow from the more celebrated but overcrowded Hamptons. Chintzy inside and freshly painted, the Evans's wooden-frame house flew a Union Jack upside down from the balcony, and friends danced to a jazz band in the rain under a porch crowned with a golden American eagle. Noticeably, the friends were all working colleagues or media names. It could be that she has no time to meet anyone else – or that no one else interests her at present. The godparents were Ed Victor, the agent; Miles Chapman, *Vanity Fair*'s senior editor, and Sarah Lewis, the literary associate; James Hoge, president and publisher of the New York *Daily News*; and Shirley Clurman from the *20/20* television show. Inside, Harry Evans dandled the baby and talked to Mort Zuckerman whose editorial director of *US News and World Report* he then was. Very recently, in a move that is likely to make Tina Brown's position even cosier, he has joined Condé

Nast himself to oversee new projects. He combines the job with the vice-presidency of the publishers Weidenfeld & Nicolson.

Fifty-eight to Tina Brown's thirty-two, Harry Evans is proud that they have come through a lot together with their marriage intact. People who five years ago wanted to know why he should marry her can now be heard to wonder why she should stay with him. She has become one of the power women she cultivated so anxiously two years ago. Their friends believe that they are ideally suited and will stay together. And at the time of going to press, the baby's job is still safe.

The success of Tina Brown seems assured. Only her achievements are remembered, the rare failures forgotten – the abortive television try-outs for *Film '82*, for instance, when she could not catch the manner that looks natural on the screen. Alexander Lieberman believes that she is on the way to becoming one of the world's legendary editors. 'She's a superb co-ordinator with an extraordinary instinct for news and telling it with the vital charge a magazine should communicate. She's growing and learning all the time.'

Tina Brown says that all she wants to do for the next few years is to build up *Vanity Fair*'s circulation. Condé Nast may assume that she will want to stay an editor for the rest of her career, but her agent Ed Victor is not so sure. 'She's always been a sort of child prodigy,' he said. 'In some ways she still is. She's only thirty-two and she has still got several major careers ahead of her. I would predict that one day she will be a great novelist.'

The man who pioneered the literary hype by winning a record book advance for the instantly forgettable *The Four Hundred*, he paused to survey the prospect gleefully. 'Tina's like an empty plot of prime building land in the heart of Mayfair. As yet, not one building has gone up.'

I mentioned the notorious diaries which she plans to publish in her dotage, and in his eye there gleamed the ancient gleam of the property developer.

Sunday Times Magazine, October 1986

Mr Klein Comes Clean

'**R**IGHT now I have a whole set of ads I'm just mad for. There's a happy, healthy attitude. They're kind of warmer, more friendly. The people are smiling. You see teeth.'

Calvin Klein is thin inside his navy blazer and pleated neutral sports pants. Since his spell at America's famous drug addiction centre, Minnesota's Hazelden, he has taken up water-skiing, tennis, riding and sailing, and it shows. His body is toned and showered and his snow-white T-shirt emphasizes a sportsman's suntan. His eyes are American blue, the blue of the jeans that took him from a $25 million company to a $180 million company in a single year.

He sits loosely between a second-century Roman torso and a thirties' silver chair by Cartier, ten floors above the delivery trucks and massed clothes racks of New York's 39th Street. His muscles are relaxed, but his eyes are wary. He has not talked to a journalist in two years. 'You must not ask him any impertinent questions,' his assiduous PR, Paul Wilmot, had insisted nine months previously, when agreeing to the *Sunday Times* interview. 'There is to be no improper conversation. The subject will be fashion. You will not touch on sexual matters.'

Caution is in order, for the mystique of Calvin Klein goes far beyond the rag-trade legend of a Bronx grocer's son who became a billionaire and top name in US fashion. Success began the day he borrowed $10,000 from another grocer, Barry Schwartz, and set up his own label. Today Klein and Schwartz are still partners, but their annual retail turnover is $1.2 billion, including the $400 million represented by perfume sales. Across from the desk in an office lined with photographs of winners from his racing stable, his business colleague proudly displays a faded snap in a silver frame. It shows the two boys aged eight and nine, their arms round each other's shoulders. One of them is already noticeably more stylish than the other.

But the real drama lies in the peculiarly American story of the fashion designer whose identity has been submerged and lost in illusion. Only in the United States, it seems, is individuality so fluid and vulnerable to image. Only in New York can you get rid of your past as easily as if you were consigning your old furniture to the attic, and begin again as if it had never existed. In finally falling for his own act, Calvin Klein is just the latest in a great US tradition, following such heroes as Elvis Presley, Jay Gatsby, Ronald Reagan, Cassius Clay and Andy Warhol.

Right from the start Calvin Klein understood that to sell clothes in their millions you have to have something to market beside garments. His name came to mean perfume and men's clothes for women – luxe peacoats, jeans, boxer shorts, satin T-shirts, a look that he says 'doesn't scream clothes' – but meanwhile he became a master of image creation. He pioneered Attitude and Lifestyle with advertising as overtly sexual as any America has seen; in many of the pictures it was rather hard to spot any clothes at all.

Until now, American fashion designers had been backroom people behind a label, but Calvin Klein appeared, larger than life, in his own advertisements. Behind the scenes, reality was keeping pace with perception. He divorced the wife he had married at twenty-two, making generous provision for her and for their daughter Marci, and his friends noticed that he suddenly looked more glamorous. Some suspected he had been to a plastic surgeon.

The late seventies and early eighties were to New York what the sixties were to Liverpool. A provocative, flamboyant nightlife of clubs and discos generated a feverish excitement, a drug of its own. Cruising this ambivalent world with a loosely knit circle of celebrity cronies including the fashion designer Halston and Giorgio di Sant'Angelo, Bianca Jagger and the Factory acolytes, Calvin Klein became a creature of the night, acquiring through the gossip columns the status and glamour of a rock star. He invented designer jeans. His apartment was borrowed for the making of *Superman*. He gave *Playboy* an interview in which he asked: 'If you have to go somewhere else for sex, then why be married?'

Then came AIDS. The first deaths of his acquaintances coincided with indications of trouble on the business front. It was soon clear that the social ground had shifted, and that his image, so carefully planned and developed, had turned into a trap. In the throes of what must have been a bitter mid-life crisis he was forced to ask himself if the 'new morality' had the power to turn him into the ultimate fashion victim. For a while he disappeared from view, and rumours proliferated. But Klein is a survivor. What he had made of himself he could remake. He rubbed out the past, rewrote his life for the second time and cast himself as the embodiment of born-again homespun values.

The new Calvin Klein appeared, extolling family tradition. 'Love . . . marriage . . . commitment. I think it is a feeling that is happening all over the country,' he told *Women's Wear Daily*. For in September 1986 Calvin Klein had come back from a business trip to Italy a married man, his wife a poised thirty-two-year-old brunette from his design studio, née Kelly Rector.

Once again, commerce kept pace with real life. He had launched his first scent, Obsession, in 1985. Not for nothing was its code name Climax. He promoted it with a blurry blue print advertisement showing three naked bodies writhing together on a sofa. Was it one woman and two men, or two women and one man? In either case it was banned by the *New York Times*. In 1988, in a change of mood that mirrored the sudden metamorphosis in his own life, his campaign for his new perfume, Eternity, projected a kind of holy trinity of heads, symbolizing the designer's new sense of priorities.

He had written his autobiography in advertisements, campaign by campaign. Only this time the world found it a little hard to accept the new chapter, to forget the wild seventies and share the celebration of simple, healthy values that Calvin Klein appeared to have discovered at the age of forty-four. If the designer's message went over the heads of a cynical media, Eternity sold and sold. The conclusion seemed to be that if, these days, there is a conflict between the designer's life and image, it is real life that must be rewritten.

Calvin Klein has junked the old apartment with its black leather bed and its two-tone minimalism. He has sold his houses in the camp enclaves of Fire Island and Key West, given up clubs and taken to charity and horse events. He has gone right off black and chrome and talks about his new feeling for wood and natural texture. He has taken a $7 million East Side Georgian town house and put in Mission furniture. He has bought a Long Island beach house on tranquil Georgica Pond with a porch and a three-hundred-year-old plank floor, where he commutes by helicopter to join his wife after the working day.

'He bought the place for $6 million and pulled it down,' says a recent visitor. 'Then he spent another $2 million building it up again, and a further million making it look truly simple with whitewash and bare floorboards. You're sitting on a sailcloth chair looking at the wall, and then in comes a butler, the image of Calvin Klein himself, dressed in full livery!'

The make-over goes deeper. In May last year, without giving so much as a single press conference, he courageously cut chemical dependency right out of his life and earned the enduring nickname of Calvin Clean.

'I had a terrible problem with Valium. All I thought was I can't go on living like that. I had to change. And there was only one way to get off it, and that was with professional help.' Under pressure from Kelly he tried to do it on his own. She scooped him off the island where he had isolated himself and checked him into Hazelden, also rehabilitation clinic to Liza Minnelli, Steve Cauthen, Kitty Dukakis and Lord Stockton. 'For over a year I've had absolutely no drink or drugs, and I'm feeling great. I'm able to enjoy the things that normal people enjoy, and it moves on to my work, my relationships, my family, everything.'

In a famous story told the length of 7th Avenue, Calvin Klein's rise began back in 1968 when an executive of a famous department store stepped out of the lift on the wrong floor and noticed a rack of his clothes. The following day the young designer wheeled the rack all the way uptown to show them to the president of Bonwit Teller, and won a $50,000 order.

'Absolutely true! I wanted those clothes to look perfect. The only way I could see that they would not be crumpled was for me to wheel this rack there myself. Much as I've tried to ease up, it still gets me crazy when someone creases a jacket. I don't see it in its proper perspective.'

He is still the anxious perfectionist in his twenty-sixth year of therapy, convinced he still has psychological needs that can only be answered by a professional. His clothes closet is a temple to clothing. His staff of five press his jackets the minute he takes them off. Each pair of jeans and sports pants are bought in two or three sizes in case his weight changes. His clothes are sponged at home and never sent to the cleaners. He still flies to London for three hours of fittings at Anderson & Sheppard, the famous Savile Row tailors who dressed Fred Astaire and Gary Cooper, and flies straight back. Once he went without checking they would be open. He arrived, it was a bank holiday and they were closed.

If his chemical dependency rose in the early eighties, sales of designer jeans were slipping. The year 1986 was marred by continual press rumours that his health was bad.

He married Kelly in the autumn – but for a while they continued to live separately, each in his or her luxury apartment. Colleagues noted that Calvin appeared to be under stress, particularly when the Wall Street crash of 1987 put paid to the sale of the company to Triangle Industries. He did not seem able to make up his mind about the direction the new collection should be taking. Her opinions were much in evidence: one staffer grumbled, 'It was as if we were designing Kelly's personal wardrobe.' The fall collection was roundly panned before Kelly left to begin work on the beach house.

'I've taken a few left turns,' admits Calvin Klein, 'and I've come back to what I love to do. My new collection is very commercial.' Barry Schwartz predicts a record year.

A preppy and athletic graduate of the Fashion Institute of Technology from Westport, Connecticut, Kelly Rector came to Calvin's studio from Ralph Lauren's in 1981. The week she flew to LA to spend time with Warren Beatty, said colleagues, was the moment she really registered with Calvin Klein for the first time. They were married in Rome, on a fabric-buying trip.

'We just thought it would be romantic to run away and get married, and come back and say hi there!' says Calvin. 'Mrs Reagan, who's a friend, fixed it for us and we were married from the ambassador's residence.' Romantic? When the couple finished work and went out to dinner, they were joined by the office team. If the impression given was that they wanted to get married secretly, that was immediately contradicted by the interviews they gave to *Women's Wear Daily* and to gossip columnist Liz Smith. But the presents Calvin gave his bride were fabulous: an apartment, a fur coat, a $50,000 hand-sewn Hermès saddle, two showjumping thoroughbreds, True Blue and Gratis, a pearl necklace from the Duchess of Windsor's collection, and the ring, inscribed by the Duke with the word 'Eternity', that lent its name to the new scent and gave the designer his first positive publicity for months.

All that is not to discount the relationship. 'Calvin really loves Kelly,' says a friend who knows both well. 'It's finally dawned on him there's a better way to live.'

But a certain gossip writer had another view. 'He loves Kelly so much, they marry, and a year later he's in such bad shape he checks into a drug clinic. I don't buy it.'

They have been New York's most handsome couple ever since their début there in January 1987 at the Council of Fashion Designers of America's gala event at the Metropolitan Museum. He wore a barathea evening suit from Anderson & Sheppard; she wore Calvin's long black silk with her hair in a chignon, and diamonds from Van Cleef and Arpels. They presented Marlene Dietrich with her Lifetime Achievement Award, but for once the famous actress was upstaged as everyone craned to see the newly-weds.

'Kelly could be a Blaine Trump or a Gayfrydd Steinberg,' says a gossip writer, naming two of America's most visibly rich matriarchs. But then Kelly spends weeks of the spring and summer away, competing in Class A competitions on the Amateur Owner Hunter circuit, travelling to cover events in Florida, Virginia, Washington and Connecticut between December and July.

They have begun inviting friends to the new house. The weekend after the death of Steve Rubell, club-owner and key figure in Klein's previous life, they had their first house party for the East Hampton Classic, one of America's most social racing events. 'It's sad. Steve won't be there,' said Calvin Klein, with deep feeling.

Neither would Andy Warhol, Jean-Michel Basquiat nor Giorgio de Sant' Angelo, to name just three of the Klein set who became casualties of the decade. For Calvin Klein's present is peopled with the ghosts of the past and the lifestyle he once made so famous. The guest list included only one name from the old days, Bianca Jagger, but the others told everything about the Kleins' new image.

They assembled for the weekend, the billionaires of the nineties, wheelers and dealers as solidly financed as most are resoundingly married. There were real estate broker Martin Raynes and his wife Patty; Jim Robinson of American Express; Edgar and Sherry Bronfman of the founding family of Seagram, the liquor company; Brian McNally, owner of talked-about New York restaurants, with his wife Ann; and *Rolling Stone* publisher Jann Wenner and his wife Jane.

'You know, I'm at a stage of my life where I don't need to prove anything,' says Calvin Klein. 'I'm just doing what I want to do, and it's a great place to be. I'm working at a feverish pace, I'm having such a good time! But my goals are no longer just geared to success. Now it's about my life, about living, about time away from work, about my wife who I love so much.'

Love. Marriage, Commitment. Normal. Having fun. Getting things into perspective. Feeling great. Having a good time.

This week Calvin Klein is in London. On Tuesday at mid-day he'll be making a personal appearance in the perfumery department of Harvey Nichols before the showing of his fall collection. He's promoting Eternity, symbol of his new-found lifestyle. He'll be creating the perception, demonstrating a happy, healthy attitude. He'll be warm, friendly. He'll be smiling. You'll see teeth.

How Andrée Saved the French from Good Taste

ANDRÉE Putman comes out into Regent Street like Maria Callas making an entrance at La Scala, Her chin is up, her Lotte Lenya face is crossed with a diagonal of hair and she holds her cigarette at arm's length as though demonstrating how to smoke. All over the world she is instantly recognisable as a Somebody, a gift that guarantees her immediate attention, a porter or a drink; out of the clogged traffic a gold taxi appears and draws up, watched open-mouthed by a knot of people who have been trying to wave down a cab for the past ten minutes.

'How did you manage that?' asks her lunch date, Richard Stewart-Liberty of the Liberty emporium dynasty, as he takes his place beside her. 'Or do golden taxis always appear just when you want them?' 'They are not *always* gold,' says Andrée Putman. 'That was English courtesy, no?'

She is the Diana Vreeland of interior design, the arbiter of French taste. Her company, Écart International, precisely re-executes designs from the early years of the century, designs which, for a variety of reasons including their unsettling nature, had disappeared without trace. And trace, spelled backwards, provided her with the name.

In its seven years the Écart agency has carried out some of the world's most exciting and publicity-catching commissions, including the apartments and salons of Karl Lagerfeld, Yves Saint Laurent, Valentino, Isabelle Adjani, Helmut Newton, the former French Minister of Culture Michel Guys, Paloma Picasso, the 'Mafia' publicity company's offices, Bergdorf Goodman, Bloomingdales, Morgan's Hotel . . . . Andrée Putman was introduced to this country by Joseph Ettedgui, and will organize for Liberty an exhibition of Écart International's masterworks, including pieces by Eileen Gray, Fortuny, Mallet-Stevens and Philippe Starck alongside her own designs for lacquer trays, ink-splash stationery and crumple print fabrics.

Her voice, a dramatic husky whisper, heavily accented, turns every remark into a pronouncement. Now the business lunch is over. It is past three o'clock and everyone agrees they don't have time for coffee. Women are picking their bags off the floor, men are flicking through their credit cards, when Andrée Putman removes her cigarette from her mouth and makes three announcements. 'A Meal.' 'Is Not a Meal.' 'Without Coffee.' Coffee is brought.

Giving food and conversation their due consideration is part of her style and her Frenchness. In an obvious way she is the epitome of tough Gallic chic, so that it is usually only in France that she is recognized as an iconoclast and a revolutionary spirit. 'Of all nationalities, the French are the most self-satisfied. You always heard "One cannot eat in England", "One cannot open one's eyes in a German apartment", "No one makes love like a Frenchman". I must tell you I *adore* all those things a good Frenchwoman is supposed not to.' Invited a few years ago to write the introduction to a book called *French Style*, she produced an essay that provoked her American editor into demanding a rewrite and remarking that it was 'the meanest thing' he had ever read about France.

The French, she says, need to be unlocked from good taste and fashion. 'Good taste, to me, is a prison of boredom. What I esteem highly are *les fautes de goût* – the stupid little pin with the best dress. The postcard that the Vicomtesse de Noailles pinned to her wall alongside her Goyas and Picassos.' She touches, on one wrist, the tin bangle given to her by a child, which jostles a lifetime's collection of ebony, brass and ivory cuffs. Nothing is too incidental to escape her eagle eye. She notices with delight a Swan Vestas matchbox, the red hubcaps on the wheels of a black car, the subtle lighting in a restaurant, the plastic shoes of a woman who passes in the street. 'I like poor art, like Le Facteur Cheval, very terrible objects made by a coal miner out of broken plates and cups. I like bizarre quilts made out of fabrics not matching. I detest rustic things, heavy provincial plates and furniture. I hate rich American women who buy ten of each dress and change their entire wardrobe by the season. And I have a great disgust for those rows of polished shoes in special cupboards – such a pompous way to live.'

Her views on fashion are radical. Her own clothes – Saint Laurent and Chanel and Azzedine Alaïa and Prisunic – she throws over a rack in her Left Bank loft. 'They are black and they are white. They mix. Solved for ever.' As much a part of the environment as furniture they should, she says, be sold in the same shops. 'I tried that in Paris in 1972. No good. Now, in London, Joseph is doing it with Pour La Maison in Sloane Street. He told me yesterday "You did it first, Andrée, but you did it too early."'

Her contempt for the purely fashionable came with the realization that inspired Écart, that distinguished work could be lost for ever just because it was too radical for the bourgeoisie of its day, and was never recorded when it was new. 'Good design is good design. It doesn't become bad design six months later. Fashion is *purgatoire*,' she growls, suffocating a Gauloise in a great black ashtray like a bathtub. 'And, like purgatory, it comes back. The uglier it is, the more you will see it, like it had to be punished once in a while.'

In the Putman philosophy there are only two kinds of good design. 'One stands outside fashion. It belongs to the eternal beauty of the classical. It may be Cycladic art but you will hear people say, 'How modern!' The other enters the hell of fashion. It is in, it is out. It may be lyrical, beautiful, but something forever stamps it with the date when it was made. For instance Gaudi, so sincere, but always 1900.'

She grew up wealthy, 'precious' and intellectually cosmopolitan. Her mother, had she belonged to another family, would have been a professional pianist. Her father was a linguist who translated Pushkin and Shakespeare. The twenty-year-old Andrée declined to spend a further four years studying music and joined instead a glossy décor and food magazine called *Féminin*, marking her independence by sealing off the two rooms where she lived next to her parents' apartment and clearing them of all but a bed, a table, a chair and a few paintings. 'It was my reaction to over-considered good taste. It was as if I had had an over-rich meal and had decided to live on carrots and herb tea.'

Today she lives in a former bottle factory on the Left Bank above her son and daughter, who are grown up and self-contained. She is in the throes of moving to a still larger, still more flexible space where she will take her own museum-worthy pieces: Sarah Bernhardt's sphinx chair, a Corbusier chaise longue, a Herbst chair, a Drian desk, a Bolide lamp. Everything is black, white or grey, a hallmark of Putman style. 'The most beautiful things are very calm. They give themselves to you little by little. A house is a shell and it should not enter into competition with what comes into the room.'

Throughout her career her taste has remained a constant. As stylist for Prisunic, the French chain store which established good modern design for the cheaper end of the market in the mid-sixties, she introduced plain white tableware, lithographs by living French artists and original metal chairs by Italian architects.

Working with creativity director Denise Fayolle, now with the Mafia advertising agency, she produced a new catalogue that revolutionized the store's image. 'Suddenly Prisunic became known for a clean and simple look,' says Michel Cultru, who left Prisunic to become head buyer for Habitat in France. 'Andrée has a very strong, strict approach which she applied without compromise. Not being part of the company was characteristic: it allowed her to be unpolitical and direct, to get exactly what she wanted.' In London, Terence Conran was one of the first to notice the Prisunic design concept and to draw it to the attention of Marks & Spencer through an interview he gave to the *Sunday Times*.

While the executives of Marks & Spencer were being flown over to Paris to take a look at Prisunic for themselves – and to return congratulating themselves on the British store's better sizing and quality without having noticed the essential stylishness of the goods they had been examining – Andrée Putman was moving on. With contacts everywhere, an inveterate party-goer with no need to earn a living, she was in danger of skating on the surface without getting involved enough to make a permanent mark and establish her design identity, strong as it already was. As a contributing editor to *L'Oeil*, the key design magazine of the sixties, she was, says a friend, 'Paris's resident dilettante, going everywhere, knowing everyone'. Social life took precedence over work, but not for very much longer. She was married to a Dutch painter, a man she describes as 'effectively paralysed in his work by having as friends most of the brilliant minds of his day'. Her days in photographic studios ended up in evenings with Ionesco or Beckett, but she says that she only came into her own with Écart, after the separation.

'My husband had given me the idea that I should die the second I escaped from him. Instead life became unbelievably exciting. Success came rather quickly.'

Like Chanel, Putman is too much of an individualist to mind being copied. 'When I see a collection of baskets like mine, or hundreds of boxes laid on a table, or white tiles with a Greek border in the bathroom, it is somewhere touching. But as time goes on there is less and less I want to collect. I am paring away.'

She is enormously receptive to people with all their quirks and eccentricities, perhaps because she sees designing a house for a client to be like painting their portrait. She is always sympathetic to craftsmen whose work she admires. She built her best-loved house, a cottage in Haute Provence with three-foot drystone walls overlooking the sea, *'tout simple'*, with the village mason. 'Once I went to see how it was going, and I said, "What about the windows?" He said, "Oh, we can fix a few if you want," and I said, "Yes, I want." And in the end it was the best-looking house.' It had to be sold during the divorce and she still misses the Proustian smell of new-mown hay, the garden where she walked barefoot and the perfect bathroom. Like Colette she has an almost physical passion for certain houses and objects.

Although her interiors always have the Putman stamp, she works strictly to the client's directives. 'Sometimes they don't say much. Karl Lagerfeld, for instance, told me only three things. He said that he wanted to be very quiet, that he has four thousand books and wanted them all within reach. And he said he wanted to come in from the rain and put his muddy boots on the sofa.'

She solved the boot problem by finding an old shop selling simple, washable cotton blankets 'all wavy and patched in grey and black, and when they ran out of grey they used yellow or red to finish. They went on the sofas.' She designed movable bookshelves 'by developing an interesting association of baked pewter paint for the verticals and grey wood for the horizontals, all on wheels to go from room to room.'

She likes a house to be 'flexible' – by which she means that spaces need not be divided and labelled as dining room, bedroom, drawing room. There is no bedroomy feeling in her own apartment, where the leather bed, loaded with lace and embroidery cushions, is divided from the sitting and eating areas only by a sheet of mosquito netting: like the ghostly bed of a sleeping princess, it has an other-worldly look to it. Every piece of furniture takes up a temporary position and may be moved at any moment. Guests who return to the Putman flat a few weeks after their first visit stand bewildered by the door as they plot their course across the wide open spaces to a new place to sit down.

'I always like to have five or six different places to eat. I take old friends to the kitchen. With my daughter or son I perch by the window and we eat off dolls' tables, looking at the view. Once in a while I would like a huge dining room, but I don't often play that particular game. What usually happens is we eat in the conservatory, and I pull up the right number of chairs, each different, which I like better than having a matching set.' At Andrée Putman's parties the food is delicious and produced in enormous quantities to feed the extra people who always come in at the last moment.

She has moved on from the francophobia of her formative years, recognizing a revival of design standards which is partly international, partly the result of imaginative people in top positions. 'Three extraordinarily distinguished men have been Minister of Culture. André Malraux followed by Giscard d'Estaing's Michel Guys and Mitterrand's Jack Lang. Monsieur Lang noticed recently that the desk lights in government administration offices were appallingly ugly and depressing. So he threw it open to competition – the winner will immediately sell several hundreds of his designs to the government.' The competition was part of the recent Paris exhibition *The Empire of the Office*, and was intended to produce an inexpensive office system for people born in the 1960s. As one of the judges, Andrée Putman helped choose the lamp designs of Sacha Ketoff and Sylvain de Buisson, both of whom have been invited to make designs for Écart.

Although she has founded Écart on the revival of early twentieth-century furniture designs, Andrée Putman is not in the least sentimental about the past. 'I have never been interested in nostalgia. You must keep design timeless. New designers are just as important to me as those of the twenties.' She says she can never remember there being so many important design events and openings as there are at the moment – 'from the smallest galleries to the Beaubourg, or in Bordeaux, Lyons or Marseilles – and all of them events of real quality'.

How, I asked her, should one live in the eighties?

She put on a pair of enormous black sunglasses and looked around the studio and its one or two glassily elegant pieces. 'Lightly, like this. Like one can pack up and go in ten minutes.'

Gianfranco Ferre Is the Nonconformist

HIS large black Mercedes blocking a tiny back street, Gianfranco Ferre is arriving for dinner at one of Milan's most famous Tuscan trattorias, the Torre di Pisa. A reception committee of maître d' and waiters rush to pull back the inconveniently small double doors for this massive, bearded man, and Signor Ferre is ushered through the rain under his chauffeur's large umbrella. He emerges from the tiny boxed entrance with relief and subsides into a shadowy corner with a wheezy sigh.

Out in the crowded kitchens, the head chef hears of his arrival. Pushing his copy of the *Corriere della Sera* to one side, he swings his feet off a chair and rubs his hands together. Signor Ferre is a man worth cooking for.

Among the diners, too, there is a small stir of appreciation. Gianfranco Ferre is one of Milan's most recognizable celebrities, seen daily in one of his three favourite restaurants or beaming on every new production from his box at La Scala. Now, as the heads turn, a stirring in the depths of his beard signals a rare, shy smile. Pushing his toitoiseshell glasses up his nose with a cigar-size finger, he glances over at the next table, where brightly clad couples noisily taste food from each other's plates.

'Copy of a second-rate copy of a Valentino,' he murmurs in his gusty, creaking voice. 'Bad-taste Milanese eating the wrong food.' It would be a mistake to take Signor Ferre for a teddy bear.

Placing a hand over his heart – covered in fine grey suiting and crisply striped black-and-white cotton – he gets down to the serious business of food. The maître d' sidles up, all anticipation, with a waiter in attendance. The menu is proffered and dismissed. Formalities over, the maître d' asks, 'What d'you want?'

Signor Ferre leans back in his chair and asks four or five questions. After due consideration, a decision is made.

'And wine?'

'I leave that to you.'

We then eat wedges of toasted bread thickly smeared with tomato and basil or liver paté, served with transparent slices of Parma ham, followed by *ribollita*, a soup of vegetables and bread that is not a soup, warmed twice and eaten at room temperature. We drink heady red wine.

'What d'you want?'

Thick asparagus, five kinds of steamed vegetables, a plate of red and green lettuces, a very small amount of pasta.

'What d'you want?'

Big slices of slightly charred tepid apple tart with a pungent, lemony ice cream. No coffee.

'Do you cook yourself?'

'What, with my three mothers in the kitchen?'

Gianfranco and his brother were brought up in a lively, cosy family villa at Legnano, a small town not twenty miles from Milan. His mother, the widow of the owner of an engineering company, and his two aunts lavished all their affections on the two little boys. Gianfranco was spoiled, adored, indulged, admired; and, as always in Lombardy, great things were expected of him. His friends trace his obsessive sense of duty and responsibility back to the influence of his mother, to whom he is still exceptionally close. When it came to homework and passing exams, she was a dragon. The young Gianfranco was a pale, shy child, an indoor boy, an exemplary student. Later, at the Milan polytechnic where he obtained his architectural degree, he distanced himself from the demonstrations, strikes and sit-ins of his radical contemporaries.

At forty-five he has never learned to drive his Mercedes, his Range Rover or the yacht in which he loves to drift across Lake Maggiore, admiring the dancing reflection of his finely restored nineteenth-century villa with its balustraded pink terraces and curling plasterwork. The house is the love of his life, full of family furniture and his antiques collections, yet he is lucky if he spends one day there a week.

He will be spending even less time there since his appointment in May as designer for Christian Dior. After his first meeting with Bernard Arnault, chairman of Christan Dior's parent company LVMH, and Béatrice Bongibault, Dior's new managing director, Gianfranco Ferre turned to his major-domo and first cousin, Rita Airaghi, and asked, 'What do you think? Is this a dream?'

The Italian designer had just been formally offered France's most illustrious and historic couture house and the most famous title in international fashion. Looking back at that moment, Ferre says, 'I'm proudest of all that Monsieur Arnault came to ask, not just to give.'

Madame Bongibault sees strong parallels between Christian Dior and Ferre. 'They share a rigorous sense of the structure of clothes and a completely modern approach.'

Ferre's capacity for work is enormous. He has been producing the couture, the fur collection, the ready-to-wear for men and women, the Oaks and Jeans collections, the recent Studio 000.1 for Marzotto, Europe's largest textile giant, eleven other lines and fifteen licensees. Four hundred points of sale throughout the world bolster an annual turnover of 520 billion lire. Bergdorf Goodman in Manhattan alone notches up a reported $1 million in his name annually.

Now his atelier will be in Paris, where he will design the couture, ready-to-wear and fur collections for Dior, while research, sketches and fabrics will be produced in Milan. He will continue all Ferre lines with the exception of the couture and his fur designs.

He never leaves the studio in the Via Spiga until 8.30 or more at night, then goes straight to a restaurant and back to his dormitory, a shoebox of a house in the Via Conservatorio. Sometimes he will tell his driver to take the road to Legnano, where he will fall asleep on his mother's sofa with his bulldog Argo, a tisane beside him in one of the gold-rimmed porcelain cups she has used for sixty years.

In a world of mighty egos and theatrical effects, Gianfranco Ferre really is different. Deeply provincial and unchanged by success, he contemplates his promotion to the world of palazzi and film stars with a shrug of his vast shoulders and a gust of laughter. One friend tells of a recent visit to New York, when, after a morning of tense interviews and important introductions, Ferre escaped from the Hotel Pierre to buy a hot dog and a large ice cream from a vendor on the street. 'Then he suddenly realized someone might photograph him. With a deep sigh he dropped the food into a trash bin and crept back into the Pierre for smoked salmon and caviar.'

Franco Raggi, renowned designer of avant garde buildings and new technological machinery, has been a friend since their days studying architecture at the Milan polytechnic. He remembers the helpless laughter with which Gianfranco greeted him one summer day when Raggi turned up for lunch aboard the boat hired by Ferre for a holiday cruise. 'He'd wanted a simple *caique*, a small sailing boat, but an associate had made the booking for him and hired the kind of boat the English call a gin palace – all chandeliers and carpets, with a huge crew and a French maid in uniform. He couldn't take it seriously.'

There is nothing of the provincial or the shrinking violet about Gianfranco Ferre's fashion. Instantly identifiable as Italian, it is clear-cut, confident, powerfully feminine. Even when he made his début fifteen years ago, it was immediately clear that Ferre had something new to offer fashion. His stark red, white, and black collections had all the drama of the Kabuki theatre. With their obi sashes with trapunto stitching, classic white shirts with exaggerated proportions of cuff or collar, precise tailoring and cross-stitching of leather into a kind of armour, his early collections were acclaimed for bringing a new sense of minimalist architecture to fashion. None the less, the comparison with architecture has never pleased the designer.

That description omits the drama and opulence of his designs – his consistent and extravagant use of fur on dresses and long evening coats, his Scarlett O'Hara silhouette for evening, the tactile richness of his taffeta raincoats. Presentations of his collections are among the most theatrical in the fashion world. Ferre has energized and modernized a kind of 1950s' Dolce Vita style, an all-out movie-star fantasy. He has recently softened his masterful tailoring with dressmaker's curves and a more sinuous line, achieving a new level of excellence.

With his latest collection, a circus of vivid animal prints and ringmaster red, he has redefined glamour as a modern attribute. He was cued to put his marker on fashion history, and Christian Dior seized the moment. Says Franco Mattioli, chairman and equal partner in Ferre's firm, whose idea it was in 1985 that Ferre should extend his formidable talents into the couture, 'If Ferre were a racehorse, this year he would win the Grand National. The shows for winter are *bellissima!* Extraordinary!' The new era has been marked with the purchase of the Palazzo Gondrand, an art nouveau monument to be immaculately renovated over the next couple of years by Marco Zanuso.

On a Monday morning at 9.30, the staff is already hard at work in the Via Spiga showrooms designed by Ferre. They are busy in the black library and video room with its steel superstructure and mobile library steps, in the designer's semicircular office with its display of eighteenth-century Japanese and English helmets, at the startling yellow abstract reception desk, and even in the luxurious washrooms downstairs, where models are changing beside the bowls of potpourri and in the cabins with their twin lavatories and bidets. In her mirrored office, Airaghi is on the telephone arranging a private dinner party for Liza Minnelli, a long-time friend and client, on the eve of her gala concert in Milan.

'I ask her, "How private can it be, with Frank Sinatra and Sammy Davis?" This dinner, Gianfranco will attend,' adds the ex-schoolteacher with just a touch of asperity. 'I usually have to push and pull!' It falls to the self-assured *directrice* to manage all the social aspects of the dealings with celebrated clients: Denise Hale, wife of a financier and former wife of Vincente Minnelli; the Patinos and the Gettys; Barbra Streisand; Princess Michael of Kent; and Milva, the Brechtian singer with long red hair, who is famous for her spectacular appearances in Italian concert halls.

'At first I just kept things going when Gianfranco was away,' says Airaghi. 'Then in '78, when Ferre presented his own label collection for Mattioli, it became a full-time job. I mean full time! Nights! Sundays! Whole weekends!'

The designer, she says, is first and foremost a realist. 'His projects are practical. He goes to work with everything in his head – market requirements, manufacturing schedules, financial limitations, development of themes, advertising. When packaging experts brought in their mock-ups for the fragrance, for instance, and he didn't like them, he took up his scissors, paper and tape and made them a model there and then.'

In the studio his apprentices show Ferre's sketches, two for each garment. One is a whirl of abstract movement, the other a blueprint with precise measurements jotted in the margin. He is one of the few couturiers who can explain, and therefore teach. A professor of clothing design at Milan's Domus Academy, he was, until Bernard Arnault's call, considering Vienna's request that he fill the famous art school's fashion teaching post recently vacated by Karl Lagerfeld.

His studio staff averages twenty-five years of age and receives arguably the most demanding of design educations available: hence the bellows of rage that occasionally echo down the black rubber corridors.

'He's very tough until you get into his method,' says Andrea Gallieri, thirty. 'He wants direction, logic, discipline.'

'The first month he lets you express yourself freely,' says Alvaro Roche, twenty-four, from Venezuela. 'Then he gets very angry. He never forgets your mistakes, but he never gives up on you. You must keep trying and trying until you can show him you've got order and proper targets.'

Ferre enters in a navy Shetland sweater pinned with his lucky gold safety pin, his arms full of fabric samples, and says with dignity, 'I do not teach how to design clothes. I explain the logical analysis required to understand how to make dresses.'

Before he met Mattioli – even before he designed accessories – Ferre spent much time travelling in India designing and advising the new fashion industry. The dazzling continent, with all its crafts, traditions and colour schemes, was a revelation to him. He says the relation between the people, the climate and the environment laid the basis of the logic that carries him from a historical appreciation of the differences between races to the ultimate refinements of the *alta moda*.

As always, it is the technique behind the vision that interests him most. He tells of the carpetmakers he watched operating on three floors of a ramshackle building, working to the rhythms of the manager's song.

'The song provides a coded set of instructions that the weavers can follow blindly, without counting their knots. Only on each floor I noticed they were making carpets of different colours. And I found that each floor of workers had a different colour interpretation for the words of the song. Typically Indian. Simple and complicated at the same time.'

Fashion's most famous epigram, Diana Vreeland's 'Pink is the navy blue of India,' has made its way into the annals of fashion literature. It was in the course of a conversation with Ferre that she made her remark, in response to his description of the Delhi railway station, with its turquoise floor and its crowds of men in khaki and beige with brilliant turbans in every shade of rose. History has failed to record Ferre's eminently realistic reply, so typical of the level-headed couturier from Lombardy.

'Naturally,' he replied, in his air-blown, leaky voice. 'Pink is the navy blue of India because it's the cheapest of all dyes.'

American *Vogue*, July 1988

Seems So Long Ago, Nancy

*E*MERGING from the downtown glitter of LA past pint-size chateaux into the low hills of Brentwood, the visitor's cab climbs west into a barricaded parkland and a maze of high-walled lanes. Here, in mansions far from the show-piece frontages of Beverly Hills, the coast's real money hides itself away. The residents of Bel Air prefer to build their porticos and colonnades discreetly, deep inside thirty feet of brick, wire and opaque foliage.

Through the electric gate the Reagans' tarmac drive rises between evergreen hedges bristling with closed circuit television cameras. In the baking parking lot four secret servicemen stand shoulder to shoulder in tight grey suiting, beefy faces indistinguishable behind reflector glasses and Burt Reynolds moustachios. Wires dangle from their ears. It is hard to make conversation with someone who is receiving intermittent commentary through an earpiece. We stand in silence. Somewhere behind the antique wood front door, Julius and Claude are already toiling over Mrs Reagan's hair and make-up, but no movement is visible through the slit windows under the functional porch. The distant racket of an electric drill from beyond the perimeter wall announces the imminent occupation of the Kirkeby mansion next door, television home of the Beverly Hillbillies, by its new owner, the entertainment mogul Jerry Perenchio.

The Reagans' is an unimpressive house by neighbouring standards, notwithstanding its price of two million five. The swimming pool is small, the grounds extend to only an acre and a half. It is hard to see where the six bathrooms can be fitted in under the single-storey brown roof, or where Mrs Reagan tucks away two live-in servants. But one of America's finest hospitals, the UCLA Medical Center, is only a five-minute ambulance ride away, and the rambling ranch-style layout of the property loosely encompasses a separate security command unit with round-the-clock staffing, multi-screen viewing wall and extra parking facilities.

The Reagans' new house was bought by a group of eighteen friends, to be leased and then bought back by Ronald Reagan on the opening of the presidential blind trust. These friends, known as Wall Management Services Inc., are a recurring feature in the Reagan fortunes. Many of them are still the early supporters, the self-made millionaires who provided the backbone of Reagan's kitchen cabinet, tyre company and car dealer presidents who once donated the Sacramento property where the Reagans built a house when he was Governor of California. Ronald Reagan will not know how rich he is until the trust is opened. He does, however, receive an annual pension of nearly $100 thousand, together with a lump sum of one million twenty-five thousand. Today the ex-President is writing his memoirs and is available to speak at your lunch club: just ring 0101 213 284 8940.

A dusty four-wheeler loaded with equipment brings the photographer's girl assistants to the parking lot just as Mrs Reagan's press representative, Lisa, emerges from the door with a clipboard. Linda and Lorraine are rangy, casual, bum-chewing blondes in sweats and jeans. The PR checks her watch.

'Herb'll be here any minute,' smiles Lorraine.

Herb Ritts arrives in a toffee-coloured Jaguar, wearing shorts and sandals.

The PR sniffs. 'He coulda worn something halfway smart,' she mutters. 'We're not going hiking, boys!'

Party complete, we trudge through the house to the patio, craning our necks to catch the corner of a bathroom matronly with Redouté rose prints, and a sliver of library in Mrs Reagan's favourite colour scheme, coral and olive. Out on the terrace Linda and Lorraine flop around on the new cream canvas chairs while the PR bristles.

Julius, the hairdresser, emerges from the house with a pleated dress on a hanger. 'She'd like to wear this,' he tells the photographer.

'Fine. Will she let us do a shot sitting on the grass?'

An ironic smile slowly spreads over Julius's face. 'I do not think so,' he murmurs softly.

'It's no big deal. But we have a few things here. I dunno if she'd want to take a look.'

Julius takes the box of sunglasses indoors, and reappears directly. 'She don' wanna wear sunglasses. She says it makes her feel too like Madonna.'

Herb Ritts is deadpan. 'Tell her she doesn't have to worry about that.'

Silence falls once more. Sprinklers freshen the sea of white petunias, security men look casual behind bushes. 'Didja bring the radio?' Herb Ritts asks Lorraine. 'I feel like a little rap music.' We glance through the drawing room windows: reproduction chairs nailed with green leather seats, a pot of orchids. Chinese coffee tables with symmetrically arranged bibelots.

Herb Ritts leans against the glass. 'Homey, isn't it?' he says. 'D'you think they have microphones out here on the patio?' The security man wears an abstracted look. He taps the earpiece of his two-way radio and tells the PR, 'Mr Reagan's limousine approaching.'

Suddenly there is movement by the French windows. Julius and Claude emerge, and hold the doors open. A brass button glints, polished court shoes tap on patio tiles, and Mrs Reagan is among us. Here is the honeyed halo of puffed-up hair, the big fragile skull like a bobbing chrysanthemum on the brittle tiny body, the swinging skirt. Her lips are set in a vulnerable smile and her eyes hold a mute-appeal, like those of a pretty animal. Her face is taut and youthful and she moves with extreme caution, like a mountaineer who fears an avalanche. Lisa makes introductions. Mrs Reagan smiles, indicates the view, responds to questions. The encounter generates no electricity. We feel neither welcome, nor unwelcome. The moment passes unmemorably.

A certain awkwardness brings us quickly to the job in hand. Sixty-six, Nancy Reagan stands primly to attention before the camera, hands clasped behind her back, like a little girl being photographed for the first time.

'Well now . . .,' she says softly. 'You won't get too close, will you? You're going to retouch, aren't you?' She laughs nervously.

Herb Ritts makes reassuring noises. He positions himself with his camera on the far side of the lawn, and takes a short run at Mrs Reagan across the grass as he shoots. Briefly, he has all of the servicemen's attention. When he reaches a radius of fifteen feet from Mrs Reagan she gives a little scream.

'Ooh! That's close!' she cries. 'Ooh!'

'How are you enjoying retirement, Mrs Reagan?'

Her eyes grow large as saucers. 'Retirement?' she asks, incredulously, in her modulated, hesitant voice. 'This isn't . . . .. I mean, if this is retirement . . . .' She laughs, a surprisingly deep laugh in another register. Life is busy: she lunches sparsely with friends such as Erlenne Sprague or Mrs Jorgensen at the Bistro Garden or

Chasen's or Jimmy's, attends designer fashion shows, sits on the Revlon board, sets up television and radio spots on the *Just Say No* programme for her drugs foundation, and goes on the lunch circuit to talk about drugs and cancer. For three years she has been collaborating with author William Novak on her autobiography, published this month by Weidenfeld & Nicolson. 'And I try to get this house fixed up. It's a little different than being in the White House. There, if you want a plumber, you can always get a plumber!'

Reports intimate that Mrs Reagan hated leaving the White House. She says, 'I put a lot of Me into that house. The last two months were terribly draining, emotionally, physically, every way. And of course we had to find a house before we left.' Her big brown eyes roll helplessly. 'Else, where would we have gone?'

It took nine flights by Air Force transport planes, thousands of man-hours and $4 million to prise the Reagans, their papers and official gifts out of Washington and into Bel Air.

Mrs Reagan is visibly eager to get the photographs over and return indoors.

Somewhere behind the French windows, Ronald Reagan is changing into cotton knits for his six o'clock exercise routine. Her man is home, and she's eager to be with him.

Briskly ushered back through the house to the parking lot, we are confronted by Mr Reagan's secure Cadillac, recognizable by its forest of antennae. The glossy bonnet encases the big '78 engine, one of the last built with the capacity to shift the extra 8000 lb of weight added by the armour-plated body, the bullet-proof petrol tank, the specially reinforced tyres that can't be shot out, the two-inch window glass. Five security men stand in a group around it. Herb Ritts cruises past them, hands full of arc lights and tripods, looking up into their faces. 'My car still here?' The front door closes quietly behind us. The security men fail to smile.

On the thirty-fourth floor of the Fox-Plaza Tower, 2121 Avenue of the Stars, in her chintzy office within the Ronald Reagan Foundation, Mrs Reagan wears a trim navy suit with short sleeves, patent belt and white collar tucked with a spotted cravat. She perches on a tiny sofa beside a glass table, clasping her hands as she remembers the bad times. 'When I think of how quiet things are in Washington now, and what we stepped into! And before that, the years when Ronnie was Governor of California were turbulent years, with hippies and rioting and burnings on the campuses.' She does not slump. She sits bolt upright. 'Then we got to the White House and there was the shooting, and my husband's cancer, and my own cancer, followed a week later by my mother's death. I didn't have time to grieve for her, because, practically as soon as the services were over, they told me the Gorbachevs were coming, and I had to get ready for that.'

Since the role of First Lady is played without power or immutable duties, image is all. Nancy Reagan has shared with Imelda Marcos the worst press a political wife can have. 'By the end of Reagan's first hundred days,' wrote journalist Julia Reed recently. 'Nancy Reagan had struck so many false notes . . . that only the attempted assassination of her husband could give her a brief reprieve.' Too early in office, she was branded as a Marie Antoinette. She is not remembered for her support of the Foster Grandparents programme, or for being the first First Lady to speak at the United Nations. She is not remembered for paying tribute to Russian religious art or for hosting a Moscow dinner that mixed the Soviet *nomenklatura* with outspoken dissidents. She is remembered for excess, for being the First Lady who spent a fortune on refurbishments and acquired a $209,000 dinner service for the White House the week President Reagan revealed that he regarded tomato ketchup as a third vegetable: who was dubbed 'First Lady of the Freebies' for her habit of borrowing designer clothing, mink coats and diamonds from the makers; whose private squabbles with the independent and fearless Raisa Gorbachev stole headlines from the peace summit; whose own daughter pointed up her shortcomings as a mother in a novel that remained on the *New York Times* bestseller list for two months.

Nancy Reagan tells her side of the story in her book, *My Turn*, a title which suggests more than a touch of retributive zest.

'For all of those eight years all kinds of things were written and said about me, and I couldn't answer! Because it wasn't right, it wasn't appropriate. And I thought after two terms of office it was really *My Turn* and I should put the record straight for my own sake, my children's sake . . .' the large brown eyes appeal for sympathy '. . . even for history's sake.'

Behind Nancy Reagan's lovely skin, cool smile and immaculate clothes, wrote Helene von Damm, the President's secretary and personnel director for twenty years, is a demanding, persistent and aloof personality. In her book *At Reagan's Side*, von Damm dubbed the First Lady a 'schemer' who, by her second term, had learned to use 'all of the weapons in her arsenal', including 'badgering the President mercilessly', toppling certain staff members out of office and using 'savvy Washington friends to act as conduits for her views to the press.'

'I wasn't a dominating First Lady in the sense that it's been said,' responds Mrs Reagan, softly. 'The wife of the President is there mainly to look after him. Nobody else will. They all have their own agendas. And that's where I stepped in.'

Mrs Reagan watched to see if the President were being over-scheduled, but her vigilance on his behalf didn't stop there. She has admitted on CBS news that she would home in on a person she considered was 'end-running Ronnie' and take a hand, beginning by warning her husband – a man, wrote Helen von Damm, 'incapable of a Machiavellian thought'. Hearts would sink as the familiar four-inch heels came tapping along the corridors of power: the First Lady would glance in, scold over untidy piles of papers and order the putting to rights of misplaced chairs or dirty ashtrays. In the White House she instigated new routines such as 'test dinners' for banquets. The highly qualified staff, men and women at the peak of their professions, would be required to go through their paces twice, so that she could sample each elaborate course in advance. Today she still persists, 'We caught a lot of mistakes that way – tastes that were wrong, wrong presentations.'

The Reagans' own daughter Patti, who dedicated her 1986 fictionalized account of a President's family life to 'all Vietnam vets', tellingly portrayed the home front of a First Lady whose maternal impulses were frequently expressed in two questions: 'Can we please change the subject?' and 'How can you do this to your father?' Walking past the window displays in Tiffany's one afternoon, the fictional Elizabeth, heavily into women's lib and campus demos, is given pause by her mother's pronouncement, 'Someday you'll be married and your husband will buy you lovely things like this.'

Nancy Reagan's predicament was to be a small town woman with small town values, a bit-part player thrust into the fierce scrutiny of the leading role. Nothing in the eight years of her husband's Governorship of California had prepared her for the White House.

'I never thought the things that were said about me would be said about me, ever. That whole thing of refurbishing the White House . . . it never occurred to me that it was a PR situation. I was the most politically naïve person.' Opposed, she resorted to small town retaliations: public snubs, dropping names from invitation lists, sending people to Coventry. World events took shape on her doorstep and left her unmoved. The tide of human affairs swept over her and left her priorities intact. She once said, 'If Ronnie sold ball-bearings, I'd hustle ball-bearings,' and her view of her position as First Lady was no different from that of any corporation boss's wife. 'I enjoyed planning state dinners, working with the chef and deciding on the tables and the flowers. But, again, your main job is the President. Nobody knows him better than you do.' Eager to fulfil the role of President's wife as it might have been defined by a fifties' woman's weekly, she couldn't wait to redecorate the White House, to set immaculate standards of appearance and ambience, and always to support her husband in all he had to do. And her appearance always was immaculate. She adopted the little bright dress or suit, favouring the stars of the American couture by turn, and demanding from each the same youthful, understated silhouette; the trim buckled waist, the round neck to frame a glittering necklace, the jaunty pleated skirt just covering the knees. She endorsed Reagan red so that distant figures in big rooms would know the moment she had entered beside her husband. She maximized the formality of each occasion, restoring the gilded frame of the presidential formality that predecessors had taken down a notch. New York and Washington followed suit. It was the decade of fast money and excess – Reagan excess.

The President's eldest son by his first marriage, Michael Reagan, once said his father would not have reached the White House but for Mrs Reagan, and when, disenchanted by four tough years in office, she wanted the President to step down, he wavered.

'I wasn't so keen about another term. My husband was. It was a matter of persuading me, and because he felt so strongly about it I went along. He had to convince me. And as it turned out, he was right. The summits came about during the second term. But,' she laughs, 'I've always believed if you have an unhappy husband you have an unhappy marriage.'

The daughter of a New Jersey car salesman who abandoned his family when she was born, she was brought up by an uncle and aunt, moved to Hollywood and took minor roles in eleven forgettable movies. She frequently says, 'My life began when I married Ronnie,' and nothing she has ever known has been so important.

When she speaks of her children, her years in office, her book and her drugs campaign, her responses are lukewarm and limited. It is only when she speaks of her husband that real feeling breaks through, and you recognize the dynamic that motivated and ran the world's most powerful man – the disarmingly affable figure-head who left office, according to three national polls, the most popular President in US history. It is an extraordinary, exclusive relationship, for she appears to be not only a one-man woman, but a one-person woman.

In their marriage there is a publicly doting quality on both sides that can be regarded as heartlifting or gut-churning. The whole world watched Nancy Reagan at the foot of the steps to Air Force One to greet her husband on his return from the Iceland summit, jumping up and down with excitement as he came down to embrace her. As they kissed, the tip of one high-heeled shoe kicked up in ecstasy. There is the President's habit of referring to his wife as 'Mommy'. There were the love songs they sang unabashed to one another, microphones in hand. There were the President's words to the media as he left hospital after removal of a polyp, 'Nancy, are you doing anything tonight?' Recently, there was the joint televised appeal to the young to 'Just Say No to drugs'. The two senior citizens sat on a sofa holding hands like teenagers.

'I was very lucky,' says Nancy Reagan. 'I married a man who's . . .' her voice falters. 'We've always had a close marriage, and I don't think we could be any closer. I couldn't ask for anything better.'

When she talks about 30 March, 1981, the day a young man named John W. Hinckley Jr shot down President Reagan, DC police officer Thomas Delahanty and press secretary James Brady in front of a downtown Washington hotel. Mrs Reagan has to fight back tears. 'We came very close to losing . . .' she cannot finish the sentence. 'And you find yourself talking to God more than ever. You turn to anything – your friends, your religion. Somebody told me this astrologer knew it would be a bad day for Ronnie and she would have told him to stay home. So I thought, oh my gosh! maybe in the future she could tell me if he should avoid personal appearances on certain days. That's all there was behind the stories about our faith in astrology.'

The Reagans will share the rest of their lives with a permanent security staff of between thirty-five and forty, on shift duty round the clock, a prospect she regards with equanimity.

'After the shooting, I thought about the security differently than a lot of people would. If it wasn't for the secret service I wouldn't have a husband. So it doesn't bother me. I'm happy to have the protection.'

Eventually the public learned to appreciate her courage, both over her husband's shooting and over her mastectomy. Her drugs campaign and the *Just Say No* projects won her a belated popularity, although not so much nor with so little effort as Barbara Bush's throwaway remark. 'There's nothing more boring than women who fuss with their hair and feet.' Mrs Reagan's attempt to get a drugs treatment centre built in California recently ran into difficulties when the well-heeled inhabitants of Pacoima, with its shaved emerald lawns and freshly painted rancheros, rose up in arms against what they saw as a possible invasion of drug-crazed hippies. They Just said No, and Mrs Reagan has had to accept it. 'I certainly never intended to go into a community and upset them. So we won't do it.'

The press secretary puts her head around the door and brings the interview to a close with a crisp 'Your meeting, Mrs Reagan.'

Nancy Reagan smiles and rises to her feet. We follow the small trim figure past the sealed-off reception area with its desert flower arrangement and framed photographs of Reagan with Mrs Thatcher and Sister Theresa, and along the corridor to the door of the conference room, which stands ajar. Mrs Reagan pushes it open. Framed in the doorway is Ronald Reagan in a well-cut dark blue suit. His hair is a bright ginger, his cheeks are rosy, his quiff is manicured into place. He looks exactly like a waxwork. As his wife enters the room he leads the room into song. 'Happy birthday to you, happy birthday to you . . ..'

The room is full of clean-cut American youth in full song, the chunky, suntanned males and the bright, busy females of the Reagan Foundation. Mrs Reagan stands, hands stiffly by her sides, a tense smile on her lips, until the singing ends.

A little desultory clapping ends in a pause. Nancy Reagan appears to be at a loss. She smiles and smiles and looks helplessly at her husband. There is a sense of opportunity missed: the moment turns null and void. Then the ex-President rises easily to the limelight.

'Well Nancy,' says the intimate, woolly voice, and everyone cranes forward to hear. A long pause is followed by the homespun punchline. 'You've made me late for the barber!'

Loud laughter.

A secretary offers her a white-handled knife, and she turns to an iced cake placed on the conference table with cards and an enormous gift-wrapped box.

'It's a little vanity stool for her private bathroom here,' whispers the PR.

A secretary lights four lonely candles, and Mrs Reagan puffs them out. Only when she is cutting the ribbons with a pair of silver scissors does she quietly say, 'Thank you. I thought all this ended when we left the White House!'

Aides lift the chrome stool off the table, and trot backwards and forwards with paper cups of champagne. After some thought Ronald Reagan lifts his hand. 'I intend to make a toast.' Relieved, all heads turn to him. The old actor reaches out, bringing his wife to his side, and slowly raises his glass. He looks down into her eyes and allows a profound silence to fall. Then he delivers. 'Here's to you, kid.'

Everyone laughs emotionally. Nancy Reagan looks up at him, bedazzled. He drinks, encircles her tiny body with his arm and leans down to kiss her. She reaches up to him on tiptoe. She whispers 'Thank you,' and her eyes are full of tears.

Ronald Reagan has his audience in the palm of his hand. Pausing significantly again, he throws in a second reference to the barber and milks another unsteady titter from the onlookers. His wife dabs at her eyes with a polished fingernail. In a nearly normal voice she says, 'I'll see you later.' He considers, head owlishly on one side, then nods slowly three times before breaking into his most affable, crooked grin. He speaks with tremendous emphasis and a theatrical fall in his voice, dwelling a second on each word.

'Yes. I think so.'

And finally departs with the famous Reagan wave.

The timing was perfect. The room was awash with emotion.

'Only Ronnie.' says Nancy. 'Only Ronnie.'

British *Vogue*, November 1989

Karl Lagerfeld: An Empire Complex

A T 10.30 on a Monday morning, the day before the Chanel couture show, five flights above the Rue Cambon, on the atelier floor of Chanel, waves of laughter and talk indicate the presence of Karl Lagerfeld to supervise the final fittings. Behind a door marked MADEMOISELLE Privé – ghost of Coco! – one of the world's richest and most prolific couturiers sits at the centre of his court. Princess Caroline of Monaco is on his right and Chanel chairman of the board Alain Wertheimer is on his left.

The room is in a frenzy of activity, awash with trays of buttons and jewels, piles of hats and regiments of shoes. Some twenty-five members of the staff are continually turning to Karl Lagerfeld or his right-hand man, Gilles Dufour, who pushes his spectacles up his nose and says apologetically, 'Toujours party! It's no temple here.'

Behind his enigmatic sunglasses and emblematic ponytail, the designer is in mid-exposition. If all his brusque pronouncements could be collected in a book, there would be nothing left to say about clothes.

'Good taste is like a red light. Everything stops dead!' he raps out. 'There's a last-minute element in fashion you can't predict. Look at Inès. Couture head, flea-market body!'

His muse, Inès de la Fressange, looks up with a smile. The flea-market body, today, wears her current street uniform of a red velvet Chanel jacket, gaudy as a Christmas tree with chains and glitter. Otherwise, she's wearing only orange wool tights.

'Ça suffit!' he calls suddenly, and a handful of chains are removed from the neck of a navy chiffon dress paraded before his table. 'The aim is to simplify without depriving!' He indicates a small bow and white camellia instead, leans back, and warbles the refrain,' . . . always something there to remind me'.

There is nothing the inheritor of the Chanel mantle doesn't understand about parody and inversion. He only accepted Coco's empire the second time it was offered, after Alain Wertheimer tracked him to London at the end of 1982 and trapped him into a long talk one Saturday morning.

Karl Lagerfeld puts out a hand to the bespectacled young president next to him. 'I told him what I proposed to do would make people furious and take years.' What he did was thumb his nose at the Chanel legacy, sending it up with micro skirts, clanking chains and camellias dripping from hems.

'I knew he was the one,' explains Wertheimer, carefully. 'People had tried before to revive Chanel with respect. But you can't stand still, in fashion or in business.' He accepted the controversial stipulation that the German couturier would never be an in-house designer, and backed his offer with the kind of money that would keep the house going through the longest possible rough ride.

'Lacroix?' says Karl Lagerfeld, with a twist of the lips. 'That's pocket money!'

Chanel today is all understated perfection. This year the girls are olive-skinned, hardly grown, and crop-headed. 'Argentinian high-society look,' he explains to Princess Caroline. 'Like very well brought up boys. Sexless. Divine, no?'

Princess Caroline, glowing with winter sunshine, stretches her long tanned legs and laughs, shaking glossy brown hair off the shoulders of a strict little brown suit. 'Always the puritan!' she exclaims. 'He says I look best like a governess, my hair pinned back sternly. He only really likes me in the black dress I had last year, with tightly closed white collar and long buttoned sleeves.'

Suddenly Lagerfeld barks out, '*Pas comme ça!* Too naïve, too dramatic!'

He rises and circles the table to remove a cartwheel of camellias and replace it with a plain navy scarf tied at the nape. Victoire de Castellane, the newest addition to the inner circle and Gilles Dufour's niece, steps forward hurriedly and takes a Polaroid.

Princess Caroline first met Lagerfeld when she was sixteen and being photographed in his Saint Sulpice apartment. 'He's unique as a friend. He keeps you on your toes! He sends a catalogue, and you must rush and see the exhibition. His friends are continually ransacking the country to find something unusual he doesn't already know about.'

At fifty, Lagerfeld is the creative force behind three fashion empires: Chanel, Fendi furs and his own two signature collections. He understands fashion as a historian – 'Dresses are only interesting as part of everything else that's going on' – and he runs his empires like Napoleon. For Chanel, he designs the hats and shoes and jewels, designs and photographs the advertising campaign and the show programme and even writes the poem for the frontispiece, a new couture fad.

Lagerfeld's annual income is probably in excess of $4 million, and his kingdom rolls out its frontiers further each year. In addition to the apartment on the Left Bank, he lives in a cream wedding-cake villa deep in pine trees at the edge of Monaco's turquoise sea: he is a tax-free resident with two more apartments in Monte Carlo for an overflow of visitors. He is also restoring a château in Brittany, whose reconstructed formal gardens have just been planted with seven hundred old French roses. In Rome he occupies a classical stone house next to an ancient convent, full of the sound of bells. The recent addition of La Mée, a historic house near Melun, causes his old friend the florist and gardener Moulié Savart to scratch his head in bewilderment. 'It's like Fontainebleau!' he says. 'He bought it but he never goes there. How could he? He hasn't the time.'

Since Lagerfeld scattered his art deco collection to the four winds, along with his beard and monocle, and abandoned the Vienna Secession style, all these houses have been filled with eighteenth-century masterworks. He has furniture by Cressent, Delanois and Foliot, paintings by Nattier, Boucher and Rigaud. When the contingent from the Louvre spot him across the salerooms of Drouot, they draw their fingers across their throats and go back home.

Like royalty, he displays a kind of consideration that hardly belongs to the 1980s. In case he should disturb your bath or reading, a call comes through during office hours: 'Will it be convenient for M. Lagerfeld to ring you tomorrow at 6 pm?'

Seated again, he rummages in a bag at his feet and brings out one of his scrapbooks to show wallpaper samples for La Mée. These weighty drawing books, crammed with Polaroids of friends, telephone numbers and pictures torn from magazines, illustrate the way his whole life has become a collage of creative expression in decoration, design, historical research and social interaction. Now he's sketching the seating plan for his birthday dinner for Princess Caroline tomorrow.

'Stress?' he barks, as if he has never heard the word. 'Don't name it and you won't get it. You can say I'm a professional dilettante. What I enjoy about the job is the job. I recharge my batteries by doing the next job. I *burn* to work. It's my drama!'

*

The next afternoon, an hour before his show, Karl Lagerfeld eats hamburgers and fries and drinks Coca-Cola at a hidden table in the Plaza Athénée, observing with interest the progress of the prostitutes along the inner promenade.

'The quality of the hair is something else, no?'

Chivvied by Gilles Dufour, he returns backstage at the Champs-Elysées Theatre at three, pausing only to sneer at a Valentino suit in a hotel showcase. 'It's not even funny.'

With the murmur of the audience on the other side of the screens becoming ever louder, there are seventeen outfits yet to arrive. Dufour, harassed, patrols the clothes rack with a furrowed brow, looking at his watch. He gets his hair combed and sprayed by one of the hairdressers, then can be seen brushing it out again in a corner.

Lagerfeld, arm in arm with his old friends, Jacques de Bascher and Patrick Hourcade, stops to chat with Salo Paquito, the Spanish tailor, and with Colette, the dressmaker, both apprentices in the couture at the age of fifteen. Brahim, his personal secretary and driver, comes and goes with Aubusson carpets from the château and packages from the house.

The show should have started, yet the couturier remains completely relaxed. He gives brief television interviews in three languages, then settles down to discuss his childhood.

'A half hour before the show!' breathes Inès. 'You would not see this anywhere else!'

Brought up in a bleak castle outside Hamburg, the son of a canned milk manufacturer, the child compensated for his isolation by reading his way through his father's library – 'Thank God, a good one.' His mother, a Thomas Mann heroine dressed in Lanvin, requested nothing from her children but that they remain completely quiet during her three-hour daily violin practice. 'If I started to tell a story, she would get up and leave the room' he says. 'I learned to reach the punchline before she reached the door.' A tyrant in lederhosen, the ten-year-old roamed the house looting pieces of furniture and paintings for his room.

Suddenly, the drivers arrive. Two racks of clothes are rushed into the dressing room. Transformation! Gilles Dufour shouts, *'Premiers passages, s'il vous plaît,'* and everyone runs. Lagerfeld takes charge of the wedding bouquet and warns the models, *'Tranquille.'* He has absolutely no interest in nerves. Today he has already written seventeen letters, bought three chairs by André Dubreuil, been to the hairdresser, and bathed and changed at home. He wears a roomy Matsuda jacket, a white shirt with a printed collar, a gold stickpin in his tie. Just as soon as he can make his way through the crowds after the show he will be on his way with Brahim to see an exhibition of pre-war ballet design at Boulogne-Billancourt. By seven he should be back at home in time to supervise the birthday dinner.

The models line up for the opening Stravinsky music in yellow, mauve and lime, Inès in all three. The show is on.

As it ends with a roar of applause, Lagerfeld makes his triumphal progress down the catwalk looking neither over-whelmed nor over-elated.

Gilles Dufour is cross with tension. 'He is *too* casual. Just a little worry would have been becoming. Is he bored? To tell the truth, I think he is more interested in his photography these days.'

Behind blue wooden gates built for a coach-and-four, across a cobbled courtyard and under an arch, up a stone staircase flickering with scented candles and hung with tapestries, a pool of light falls on an immense desk in the recesses of an eighteenth-century study straight from a painting by François Guérin.

It is four in the morning, less than twelve hours after the show, and a man with greying, shoulder-length hair sits in freshly laundered white piqué, covering page after page with a rapid scrawl. It could be Charles-Maurice de Talleyrand writing, 'War is much too serious a thing to be left to military men' – but for the pile of envelopes addressed to Princess Claude of France, Susan Gutfreund and Marie-Hélène de Rothschild. Slowly he takes a new sheet of paper, doodles the movement of a chiffon skirt, transposes it into a wool coat and adds a hat.

Karl Lagerfeld has begun a new collection.

American *Vogue*, April 1989

Socialites Against Heroin Addiction

B Y 10 am, anguished counselling sessions are under way in the Chemical Dependency Centre's residential houses in Maida Vale and Clapham. But the only anguish over in Fulham, where a group of polished young mothers are converging on Patrizia Wigan's house, is due to a lack of parking space. Having massaged their cars into slots three or four streets away, Lady Northampton, Lucinda Stafford-Deitsch and Princess Helen zu Oettingen-Wallerstein are the earliest to enter the pink-painted playroom for the second committee meeting of Wigan's mother-and-child fashion show in aid of the CDC. A few shivering white figures animate the tennis courts of the Hurlingham Club beyond the French windows. Inside, there is a strong bouquet of dog and Nescafé.

Patrizia Wigan, Austrian designer and owner of the two children's clothes shops in the King's Road and Walton Street, dispenses mugs and perches on a child's chair, brushing glossy blonde hair off her face.

'Terrible dramas since we last met! My nanny's on holiday and I had to sack the substitute! One of my best machinists was injured by a car and won't be back until after the show! The daily's off, having a baby!'

Mary Troughton, Caroline Eckersley and the Hon Mrs David Russell arrive in an array of ski sweaters, leather pants and tight skirts, followed by Astrid Wyman, former wife of Bill. Kathy Millington-Drake, once the prettiest nurse in the famous Minnesota de-tox centre where she became engaged to the Chemical Dependency Centre's founder Tristan Millington-Drake, enters with a box of invitations. Publicist Lindy Woodhead sweeps in wearing mink, bewailing a champagne headache from the previous night's Wishing Well Ball.

'When the invitations arrived they were tiny, flimsy and

crooked,' says Kathy Millington-Drake. 'We had to begin again from scratch. I've got the raffle-tickets, too. Catch!'

Promising to be the prettiest charity event of the spring, the show is to be staged in the presence of CDC patron HRH The Duchess of York. The audience will pay £35 a seat to watch eighty children preview Patrizia Wigan's summer collection of sailor suits and smocked lawn party frocks, shepherded by a dozen mothers dressed in her new line for adults. On D-Day, 20 February, the children will enter adorably from striped bathing huts with a bobbing cloud of pink and white helium balloons beneath the ornate plasterwork and glittering chandeliers of the Savoy's Riverside Room.

'The first thing to say is that we've "walked the course" with the Duchess of York's private secretary,' says Patrizia Wigan. 'She'll arrive at 10.50 and we'll be ready to receive her in the Manhattan Room.'

'We've got to talk about seating,' says April Russell. 'Is it first come, first served, are we going to number the seats or what?'

'The mothers will have to be quick off the mark about their tickets,' says Lucinda Stafford-Deitsch. 'It's no good saying, "Yah, okay" with a week to go, and then complaining they're in the back row.' 'The grandmothers are going to be pretty irritated if they can't see their darling grandchild.'

'In case one of the children falls off the catwalk, are we insured?' asks Helen zu Oettingen-Wallerstein. 'Suppose the child is crippled for life. . . .'

The ladies arrange seating, flowers, food for the technical staff and times of fittings and rehearsals with the minimum of fuss. Mostly in their early thirties and married to bankers and stock-brokers, with a couple of well-nannied children and two homes to run, they are already experienced committee members. With-out any kind of business training, they regularly raise sums of which any businessman would be proud. In the guilt-inducing eighties these women are under peer pressure to support a charity, any charity, if they don't do a full-time job. 'It's tit for tat,' says one. 'If they've sat on a committee for you, then you're expected to do the same for them.'

As the committees proliferate, they involve the same set of people in all the big bashes of the social calendar. As the network strengthens, only weddings and coming-out dances are exempt from the charity tag.

'Remember to submit the artwork immediately. The complete dummy thing has to go to the art man soonest.'

'Because of security I just actually think. . . .'

The style-appeal of this event suggests a more fashionable cause, perhaps a new dancing school or a facilities wing for a children's hospital, for chemical dependency lags well behind cancer victims, children and animals in the benefit stakes. But for the next seven weeks these mothers will be rushing back from holidays in Antigua and Gstaad for their children to be fitted, have their hair cut, buy navy party shoes and attend rehearsals, all for anonymous victims of the drug culture.

Heir to the good works and social consciences of their mothers and grandmothers, the committee members have long supported charities such as Save the Children, the NSPCC or Amnesty International without having the slightest connection with a starving or battered child or political prisoner. This time, the object of their concern is not 'someone else' with whom they will never connect. For every member of the committee has had some sort of a brush with drug addiction.

The founder and executive director Tristan Millington-Drake gave up a fat salary at Inchcape, once the family business, to blow his returned pension contributions on the counselling course at the Mecca of addiction centres in Minnesota. 'Three out of twelve close friends at Eton ended up with serious drugs problems. You could say I'm addicted myself to addictive personalities. I find them compulsive people, extreme, attractive and of above-average intelligence no matter what the level of education has been.'

The Rt Hon Cecil Parkinson, president, and the Hon Mrs Jacob Rothschild, chairman, have seen some of their own children through treatment. Another trustee, the Earl of Stockton, head of Macmillan publishers, introduces himself at the start of every speech with, 'Hullo. I'm Alexander. I'm an alcoholic.' A close relative of Princess zu Oettingen-Wallerstein died of a brain haemorrhage following a drug-induced fall. Astrid Wyman continues to win her battle against addiction, and everyone else counts one or more friends or relatives among those who've been through treatment. One mother modelling in the show said, 'My father's an alcoholic. But no one admits it.' All know the creed: addiction's an illness, it cuts through every class, you're never cured, you can only hope to arrest the disease.

Caroline Eckersley, pretty blonde thirty-six-year-old wife of Lloyd's broker Roger, will model in the show with her children. Typically for her generation and class, her own mild encounter with drugs ended when she fell in love and married.

'Out of ten of us there were those who could take it or leave it, and those who got it badly. Two turned out to have a real problem. One's dead. The other went to prison. Debs like me couldn't wait to burst out of the mould. We flirted with modelling or the music business. We got to know the photographers and did the clubs in the evening. I tried marijuana and LSD. I took heroin once but it made me feel so terribly sick I never tried again.

'Cocaine was different. It made you feel a non-stop sociable animal. I can see why it became the City boys' drug, the one shy businessmen use.'

Her experimental phase left her with a strong sympathy for the addicted. 'If young people come to me about drugs, I hope not to put my foot down without understanding. . . . There, but for the grace of God.'

As the meeting breaks up and the ladies disentangle their coats Patrizia Wigan warns, 'Tell your nannies we don't want them sitting nicely in rows against the walls while the children run wild. That's not on!'

Three weeks later the children's fittings are held over two consecutive days in the sprigged interior of the shop in Parsons Green. The nannies are on parade. Princess Alexa Romanoff's is rather famous for her badge collection, and wears a chestful of challenging slogans proclaiming 'Born to party', 'If you're rich, I'm single' and 'Expensive but worth it'.

Gemma Cummings, shop manager, holds a sailor suit and a smocked party dress. She bends over an extremely small person in dungarees and whispers, 'Are you a girl or a boy?'

'No,' replies the child with composure. 'Tis a baby.' The nanny comes to the rescue. 'Come on, Tabs! Get that dress on!'

Ralph Rogge lies on his back on the floor, kicking and shouting. 'Put that shirt on for me, honey,' says Mrs Rogge. 'Or Mummy's going to get rather cross.' Turning to Patrizia Wigan, she adds 'Sorry – we only had half an hour's kip this afternoon.'

Given the strong links between circles of privilege and addiction, how many of these children will be candidates for chemical dependency referral in another fifteen years? How does a young person with every advantage and all the right connections become a heroin addict?

Tim, a resident of Thurston House on a suspended sentence for heroin possession and obstruction, asks himself the same question every day of his life. At twenty-seven, he is good-looking in a particularly English way, with a candid face and blue eyes. From a county background, he went to boarding school at seven and on to Stowe. His high-powered workaholic father showed his family no affection, and never joined them on holiday.

'My background meant you didn't cry, or shame and public ridicule would follow. At school people thought I was arrogant as hell, but it just hid the fact that I was terrified.'

At fourteen he would disappear into the school grounds, first to get drunk and then to smoke joints. Through a classmate's brother in London, who was a dealer, he was soon buying and selling to the school on his own account. Finally expelled, he went up to Edinburgh to cram for his A-levels, and found a full range of drugs easily available.

'I always liked getting out of it, feeling different, and now I really bought into the drug culture. I was drinking, smoking joints, taking the landlady's Valium to clear the hangovers, using cocaine for parties and acid at weekends. . . . I just wanted to party, party all the time. It was '79 and I remember sitting back and watching the music come out of the speakers like strands of spaghetti and I was just happy and life was full of laughs.'

By the time he was seventeen he was stealing from the till of the wine bar where he worked to pay for the drugs that he had come to need every day.

'Then someone came into the bar and wanted to buy eight ounces of hash. And I knew some Afghani black hash had just come in and was good stuff, so I wanted to play the middle man. I went to his flat and it was very civilized. We played backgammon and he asked me, "Would you like a line of coke?" And straight after that I said to him, "That's the weirdest coke I've ever had. It's too strong". And he said, "Oh, didn't I tell you? It's got smack in it." And within a month, I'd got a heroin habit.'

Tim was nineteen and living with a wealthy girlfriend when he learned to inject himself. When family trusts stopped their money, he started asking for advances on his salary and eventually his employer rang his parents.

'I was detoxed by our GP in my bed at home and it wasn't too terrible. Then they sent me away to our house in Portugal and Mum came to keep an eye on me. And as soon as I could, I got started on the heroin again.'

From now on, events were to repeat themselves in an ever-worsening spiral. Another year or two and he was homeless, living on the streets round Piccadilly or on remand in the Scrubs.

'Mum took me to a doctor on my twenty-second birthday, and he told me I had three months to live if I carried on the same way.' Tim is 6ft 3 in, and at that stage he weighed nine stone.

'Tried to do a cold turkey all by myself in a hotel room. Then my folks had me put in a psychiatric ward. Exiled myself to Northumberland, then spent ten hours on the train every day coming down to London to buy smack.

'Tried drinking three bottles of codeine linctus straight off instead, which cost £6 instead of £150 a day. The sugar in it made me quite fat so I looked better. I thought I could cope and I got married.'

His wife left him after seven weeks. On a suspended sentence, without family support, kicked out of a treatment centre, Tim says he hit rock bottom.

'Everything suddenly fell to bits. I was just short of killing myself. And I finally said, "Please. Just help," for the very first time. I seemed to be asking the Fellowship [Narcotics Anonymous], but I think I was really asking God.

'They gave me one more chance. Then I came here, to Thurston House, and I have now stayed clean the longest I have ever managed it since I was fourteen. It's not very long. To be precise, 104 days. Would I be prepared to spoil that record?

'Not today. No. Not today.'

Following a long day of rehearsals and a frantic finale in the Parsons Green workroom, Monday, 20 February begins at 9 am at the Savoy with the Millington-Drakes unloading boxes of programmes from the boot of their car, while eighty-four children arrive in twos and threes to throng the dressing rooms backstage. The sound system is being tested with deafening bursts of music while stylist Penny Graham organizes the children into groups. Show producer Nicholas Miller is telling the mothers, 'Relate to the children. Talk to them. Flaunt yourself only when you're out there on your own.'

Downstairs police sniffer dogs are checking out the Manhattan Room where the Duchess of York will be entertained before taking her seat for the show. Through the heavy double doors of the coffee room guests are already tucking into the Danish pastries.

Reasons for being here vary widely. Pilar von Goess, beautiful Austrian socialite whose name has frequently been linked with that of the Aga Khan, explains her connection with the cause.

'I want to start a CDC back home. The problem's enormous in Austria. You can spot the dealers hanging round school gates, offering the first three times for free. My cousin Pipi Hanover and my friend Isabel both died of an overdose.'

A man in a pinstripe suit asks, 'What's the CDC? I've taken the morning off work simply and solely to see my daughter.'

Tristan Millington-Drake stands near a board displaying photographs of Thurston House before and after restoration, fielding questions.

'I realized there was a gaping hole in the market,' he tells the man in the pinstripe suit, '. . . a need for a charitable outfit which would provide referral services, counselling and after-care at low cost or free. And a desperate need for halfway house accommodation in central London.'

To a journalist he says, 'I've a private income, yep. Put it this way, it helped. These days I'm paid a wage, but it's not a City salary by any stretch of the imagination.'

'You're a saint!' says a grandmother.

'We look for a small percentage of paying patients to subsidize those who can't. We've four paying residents at Thurston House at the moment, and we get a substantial income from the DHSS for the other seventeen.'

By 11 am the children are tidy, starched and fidgeting. The Duchess makes her entrance in a tight black leatherette suit with her long red hair tumbling over her shoulders. She takes her seat in a ripple of polite applause.

Lord Stockton, whose own children are in the show, was to have made the welcoming speech. In the event, worried by a recurring cycle of behaviour patterns, he has checked himself into treatment for a refresher course. Before he left, he prepared a video which is now screened on both sides of the catwalk. He begins in his accustomed way with, 'Hullo. I'm Alexander and I'm an alcoholic. . ... I'm sorry I can't be with you today.' He hopes that by the time the children here today have grown up 'this illness won't be the scourge it has been in the past'.

And then the music begins and the show is on. Some children burst into tears and refuse to walk out on the stage, while others, mesmerized, forget to leave it. While nannies, dressers and mothers work frantically backstage, vignettes such as 'Deauville in Springtime' and 'Bohemian Rhapsody' follow each other serenely out front. All the children assemble on-stage for the presentation of the bouquet to the Duchess as five hundred balloons float to the ceiling in a flourish of Viennese waltzes.

It takes a few days for Anthony Wigan, CDC treasurer, to work out the sums. In hard cash terms, the Wigan company spent £16,000 and the CDC contributed £4000.

'The Wigans found they had to put in more than they had

expected,' says Lindy Woodhead. 'But that £16,000 would only have bought a double page spread in *Vogue*, or paid for printing a catalogue of the new range of clothes for mothers. This way, we could count on the presence of the charity's patron, the Duchess of York, and we were able to mount a show that would cost £30,000 if we had not been given subsidized rates, discounts and donated raffle prizes.

'The point is people love to see their children on-stage, and four hundred people thought it was worth paying £35 a ticket. Patrizia Wigan is better known where it counts, and everyone had fun. That can't be bad.'

The proceeds as far as the charity was concerned were £16,000 net. The committee had hoped to do better.

A few weeks after the fashion show, residents and counsellors crowd the steps of Thurston House to say goodbye to Tim. He waves as the car pulls out from the kerb. It is driven by his wife.

As each resident leaves, he is replaced by another patient from one of the treatment centres. Kenny looks like a young Sid James, and came to heroin from a Catholic housing estate in Liverpool. Without money, it was a more savage world than Tim's. Kenny counts a dozen of his friends dead over fifteen years and repeats the sad litany of their names '. . . Mechy, Joey Baker, Chrissie Booth, Douglas Sedgewick . . . guys who put in Dicanol when they were full of cocaine, guys who were dead before they hit the floor . . . the lad who lost a leg when he nodded out on barbiturates with a cigarette in his hand, guys who lost part of their hands through hitting arteries in the fingers by mistake.' The death he doesn't talk about is that of a baby who found Methadone in her mother's open handbag on the floor of his room.

After all, it was a minor but mortifying event that brought Kenny into treatment this time. He bowed to family pressure the day after he had stood up at a PTA meeting and held the floor for forty minutes, shouting down all attempts to shut him up.

'Without drugs all the colour leaks out of your life. I've always found it easy to admit I'm an addict, but when I went into treatment and was told I was an alcoholic I couldn't cope. Because alcoholics are people roaring away on street corners, talking to traffic lights and that. And it grieves me because other people drink more than me but I'm always the one who's last at the party.

'I was in total mockery of the CDC until I got here. What do I look forward to? Taking the kids out and not having a can of beer in my hand. Not starting some argument with someone in the park. Not turning round afterwards and catching a scared look on their faces.'

The fashion show had done its job: when all the sums were done it had raised £4000 towards the costs of starting up Thurston House, £6000 towards the end-of-capital appeal and £6000 for furnishings and equipment. And everyone had fun.

Sunday Times Magazine, June 1989

Giorgio Armani: The Man Who Fell to Earth

*L*EASING a restored seventeenth-century Milanese *palazzo* for the brain-centre of his £550 million fashion empire, the great minimalist had already obliterated a large acreage of frescos, colonnades and rampant gilding with neutral panelling when he came face to face with a medium-to-good Tiepolo on the ceiling of his office. Right where there should have been laminated edge-to-edge lining boards and grey-beige resinated paper with suede finish, there was a startled naked shepherdess and a smiling rustic. After a bitter inner struggle, Giorgio Armani gave orders for a hole to be cut in the panelling.

Sitting at his huge sketching table, he casts an excoriating glance upwards. 'It's disappearing,' he says, coldly. 'Now we have got to get it restored.'

His staff believe this is Armani's one and only compromise. The sole owner and director of the company, his control is absolute and extends to every facet of his empire. None of his employees is permitted to wear dark tights, nail varnish or high heels. He stipulates the distance between clothes hangers on the rails of his 136 shops worldwide. When he gives one of his celebrity galas to launch a new boutique, he flies in the waiters' jackets, the chair covers, the tablecloths and the silver plate. He owns and operates a superb restaurant in his commercial bureau in the Palazzo Durini solely to prevent international buyers and press from leaving the offices at lunchtime.

Pausing impatiently beneath the Tiepolo in a navy polo sweater and white T-shirt, he prepares to give a minimal interview. He is fifty-four, and looks a decade less. His body is lean and hard. His lightly-tanned skin is tones darker than his aquamarine eyes or his polished silver hair. His profile is perfect.

'If the Armani jacket was the garment of the eighties, what will the garment of the nineties be?'

'Another jacket.' Silence.

'Would you agree your contribution to fashion history has been to harden women's clothes and soften men's clothes?'

'*Si.*' Silence. That seems to be that, really.

Except for the fact that the more Armani simplifies, the greater his power grows. He has turned understatement into mega-style. He is the biggest-selling European designer in the USA, which accounts for only 30 per cent of his total annual turnover. He is midway through an expansion programme which will give him a total of two hundred outlets in Japan, and make him the country's most important European fashion designer.

In Italy, through seventy-five shops, he outsells every designer but Valentino. In extenuation, Armani has explained that Valentino has cornered the market in Arab princesses. Valentino has more graciously responded that Armani and Yves Saint Laurent are the only other two designers who do not oblige women to go naked until dinnertime.

While Valentino dresses Princess Margaret, Nancy Reagan, Sally Aga Khan and Queen Noor of Jordan, Armani designs ready-to-wear for working women, the kind of working women who can afford upwards of £800 for a perfect suit, or up to £8500 for a beaded evening jacket: Diana Ross, Anjelica Huston, Lauren Hutton, Michelle Pfeiffer and Tina Turner – off-stage. He also dresses Harrison Ford, Robert de Niro, Michael Douglas, Steven Spielberg and the ultra-fashionable corps of Italian security men. The half-price Emporio Armanis are the uniform of the *paninari*, the *motorino*-riders who hang out at the Piazza San Babila.

When he started his own label in 1975, in an office a couple of feet smaller than his current bathtub, he had spent six years designing menswear for Cerruti and was already the best men's industrial tailor in the world: the Armani collar remains the *ne plus ultra* of pattern-cutting. He is one of the top international designers to have changed the face of synthetics in the eighties, developing fabrics so sophisticated that they baffle the copyists and put the designs out of reach of the mass market.

If Armani has a motto it is that elegance need not involve dressing up. Unlike other designers who count the landmarks of their development in changes to the status quo, Armani can measure his progress in a series of subtractions. He invented the power suit for women, eliminated the details, removed the structure, took out the stiffening, and made the first crumpled linen blazer. And lo, jacket-lust spread throughout the land, and women never looked quite the same again. So conclusive is

Armani's lead in this category that it sometimes seems he has taken out the copyright on women's jackets.

What had begun to happen to women noisily in the sixties finally happened quite quietly in the eighties. Their relationship to men changed as a result of self-analysis, economics and rejection of rigid social structures. Each fashion collection required a redefinition of what women had become.

While most couturiers were grappling with these problems, Armani simply took for granted that working women needed a parallel to men's suits, a dignified and readily accepted way to dress that didn't require complicated decisions at 7.30 in the morning. The whole Armani mystique begins at that point.

In a world of extremes his women's style can be criticized as bland, and because Armani treads quietly, he may never become the legend he says he wants to be. But if he is a modern designer in a way the others are not, it is because an Armani woman is an objective conception, not subjective. A woman in a YSL suit is a woman in a YSL suit, but a woman dressed by Armani is a confident, capable woman at a desk, in a restaurant, on the telephone, seen at moments in her life when she is not thinking about herself.

Asked to comment last year on the number of mature American matrons shoe-horned into Lacroix mini-poufs for the opening of the Armani boutique on Rodeo Drive, Armani swallowed and managed a fairly diplomatic: 'Women can follow fashion too closely.' He says, 'I design for women who are content not to overstate their importance in the world or pose as princesses or ball-breakers.'

Before every show Armani collects his models together and gives them a tongue-lashing. 'I tell them to remember that the audience is not there to sleep with them. I tell them the point is the clothes. I tell them not to walk in a sexy way.'

'Do they obey you?'

'All except for Dalma.'

Armani suddenly places one hand on his hip, throws out his other arm like the spout of a teapot, and parodies the famous model's voluptuous, pneumatic walk by bouncing and swivelling in his chair, laughing loudly.

Since the death in 1985 of his intimate friend and business partner, Sergio Galeotti, Armani has not laughed a great deal. In those five years he has become one of the world's most generous contributors to funds for AIDS research. Galeotti, whose bellhop grin beams out of a number of heavy silver frames in Armani's

apartment, used to tease him out of his moods, telling him;
'You're young, you're beautiful, you're rich. What else do you
want?' Back when the thirty-eight-year-old Armani was just a
freelance designer, it was the ambitious twenty-seven-year-old
architectural draughtsman who boosted his confidence and persuaded him, a few years later, to form his own company on
$10,000. The Galeotti decade saw the company establish itself as
the best-known commercial label in Italy, so that after his death
there was intense speculation, both inside and outside the
company, about the future. Could Armani carry on alone without
the commercial navigation and merchandising skills of his
partner? As it turns out, the answer was a resounding yes. With
his private life in ruins, Armani reorganized his business, took the
financial reins into his own hands and taught himself everything
he needed to know about business management in the course of
a single year.

Although he says that living alone is the hardest thing he has
learnt, these days Armani does just that in his immense two-
storey apartment at the centre of the *palazzo*, its balcony facing
the back of the Accademia di Brera over the structural black lines
of his steel gazebo. If his evenings are empty, his daytime world
is one of constant companionship, a time when he is perpetually
surrounded by familiar faces. He prefers to work with people he
knows well. He likes to employ his relations. His capable sister,
Rosanna, is president of the Italian press office; his bright niece,
Silvana, responsible for the styling of the women's division of the
younger and lower-priced Emporio Armani. In common with
more pronounced and famous recluses, he only moves out of his
lair when accompanied by his team. 'I am terrified of being alone,'
he admits. 'Even in the afternoon I put on all the lights, switch
on any programme on the television.'

At the weekend, when Milan is empty as the Gobi Desert, he
travels to one of his three holiday houses. At this time of year it
is usually the autumnal, shuttered pink villa on the river Po in
Broni, with its set of new bicycles for visitors. In the summer it
might be Forte dei Marmi, built as an English country house by
the sea, or the futuristic poolside cement and glass of Pantelleria,
set in volcanic coastal hillsides in the south of Sicily and ready-
supplied with ten water-scooters.

It doesn't make much difference where it is. The interior setting
of neutral walls, wooden floors and geometric lamps is uniform.
So is the cast of characters from the company, a regular coterie
from the Borgonuovo and the Durini supplemented by the

occasional saleswoman. She will be singled out for reward at the gruelling sessions when Armani interrogates his commercial director, Pino Brusone, on the month's sales records, shop by shop.

'Since Sergio's death,' says Gabriella Forte, vice-president of the Armani corporation, 'it has become impossible to separate the living human being from the business.'

There are so many legends about Armani's perfectionism, his remoteness from ordinary life and obsession with detail and hygiene that it is hard to separate the apocryphal from fact. It is not true, for instance, that he works in surgical rubber gloves and will never shake hands. It is true that in his clinical, tiled kitchen every glass, knife, fork and spoon is seal-wrapped. It is true that his five beloved cats eat their dinner off plates set down on freshly laundered, white linen napkins. It is true that Armani, like the Queen, never handles money: for the last twenty years his bodyguards have always carried the cash.

'But Giorgio is growing up,' says Gabriella Forte. She noted to her surprise that the last time they ate together in a restaurant, Armani actually opened up his wallet, produced a card and signed for the bill. 'He is very proud of his credit cards, and I notice when he goes abroad he now takes responsibility for his passport.'

It is a paradox that the man who has done so much for worldly women should live at such a distance from the everyday.

'Sergio protected me from everything,' explains Armani. 'The outside world was like a foreign country to me. I was allowed to be a designer. Then he died, and I had to confront many problems. I had to defend myself from my lawyers, deal with the press, get to know the people who worked for me. There are so many aspects of the business to take care of that now I feel more like a manager.'

Armani's insecurities were always clear to those who adored him. He grew up in wartime, an unnaturally tidy child plagued by a recurring nightmare after being slightly injured by an exploding grenade. His father was the transport manager of a company in the dull industrial town of Piacenza, eighty kilometres from Milan. All three children yearned for escape and glamour. His sister Rosanna became a model. His brother, now something of an invalid, worked for La Rinescente, the big department store where Armani served his own fashion apprenticeship after army service and two years of medical school.

Although he says he has lost confidence in the future and long-term strategies no longer interest him, he remains too much of a realist and businessman to be believed. The management and maintenance of Planet Armani need constant tinkering, and there is only one captain. Taking on the forward programming that was once Galeotti's province, he is enormously concerned about the Japanese expansion, the new boutique in Paris, and the twenty-three licences for which he designs each item personally instead of delegating in the manner of most fashion barons.

'Giorgio Armani's point of view has produced an enormously successful formula,' says Gabriella Forte. 'Because every decision goes back to him, the image has a clarity that transcends what you think of it. What I am doing today I do only because he thought about it five years ago.'

Besieged by pressures, the designer who feels more like a manager displays a certain intransigence when the untidy world fails to fall in with his code. In particular he tends to treat fashion editors much as he would his junior members of staff. He has banned the press for giving more space to the sensational than the wearable. The British fashion contingent recently complained of Armani's aggressive PR system when they were invited to dinner with him on the same evening as the gala night wind-up to the Milan shows at La Scala.

'His press lady wept on the phone and told us if we didn't forgo the gala Armani would take it as a personal snub,' says one fashion editor. 'So we all cancelled the opera and went to the restaurant. And Armani didn't show. Later we found out where he was – at La Scala!'

His staff are slaves to his charisma and even a little in love with him, but his brusque management undoubtedly adds zip to their performance. One member has compared his pre-collection manner to a rape of the entire staff.

'We have to pass a new test every day,' says one executive. 'When it gets tense, we watch out. If his eyelids start to redden, we know we have reached boiling point.'

'I am not difficult,' says Armani, with some surprise. 'But I am very direct. I now have a meeting. Goodbye.'

Upstairs in Armani's apartment a few hours later, the two Filipino cooks are clearing away the spiceless pasta dinner and hooking the canvas cat-baffler across the spotless kitchen counter. They take the lift downstairs and follow the last members of staff through the side door into the Via Borgonuovo. A hush descends on the great grey monument. For the next ten hours only Armani and his bodyguard Massimo will have access to the thirty-five enormous rooms and park-like garden.

Several hundred yards of corridor from where Massimo peruses his *Corriere della Sera*, dusty shoes up on the bare desk, the designer is pulling himself out of his private swimming pool and wrapping himself in a freshly laundered dressing gown. The pool is neither wide, nor deep, nor blue. A narrow alley of transparent water nowhere deeper than three feet, it is the minimum requirement for fifteen lengths of stately breaststroke.

Letting himself out of a camouflaged door, Armani steps through a wall of screens and emerges on the catwalk of his fashion theatre. He crosses the arena and climbs the central aisle between the seats, receding into the distance towards the private lift that will carry him silently up to his pictureless and plantless apartment.

The fashion theatre is the size of five tennis courts, with 250 seats in specially designed quilted cotton covers banked around the sub-lit catwalk. Wherever an Armani fashion show is staged, in Honolulu, New York or Osaka, his team begin by building an identical theatre and start the countdown from the arrival of the air-freight containers carrying the building blocks. For Armani's world is airtight.

Yet, at this time of night, the *palazzo* seems to reassert itself against the neutral tide of modernism. The shadowless, bland room is ghostly with the presence of former occupants, the spoiled children of billionaire industrialists. This was once their play-room, where on rainy days they took it in turns to play driver and passengers, sitting in a child-size train as it chugged on winding tracks through a papier mâché world of its own and under a painted bridge into its own bright station. The children's fantasy was complete, too. But Armani's is bigger. It spans the world.

Sunday Times Magazine, February 1990

Patricia Kluge: Hey, Big Spender!

*I*T was fall 1985 and élite America was in the grip of English frenzy. All Washington schemed and jostled for an invitation to meet Prince Charles and his cover-girl princess on her first trip to the USA to open the spectacular National Gallery exhibition, *Treasure Houses of Britain*. Chintz ran riot over Manhattan duplexes, lofts were submerged in library veneer, and for a week or two a cut-glass English accent got you anywhere.

Down in the social hot-bed of Palm Beach, Florida, where the couple were to make their grand finale, a burst of royal fever sent committee members spiralling into overdrive. Would Prince Charles want to eat English, American or vegetarian food? Should the national anthem be played when they arrived or when they left? And, most important of all, who would sit next to Prince Charles at the $50,000-a-ticket charity ball?

In the end, there wasn't really any doubt. It had to be the decorative thirty-seven-year-old English co-chairwoman Patricia Kluge (pronounced 'Kloogy'), a gracious and refined addition to Palm Beach ladies' luncheons and dress-up dinners since her spectacular marriage to the brand-new billionaire, septuagenarian John Kluge.

And then the British tabloids, previewing the royal progress, hit on Patricia Kluge's past. Within days it was all over Florida that the wife of the second richest man in America was none other than London's Patricia Rose, Soho stripper, belly-dancer and cover girl for a soft-porn mag.

Although Patricia Kluge had never hidden her feather-and-tassel days, she had not broadcast them either. So it was not until the Florida matrons read the lavishly illustrated newspaper stories – 'Di's Porn Queen Hostess' – that they knew. By general accord, the plug was pulled. The Kluges' packed engagement diary emptied overnight. Suddenly, Patricia couldn't reach anyone on the phone. For the eager hostess and generous benefactress of a score of worthy local causes, it was a cruel blow. She resigned as chairwoman and announced that, after all, she and her husband would be travelling on the night of the party. Local society doyenne Mary Sandford voiced the typical Palm Beach reaction: 'Why they asked her, I don't know. I was horrified!'

Prince Charles responded with a warmth that was immeasurably to increase Mrs Kluge's respect for the English royals, when he wrote immediately after the ball to say he didn't know what all the fuss was about, but that he was sorry to have missed meeting her. Patricia would take him up on that off the coast of Majorca two years later.

From that day she was to grow more and more contemptuous of local hierarchies, while her desire to be counted among the familiars of the royal family increased in due proportion. Following an action-packed three years in Virginia, New York and the Mediterranean, the Kluge story is about to burst on British audiences with the acquisition of a springboard into a brilliant Scottish social life. The purchase of a traditional Scottish Highland sporting estate, the £7.2 million Mar Lodge, will provide the Kluges with 75,000 acres of ancient deer forest, four hundred 'walking up' grouse a season and a house that was built by Queen Victoria for her granddaughter. But perhaps the property's most interesting aspect is that it is situated not a million miles from Balmoral. In fact it is barely ten miles down the salmon-rich Dee, or eight minutes by chauffeur-driven Bentley.

Currently the history and documentation of Mar are being thoroughly investigated as a prelude to painstaking renovation, but Mrs Kluge is hardly without a roof. Besides the Manhattan triplex there is the sparkling new forty-five-room Georgian-style residence gorgeously executed by a top American architect and designer, David Easton, a stately mansion set in a landscaped park and verdant 12,000-acre estate near Charlottesville, Virginia. On completion of the house with its eighteen-hole golf course, tournament croquet lawn, pool, helicopter pad and five artificial lakes, its housing for live-in members of the 120 staff, its projection room, visitors' bungalow, basement disco, its stables and carriage museum and amphorae gallery, its orchid house, formal and cutting gardens, its farms and new Arab stud, its cow barns with brass chandeliers, and its private chapel with the painted ceiling mural depicting Mr and Mrs Kluge strolling over a Virginian landscape to hobnob with the Virgin Mary – on completion of all that, Patricia Kluge was moved to make a statement in the royal manner.

'Albemarle is a house for the ages. The idea was to establish a family seat in the English tradition, surrounded by history. What gives me and my husband the most pleasure, now it's all built, is that we are able to leave a bit of ourselves to posterity.

'Albemarle Farm is a statement to the generations of what we stood for.' Stirring words reminiscent of what William the Conqueror probably said when he parcelled up his land for the barons.

But, at the risk of striking a discordant note, what do the Kluges stand for? Could Mrs Kluge be referring to her husband's past, or hers? If to his, the estate is a monument to a self-made man whose current net fortune of $3.2 billion is second in the United States only to that of Sam Walton of Wal-Mart Stores. A matchless poker player from a penniless German immigrant family, John Kluge turned one good card, his first radio station, into the golden hand of the Metromedia Corporation, a chain of television and radio stations to which he rapidly added the Harlem Globetrotters, the Ice Capades, Frito Corn Chips and other concerns close to the heart of fun-loving America. In 1983 he put together the buy-out deal which turned it from a public company to a private one in which he now owned 94 per cent. When he rapidly liquidized the assets and sold up piecemeal – Rupert Murdoch acquiring most of the television stations as the core of the Fox network – there were many to point out that he had paid his own shareholders one-sixth of what their equity ownership in Metromedia turned out to be worth. But that's what business is all about and, ultimately, that's what puts you on a social footing with the Virgin Mary.

Or perhaps Patricia Kluge was referring to her own agility in neatly vaulting a social divide whose English equivalent would have taken four generations to bridge. For she has progressed to the ranks of American royal without losing her poise or her ingenuous ambitions, bringing her considerable talents and energies to the great New World pursuit of living well.

It was a quality notably absent from her early life in Baghdad, which turns out to be rather different from the pictures she liked to paint in early interviews, telling American reporters, 'When you lead a colonial life you really live in a land of Shangri-La, an ideal world of uniforms and tea garden parties and balls and men who looked so gorgeous.'

That is how it ought to have been. But her father, Edmund Rose, had a comparatively minor job in Iraq until the revolution, translating local maritime and commercial law. Long before then, he had walked out on his Scottish-Iraqi wife, a devout, resourceful woman who buckled to and founded a fashion business to support her daughter and two sons. According to one acquaintance, Patricia Rose's early years were spent searching for a mentor to replace her errant father, now retired and living in West Sussex. Her life was certainly marked by her mother's grim battle to make ends meet.

When Mrs Rose brought her family to London, Patricia was sixteen, full of unspecified ambitions, conscious of her charms but unsure of how they could be turned to advantage. She sulked and flounced in the dark, overcrowded flat until her exasperated mother packed her off to secretarial school. The experiment was not a success. Patricia Rose walked in and then walked right out again.

'I went in that class and I saw pale, sallow faces,' she explained in a later interview. 'And I thought to myself, "I am not like them, nor will I ever be like them" . . . I never went back.'

It was not long before she had discovered a part of London where the faces were neither pale nor sallow. She was soon to be found demonstrating belly dancing, Baghdad's most venerable and athletic discipline, in Soho's pink-lit Labyrinth Club, where one night she met her first husband, Russell Gay. A forceful father-figure, who had climbed to the top in the demanding field of soft-porn publishing, he out-manoeuvred Mrs Rose and swept her daughter off to Hampstead Register Office. The best man was the photographer and erotic film producer George Harrison Marks, who was to cast Patricia Gay in many a starring role. A frequent cover girl for Gay's raunchy rag *Knave*, her nude photograph was soon decorating a regular column of mind-expanding bedroom advice. Turning her back on her mother's exhortations, she embraced her new role without reserve or thought for the future, kicking off the Danish Sex Fair of 1970 with a memorable striptease and pioneering the wearing of see-through blouses in top international restaurants.

'Russell Gay had a very strong personality,' said Patricia Kluge in 1985. 'I fell in love with the man, and I'm the kind of woman who supports a man in every way. It's something that happened when I was very young and in love and very naïve, and I'm not ashamed of it.' She added, with disarming candour, 'I have to say it was very amusing.'

The Patricia Gay whom John Kluge met in New York in 1976, and then in London when they had both been divorced, was already two moves away from her stripper days, a doe-eyed, willowy brunette anxious to close the door on several past episodes. She had also left London as a way of resolving an affair with the second important father-figure in her life, a man of a different ilk from Russell Gay. He was a distinguished if impoverished London doctor who helped her to find her feet after her divorce. He knew about architecture, furniture and paintings. In Patricia he found a rapt and intelligent student, eager to accompany him to country auction houses and stately homes. Together, they ate their way round Paris and pounded through the Louvre.

'He wouldn't marry her, so she crossed the Atlantic,' says one acquaintance. 'There she met John. Later, after they married, she told the press she had been captivated by his mind.'

A man of some humour, John Kluge, years older and five inches shorter than Patricia, is from a hard-working German Lutheran family who arrived in Detroit when he was eight. While studying economics at Columbia on a scholarship he supplemented a less than meagre income by working three shifts in the dining hall, running a secretarial service from his room and playing poker. It is said that he accumulated $7000 before graduation.

As he turned the thousands into millions he earned a reputation for making every dollar run for its life. David Finkelstein, a partner in his former food brokerage business, told an American reporter that back in the sixties John Kluge would always leave his hat and coat in the car when they went to a restaurant, explaining, 'It's going to cost me a buck tip to give them to the hat-check girl.' 'He isn't a guy that just pisses money away, pardon my French,' adds Finkelstein.

A radical change appears to have come over the cautious tipper when he teamed up with Patricia Rose. His two former wives, a society enthusiast and a would-be actress and movie star, had done little to encourage the wealthy entrepreneur to expansive estate building.

His first exuberant gesture in that direction had been to establish a small horse farm in Virginia based around an early American log cabin with plain wooden furniture. But mention a two-bit horse farm to Patricia Kluge and she takes it into overdrive. She starts thinking in terms of a 2400-acre Arab stud, the ex-manager of the National Stud at Newmarket to run it, stables, four-in-hands, a Belgian count and his wife to run that, and seven hundred head of Simmental cattle. And lest John Kluge should feel any hint of Rosebud nostalgia coming on in his extensive San Simeon, she has built him his very own log cabin in the woods and taught the staff to call it 'Mr Kluge's bunker'.

With Patricia to prompt him, John Kluge woke up to the fruits of excess. He has a private jet and his first yacht has proved so rewarding as a luxury base for entertaining the Prince and Princess of Wales in the Mediterranean that he has already embarked on something a little less prosaic. The second boat, now under construction in Amsterdam, will be more on the scale of the Aga Khan's latest *Shergar* and the Kashoggi/Trump *Nabila*. Meanwhile the decorator David Easton commutes across the Ocean between, Mar, Amsterdam and Virginia with such frequency that he scarcely bothers to unpack. 'You look *terrible*,' is John Kluge's inevitable greeting to the weary figure who makes monthly progress reports from all fronts of the empire.

'He runs a tight ship,' says Easton. 'He will pay an immense price for a Roman bronze, but he doesn't waste a cent.' The methods which served John Kluge so well in the past – making his employees state their own aims and account for their progress, or lack of it, face to face – is one he still applies to all his dealings and even to his wife. Basically, say friends, she can have anything she wants if she can make it work. As her husband often says, 'I do understand the difference between business and waste.'

It is a point he has had to make with increasing frequency of late. For in her unbridled enthusiasm for the good things of life, Patricia Kluge has failed to notice that élite America is in the grip of a phase of self-induced guilt and conservatism in which point-scoring has less to do with the fortune you have managed to spend than the funds you have managed to raise. Persistent rumours that $40,000 worth of Kluge plants died overnight when no one remembered to turn up the conservatory heating, and that whole larders of Albemarle caviar and meat regularly go to waste, have not helped her cause.

The series of lavish Kluge entertainments commenced with a celestial Catholic wedding ceremony in St Patrick's Cathedral, New York – 'the wedding of weddings' according to the best man, David Finkelstein. The fact that in the eyes of non-Catholics the bride had already been married once and the groom twice did nothing to subdue the spectacular effects of the occasion. John Kluge's sudden conversion to Patricia's religion surprised many of his friends, not least his second wife, also a Catholic, who had never noticed that he yearned to embrace her faith. Patricia had convinced him that it never does any harm to be on good terms with the Almighty, and it was through a Catholic business associate, William Fugazy, and his sister Irene, a member of the

Sisters of Charity, that Mrs Kluge was enabled to adopt a baby boy a couple of years later.

But it was Patricia Kluge's fortieth birthday party last year that brought her closest to the role of Marie Antoinette. In a bash for three hundred and eighty at the Waldorf-Astoria that set her husband back some $1.5 million, guests headed by ex-Empress Farah of Iran, Lord and Lady Grade, Armand Hammer and the Sangsters – in whose racing interest John Kluge now owns fifty per cent – fished in a lake of caviare for ice sculptures containing bottles of Russian vodka, two orchestras played 'happy birthday' and Chanel No 5 vied with the overpowering scent of flowers that 37 florists had worked for twelve hours to arrange.

'A belly good time was had by all,' wrote Nigel Dempster. But a well-known New York socialite who attended the ball had something more pertinent to say.

'A birthday party that size is not exactly *comme il faut* these days. It was on the scale of some great charity gala, but there was no charity to benefit. There is an absurdity in carrying on as if it were the eighteenth century. No one can be absolved, not even through naïvety.'

Patricia Kluge had hit the wrong note again and offended the very people she would have liked to impress. It began to seem as if each manoeuvre up the social ladder had been orchestrated by Laurel and Hardy. Comically and almost tragically, the Kluges have come to stand for a rising crescendo of epic drawing-room disasters.

Ever since the Prince Charles débâcle at Palm Beach, Patricia Kluge had outgrown the mores of local hierarchies and now she tended to dismiss the landowners around Albemarle as she had once brusquely dismissed the class of pallid copy typists.

The leading Virginia families, who had been ready to accept the Kluges' first dinner invitation and pass judgment for the benefit of their peers, now found to their chagrin that they were pushed to one side in favour of newcomers such as Sam Sheppard and Jessica Lange, two of Albemarle's nearest neighbours, who were frequent guests.

'Today she's not going to have anyone round her table who's not good company,' says one guest. 'She simply ignored the narrow pecking order in Charlottesville society, cut right through it, with the result that a good many established families have been banished from Albemarle. That sewed the seeds of what happened later.'

Events up to now had been in a minor key, causing mainly

localised unpleasantness or mirth. But now a storm broke which shook Albemarle House to its foundations and destroyed forever its aura of a world apart, answering to nobody.

It was always Patricia Kluge's dream to do things in the English way. She had built a stately home which was authentic in every detail and organized a life which she thought could only be compared to that of English royalty. It did not seem to her complete without the sporting element so dear to aristocratic hearts. She wanted an authentic English shoot. It was this project which resulted, last March, in a summary police raid by helicopter, forty federal and state wildlife agents and two front-end-loaders.

Shooting the American way consists of obtaining a permit which specifies a small number of huntable quarries that may be taken, and then tramping through woods with a dog, killing a solitary deer or a few turkeys. The Kluge shoots were rather different. The pheasants, carefully reared from chicks, were driven in their hundreds by the beaters towards a group of trees that forced them into the air. On the far side of the trees the shooters kept up a barrage of fire on alternate guns, one being reloaded while the other was in use. To Americans, an English shoot seems like a massacre of half-tame fowl. Within the October to March hunting season Mrs Kluge conducted nine or ten shoots. It was possible to kill six hundred birds in a day. Kills of four hundred birds were normal: one participant claimed to have witnessed a kill of three hundred and sixty ducks in twenty minutes. Neighbours Jim and AnaMarie Liddell told one journalist, Frank Kuznik of *Washington Dossier*, that the constant artillery of fire was so deafening that they had temporarily to leave their house.

To run the shoot Patricia Kluge picked a master gamekeeper with a title. Sir Richard Musgrave is a generally well-liked sixty-year-old Irish baronet, rather short of cash and apt to overplay the role of a bluff Sir Anthony Absolute. It had been Musgrave's job to stock the grounds with the 10,000 pheasants and 3000 ducks, to be protected by himself and the British sidekicks he hired, Paul Shardlow, then twenty-five, and David Amos, twenty. Keeping the natural predators in check is part of the normal course of a gamekeeper's work. Musgrave took it to unprecedented lengths.

In November 1987, seven hawk carcasses tied together with sixty-one hawk talons were dumped near a gate in the adjoining territory of Fluvanna County. A few days later an anonymous letter invited the authorities to look into the rumour that predators had been 'ruthlessly destroyed'.

The tip-off led the investigators to some rather unpleasant revelations concerning local domestic animals. It turned out that neighbours had been losing their dogs since the Musgrave team had begun 'protection' measures in March 1986. Dogs had not only been vanishing. They had been turning up days later, dragging themselves home with horrific injuries.

When the police made their move, the agents immediately started to unearth a rubbish pit on the shoot land some ten miles from the Kluge house. As they dug, they discovered many more pits – some six or seven in all. The first two disgorged the rotting bodies of more than three hundred protected birds, many foxes and some dozen dogs including a beagle pumped with shot and still wearing a collar inscribed with the name of its owner, a local policeman. The agents now had more than enough proof to bring a federal case, and they abandoned their excavations on the further discovery of a horse carcass and a piano. Musgrave, Shardlow and Amos were arrested immediately.

With the revelations out in the open, neighbours swapped stories. One man, who testified at the trial, found his dog hanging by the neck in a trap, alive, but with its vocal cords cut. It had managed to stand on its hind legs for two days. Another neighbour, Courtney Peck, had been looking for his Dobermann when the dog struggled up the drive with a snare trap on its hind leg and a bullet between the eyes 'big enough you could stick a pencil in it'. He confronted Sir Richard Musgrave, who admitted in the course of a violent argument that the injuries to the dog were the work of his assistants. Amazingly, the dog survived.

Never had the Kluges been so hated as when the story appeared in the national press. It seemed they had managed to offend everyone in America – hunters who resented the importation of methods completely foreign to the United States, conservationists, greens, animal lovers, dog owners, fox hunters whose prey had been completely obliterated within the neighbourhood, and landowners across the nation who felt the affair reflected conspicuously badly on them all. Vicious mail arrived by the crate. Virginians vowed that if they ever received an invitation to Albemarle it would hit the bottom of the trash can faster than an Exocet missile.

Patricia Kluge acted fast. She hired a publicist from New York and summoned a press conference, appearing without make-up and in the simplest of white cotton shirts and jeans. She faltered through a battery of questions with many hesitations and fluffs.

'To use the word horror is not even a big enough word. But I'm so exhausted thinking about it that my vocabulary is just stopped with that. . ... You just throw your hands up in the air and just say . . . how could this possibly be? It just goes to show what can happen. . ... To think that it has gone on without us knowing has left us just frozen in our place. How *could* this happen? None of us knew.'

Throughout the trial, Musgrave, Shardlow and Amos denied that the Kluges had any knowledge of what was being done in their name.

The three gamekeepers would have found it hard to pay the fines with which the Federal court hit them. In the event the full $11,000 was paid in cash by Mrs Kluge. After further hearings connected with visa violations, the men agreed to leave the country within twenty-four hours rather than face deportation orders. Mrs Kluge paid their air fares.

Sir Richard Musgrave came home and covered his tracks. It took the *Sunday Times* forty-eight hours to locate him at a London number, from which he waxed passionate about the 'horrific way the press has treated Patricia'. Of his own part in the reason for the bad press he had less to say.

'Why on earth would anyone want to rake all that up again?' he said. 'I'll have to consult my legal adviser. I'll ring back.'

Not surprisingly, he didn't. And the following day he apparently left that address for an unknown destination.

Peter Robinson, senior investigations officer for the Royal Society for the Protection of Birds, put the affair into perspective. 'In Britain if you let a shoot for ten or a hundred thousand pounds a year, there is an awful lot of pressure on the gamekeeper to protect the pheasants. So does he let the predators take a share, or does he go outside the law under pressure from the owner?'

Robinson has a particular reason for concern in view of the Kluges' recent purchase of Mar Lodge. 'The potential for killing protected species up there is appalling. There are golden eagles, peregrine falcons, merlin and ospreys, all of them extremely vulnerable. We are anxious to be assured that the Kluges will ascertain the law of the land and make it quite clear to their employees that there are certain restrictions and these must be obeyed. We should be extremely glad to know that they will not be re-employing Sir Richard Musgrave at Mar.'

Robert Clerk is a partner in the reputable and long-established chartered surveyors Smiths Gore, the land management experts whom the Kluges have requested to take over the day-to-day running of Mar. He is happy to inform the RSPB that they have

no connection with Musgrave, Shardlow or Amos and no expecta-
tion of their being involved in the future of the property. 'Mr and
Mrs Kluge have purchased Mar as a traditional Highland sporting
estate and future management will be directed towards streng-
thening the natural assets, while promoting a variety of land uses
and wildlife habitats.'

Patricia Kluge has already stumped around the estate in
mackintosh and boots, shaking hands with the resident stalkers
and other employees, and inviting the tenants to lunch. But when
the Kluges family arrive at Mar they will still have to win the
acceptance of their neighbours, a talent which has habitually
eluded them.

Artless as ever, Patricia Kluge exhibits a candour that can only
be damaging. Remarks such as: 'Meeting the Queen would be the
greatest moment of my life,' leave her cruelly open to snubs.
When the Kluges came to the Windsor Horse Show last year at
about the time of the trial, and one of their four-in-hands won first
prize, Patricia was poised in the carriage for the big moment when
the Queen presented the award. In the event the Queen handed
the prize to the driver, whom she knew well, spoke a few words
to him and then continued on her way without so much as a
glance in the owner's direction. And when, at the same show,
Prince Philip presented the Kluges with a conservation award in
recognition of their contribution of $25,000 to the American
branch of the Nature Conservancy, the irony was not lost on the
gossip columns.

Inevitably, the news that the Kluges had bought Mar Lodge
coincided with reports that they are to be investigated as part of
a Federal case over back taxes. Whatever the benefits of Mar – and
an informal invitation from the Prince and Princess of Wales may
well follow – a good press is not likely to be one of them.

Patricia Kluge's social ambitions overshadow her likeable
qualities, her kindness; generosity and love of everything British.
'Patricia's never hurt anyone and it seems like everyone's out to
hurt her,' says David Easton. 'I guess although you can never be
too thin you can obviously be too rich in this cruel world.'

If part one of the Kluge story concluded last year with the
Federal trial, part two is only just beginning. Will the comely
Patricia carry all Scottish society before her, the past forgotten?
Will she be permitted to entertain the Queen and Prince Philip
aboard her breathtaking new yacht? Will the royals be forced to
recognize a kindred spirit? And, one glorious Highland evening
with the sun sinking in a blaze of gold behind the heather and the

bagpipes wailing, will she at last achieve her heart's desire and enter the great gates of Balmoral for dinner? Watch this space. For as long as saucy heroines, money and class remain compulsive reading, the Patricia Kluge story will be followed with all the attention it doesn't deserve.

Sunday Times Magazine, April 1989

Christian Lacroix: Fresh Blood on the rue du Faubourg Saint-Honoré

AFTERNOON in Paris, Sunday, 26 July. In the baroque salon of a swish hotel off the Place Vendôme, the world's press are assembled to witness the fashion event of the generation. Today they will report the début of the first new couture house for twenty-five years. Not since the launch of Yves Saint Laurent in 1962 have jaded fashion editors and blasé buyers sat down to await a collection in such a hubbub of excitement. At 3.25 the twelve-foot outer doors are finally locked against a frantic mob waving press credentials to which press aides remain stolidly immune. At 3.30 the chandeliers dim, the noise subsides and spotlights beam down on the scarlet runway. In an electric silence the opening announcement begins.

'Ladies and gentlemen, it is with great emotion. . . .'

In the packed dressing arena backstage, the heavy features and beetling brows of Christian Lacroix have settled into a scowl of tension as he steels himself to undergo the supreme test of his career. His future hangs in the balance of the next half-hour, together with the fate of £5 million invested in him by Financière Agache. Now the regional song of his home town, Arles, sung by choirs of convent girls, spills out into the auditorium and the show for which he has been preparing for six months is under way. Preparing to bare his soul on the floodlit crimson stage of his public confessional, he bows his head and makes the sign of the cross.

Thirty minutes later, the audience is in uproar. Cheering spectators are standing on their chairs or pelting the catwalk with the magenta and orange carnations that were placed on each press kit. Others, such as Irène Silvagni, the new fashion editor of French *Vogue*, are weeping.

Pulled on to the runway by model Marie Seznek in her finale wedding dress, a meringue of ivory silk under a winged and veiled cartwheel hat, Lacroix confronts his audience with a face that is solemn with shock.

Photographers swarm on to the catwalk. The headlines that will be flashed around the world by nightfall are already being composed. THIS IS FASHION HISTORY . . . LACROIX IMPOSES A NEW COUTURE . . . THE WORLD OF FASHION HAS A NEW STAR. Paloma Picasso is borne through the crush to call to Lacroix '*Fantastique!*' but still he looks, paradoxically, like a man with a disaster on his hands. Only when his models applaud him does he at last remember to grin.

'We've had nothing like this since Dior and Saint Laurent,' concludes *New York Times* fashion editor Bernadine Morris. 'A new star? A new *king!*'

In an earlier incarnation, the king was style director for Jean Patou, a once great landmark in Paris couture but, by 1981, a somewhat dusty name.

In five years Lacroix revamped Patou, upping the sales from thirty dresses a season to almost a hundred. He imposed a house style that was coquettish and spectacular, producing shows that shocked and then seduced. It was Lacroix who brought back the puffball skirt, the frou-frou petticoat and follies such as the purple mink mini, saying, 'Everyone had forgotten Patou, so I had to shout for attention.'

Lacroix designed his last collection for the house in January 1987. To the despair and rage of Jean de Moüy, president of Jean Patou. Lacroix had decided that in future he would be designing for the couture under his own name. Following his meeting with Bernard Arnault, president of the powerful Financière Agache, the textile conglomerate whose crown jewels are Christian Dior and Boussac, events moved fast. Only a few weeks after Arnault had signed over £5 million Lacroix found himself installed in a magnificent *hôtel particulier* opposite the President's palace with a telex machine, an assistant, a secretary and a studio co-ordinator. The salon looks out in front over a fountain set in a ring of flowers, at the back on to a garden with lawn, gravel paths and mature trees. The fly in the ointment was the split with Patou, which was rapidly turning into an ugly divorce. Patou, who had no winter collection to show this July, are currently suing Lacroix for 85 million francs for *concurrence déloyale* (unfair competition).

'We had a very strong presentiment that the climate was right for a new couture house,' says chairman and financial director Paul Audrain, running a replay of the representations which

influenced Bernard Arnault to make the investment. 'New social
and cultural trends have put the values of the 1970s into reverse.
Ten years ago my kind of personal expression was at a low point.
Everyone wanted to dress down in jeans and T-shirts, cars became
anonymous, there was little visible difference between the sexes.
All that has changed. There is a new emphasis on sexual values
and individuality. People with new money want to express their
success and there was no new couturier to capitalize on this
particular trend.'

Audrain has an equally persuasive rationale for the business
structure which should bring in profits by the end of 1988.
'Couture is the umbrella that brings legitimacy to the money-
spinning ventures then created under its name and aura. The
couture, as Christian Lacroix is brilliantly equipped to create it,
projects the dream, the drama, the big powerful fashion statement.'

The strategy already seems to be working. Before a single
garment was shown he had signed up with the Italian ready-to-
wear firm Genny for a Lacroix collection for winter 1988. The rest
of the iceberg follows in due course: The Lacroix *de luxe*, a
menswear collection, licensing deals and the opening of the
boutique on the Faubourg Saint-Honoré.

With a staff of twenty-five they are not programmed, says
marketing director Jean-Jacques Picart, to make more than a
hundred couture numbers in six months. 'Saint Laurent could do
a thousand. But because they are running four ateliers they are
losing money. The real money here will come from the ready-to-
wear.' A ready-to-wear dress will cost from £300, as compared
with a *de luxe* at £3000, or a handmade couture equivalent from
£5000. 'But even the cheapest dress will be designed by Christian
himself.'

'This is the nicest and youngest fashion house I've worked in,'
says model Diane de Witt. 'It's like a family.' The impression
given to the newcomer is that he has walked into a web of half-
understood relationships. Many of the staff have worked together
for years, joining straight from Patou in the messy aftermath of
Christian Lacroix's departure, when the denuded salon sacked
many of the remaining workers. The key partnership is between
Lacroix and Picart, who form a creative triangle with Lacroix's
scintillating live-in partner of fourteen years, Françoise Rosen-
sthiel.

Not ostensibly part of the fashion house, she nevertheless filters
much of Lacroix's style through her own critical and prejudiced

eye for design. He shows her all his sketches, just as he will not
pass a single garment until Picart has approved it. Between the
three of them flourishes a sharp and private humour. She worked
as Picart's assistant when he ran his very successful freelance
press office and through her Picart, the fashion guru and image-
maker, met Lacroix, the art history graduate with a love of the
theatre and a limitless talent for creating new ideas from well-
worn themes.

Over lunch in the garden, ten days before the show, Picart plays
court jester in striped shirt and braces, while Françoise Rosens-
thiel undercuts and parries, a cigarette between her crimson lips.
She wears, with a ragged crop and sunglasses, a huge pair of brass
earrings and a brown cotton suit.

Where do she and Lacroix live? 'In a shoe-box under a litter of
papers.' Possessions, she says, are death. Lunch began with
smoked salmon and ended with a basket of apricots and wild
strawberries, during which interval the conversation touched on
many topics and there were several shouts of smoky laughter. Was
it possible, as the continental press say, that the British royal
family really are descended from vampires? What horrible jewels
the Duchess of Windsor owned. Had we noticed that the
'demolition' school of London furniture design had its origins in
the work of Oliver Messel and Christian Bérard?

At Patou, Lacroix's clothes were snapped up by new American
money, whacky European aristocracy such as Princess von Thurn
and Taxis and by media stars such as Bette Midler, who wouldn't
naturally turn to the Paris couture. The earliest enquiries in the
new salon have come from Madonna and Paloma Picasso.

'Success won't come by social status,' says Picart in a rare
serious moment. 'When I first met Bernard Arnault I told him,
"Don't worry, the success of Christian Lacroix will not make Dior
lose money because we will attract another kind of client."'

Lacroix considers, stirring his coffee. His face is mobile and
humorous, his voice gentle. He wears a putty Ralph Lauren suit
with a green striped shirt and old brown brogues, carefully
polished. A silk handkerchief in mustard and yellow flowers in
one pocket, precisely mismatching a Paisley tie.

'I want to get back to the position where the couture becomes
a kind of laboratory for ideas, the way it was with Schiaparelli
forty years ago. The new couture should be all about theatre. One
dress for one woman for one character; you dress the actress for
the part she is to play.

'We are all in the lifestyle game now, because you have to create your own stage. So much contemporary art and design is a parody, a joke, and full of allusions to the past. It's like that because it is the end of an era, like the end of the nineteenth century. Not such a comfortable period to live in. Everything must be a kind of caricature to register, everything must be larger than life. Design now has to be on the second level.

'I am not so interested in the architecture of clothes as in the atmosphere I can create around a woman. That's why I need strong people to construct my sketches exactly as I draw them.' An important factor in the success of the venture was the acquisition of two *premiers d'ateliers* of some forty years' experience. Mario Matignon, the *tailleur*, began his apprenticeship in the business at the age of eleven, and comes to Lacroix from Yves Saint Laurent and the Vicomtesse de Ribes, Jeanine Ouvrard, the *flou*, began at thirteen and worked her way from Jacques Fath to Lanvin and Balmain.

The day of the show, the clothes begin to move to the show venue at 7 am, to be placed in rectangular clothes-racks, each bearing the name of a model. Tacked to the wall is a list of accessories for each outfit, together with photographs.

Out front the stage is being decorated with Camargue bulrushes, while a workforce including the pertly freckled and ringleted Stella McCartney, Paul's daughter, numbers the four hundred little gold chairs.

Lacroix, in his striped cotton working jacket, confers with Picart over the running order, then moves backstage to welcome the Queen of Arles and her ladies-in-waiting. These southern girls from the oldest and most respected families in Lacroix's home town are highly educated cultural ambassadors for their city. They wear their long traditional costumes with fichus and lace headdresses, gloves and fans. Lush beauties in the Victorian manner, with waxy complexions and long folded hair, they resemble Ingres portraits and present a striking contrast to the models with their bony, boyish figures and slicked-back hair.

Lacroix moves about restlessly, checking and rechecking, while television cameramen move in to film the last half hour, their lights sending up the temperature of the room until the ladies from Arles start to fan themselves. Uncertain whether they are real royals or carnival queens, the cameramen make awkward bows before asking for a picture.

Now Lacroix has no time for anyone but his models. Coiffed and made up, they are climbing into their first numbers. In their wrap-around sunglasses and three-foot hats, they have the devastating glamour of a past era. *Couture* can get no more *haute* than this.

From the far side of the panels that screen the dressing arena from the runway comes a steady roar of voices: the audience is waiting. Picart confers with a sound assistant in headphones and ushers the press to the back of the room.

Lacroix, chewing his cheek, lines the models up behind the Queen of Arles and makes a last-minute change to a hat. The sound assistant raises his arm. Suddenly everyone is saying *Ssh*. The arm drops and a great silence falls on the far side of the screen.

'Ladies and gentlemen, it is with great emotion. . . .'

The music begins and the Queen and her maids move up the steps, pass between the screens and vanish on to the catwalk, to be seated in the place of honour by Paul Audrain. Now the music changes and with it the atmosphere. Wild, hoarse cries and a stamping beat set the models dancing up the steps, fidgety as racehorses. As the show progresses, a rattle of clapping becomes sustained applause from the audience. Running between the models and a peephole in the screen, Lacroix tries to see what's going on out front.

The Lacroix collection, as promised, is pure theatre – a striped satin ballgown with the bustle in the front, a toreador cape of pink and yellow satin, a scarlet *buster* bursting into a storm of striped petticoats.

As the girls go out in their ballgowns for the finale, the clapping changes to cheers and shouts of 'Bravo!'

Backstage, the dressers and models perform an impromptu *bulerias* together, a dance of triumph.

By the time Marie makes her appearance as the bride, the applause is wall-to-wall. Reappearing, she takes Lacroix's arm and urges him onstage. He looks bewildered. Everyone rushes to take him in hand. He is pushed, pulled, pummelled, cajoled and propelled up the steps. Despairingly, a gladiator thrust into the roaring circle of spectators, he disappears around the screens and is seen no more.

Sunday Times Magazine, October 1987

The Queening of Mrs Thatcher

*L*AST summer one of Mrs Thatcher's advisers was trying to persuade her to accompany him to the Derby.

'I rahlly don't have time,' said the Prime Minister in her breathy, hooting voice. 'I don't have to do everything, surely. Can't I leave that sort of thing to the Queen?'

By her third term, the Prime Minister appeared to take it for granted that she and the Queen divide up the nation's visible circumstance equally, as befits two women of equal importance.

The appointment of a woman prime minister in the Queen's reign once seemed as unlikely as a Papal Bull declaring God to be female. The British have now had eleven years to get used to the odd configuration of national leadership by two strong-minded women, almost identical in age. But the iconography of the female duo is still hard to assimilate. It makes the partnership unique in the world and without precedent.

Nothing has dispelled our perception of this as a tricky *pas de deux*, even now, when its days seem numbered. It is, of course, a business relationship, and both parties are committed to making it work with what grace they can muster. Although they rarely meet privately, the Queen makes a point of inviting Denis and Margaret Thatcher to Balmoral for a few days each August, when the Prime Minister has been seen to roll up her sleeves and wash the plates in the Norwegian log cabin after one of Prince Philip's barbecue lunches. 'But when she is no longer Prime Minister, there will be no more trips to Balmoral,' says a member of the royal family. 'Mrs Thatcher just doesn't belong to that world.'

The relationship, which might have proved a strain for even the most like-minded of partners, has been prolonged for an unconscionable length of time. Mrs Thatcher has already been in power for longer than Palmerston, and will, if she holds on tight, overtake Gladstone next year. While the Queen long ago absorbed every part of herself into her role, time has completed the evolution of a prime minister whose office has become merely an extension of her personality.

Gone are the days when Mrs Thatcher reigned supreme as Europe's most experienced premier, the Queen of the West, glorying in her special relationship with Reagan and confidently counting on a fourth term of office. Pretenders to her throne are springing up left and right as her courtiers ask each other whether she will abdicate to save the party. History is beginning to leave Mrs Thatcher behind, and as she goes out of style we see her in a harsher light. She has, even former supporters now acknowledge, presided over the unravelling of Britain's social fabric. Gorbachev, whom she certainly helped launch on the international arena, then seemed the willing recipient of her good offices. But in retrospect, Mrs Thatcher's role is diminished. She was used as a special envoy to the relationship that really counted, the one with Reagan, that led with such astonishing ease to the peace summits. From here, we can admire the consummate skill with which Gorbachev deployed both Thatcher and Reagan.

When Mrs Thatcher came to power in May 1979, she was a rather different person. She was as abrasive as she is today – marking papers 'Nonsense', 'Needs more briefing' and 'Do this again' – but her overbearing manner hid considerable private misgivings. She continued to feel herself inexperienced and on trial. She attended early royal audiences rather overwhelmed and nervous, finding herself face to face with a monarch of twenty-seven years' standing who had already seen the passing of seven previous prime ministers.

But in recent years Mrs Thatcher almost seems to have transcended her role. Long before she had palace gates erected at the end of Downing Street, she was apt to betray herself at unguarded moments. 'We have become a grandmother,' she told the news cameras after the birth of her grandchild, and the nation was finally let in on a comedy that had been diverting the side-rooms and corridors of Buckingham Palace and Westminster for many months. The Queen hasn't used the royal 'we' for many years, other than in the annual speech to Parliament written for her by Mrs Thatcher. The monarch prefers the more modern, if frequently parodied, 'my husband and I'.

Following the occasion when Mrs Thatcher and the Queen turned up for a banquet in an identical shade of blue, Downing Street asked Buckingham Palace if next time, to avoid an embarrassing repetition, the Palace would inform them in advance what the Queen intended to wear. The response came perilously close to a royal snub. The precaution was deemed unnecessary because 'Her Majesty the Queen does not notice what people are wearing'.

It seems that the closest and most fruitful relationships between British queens and their prime ministers have flourished on a blend of compatibility not a million miles from a sexual charge. The scholarly, wilful Queen Elizabeth I matched Lord Burghley's canny probity, and Queen Victoria relished her sessions with Disraeli, who constantly stimulated her with his battery of charm and flattery. Once the male–female polarity is abandoned, the most striking analogy that springs to mind is the one of mother and stepmother.

Personal differences between these two women in power come to light at the weekly private audience. Every Tuesday evening at 6.30, the Queen and the grocer's daughter are thrown into a forty-five-minute embrace of mutual mistrust.

Mrs Thatcher's government Daimler glides between the gates of Buckingham Palace at 6.10, delivering her a courteous quarter of an hour early. The conversation is conducted informally in the Queen's study overlooking Buckingham Palace gardens. The Prime Minister is debriefed on certain issues that have arisen over the week, and alerts the Queen to subjects likely to come up before the next audience. The Queen's role is 'to advise, to encourage, to warn'. It is in effect a business meeting for which private secretaries have already drawn up a shortlist of suggested topics. The recent agenda at the meeting following the weekend of poll tax and prison riots is likely to have caused a sharp drop in the temperature. But from the accounts of Lord Home, Lord Wilson and Lord Callaghan, the Tuesday meetings can be warm and friendly, and the conversation can stray. Lord Callaghan has talked about the 'complete frankness' of the talks he enjoyed with the Queen. 'We'd talk about anything at all – her family, my family.'

With Mrs Thatcher, the audience proceeds as prescribed. Escorted to an ante-chamber, she seldom has to wait more than a few minutes before being told that the Queen is ready. There follows a rapid walk along the red-carpeted corridors behind the liveried footman, who finally opens a door and announces, 'The Prime Minister, Your Majesty.' Mrs Thatcher enters with a deep curtsy and a 'Good evening, Ma'am'. The Queen smiles and points to an armchair. Drinks are offered and the polished door closes quietly on pomp and circumstance. Nobody interrupts. In the corridor outside, an ornate clock slowly ticks the minutes away.

The women facing each other across the study are a little alike, and not only in stature and bearing. Both are grandmothers, conscientious, authoritative, used to taking precedence. These similarities set them on a collision course, while their differences drive them further apart.

At her coronation, the Queen committed her life to Empire and Commonwealth. Mrs Thatcher is committed to winning the next election. The Queen stands for tradition, service and family values. Mrs Thatcher is a self-made woman and, more than any Tory prime minister for decades, stands against the establishment for change and enterprise. The Queen has a broad knowledge of global views and personalities. Mrs Thatcher's view is predominantly political. The Queen is pacific, diplomatic and receptive to all kinds of people. Mrs Thatcher is aggressively hard-edged, well-versed in law and science and, confronted with unfamiliar types, can patronize or briefly dry up. The Queen has always been loved more than Mrs Thatcher, and has never had to endure the kind of disapproval that the Prime Minister now faces. Inured to palaces and treasures, the Queen enjoys a robust outdoor country life, while Mrs Thatcher is a workaholic indoor person who may not have felt the sleet on her face or walked much further than her limousine in years. One is the mother of a billionaire wet concerned to immerse himself in the fabric of British life, the other the mother of an Americanized new millionaire. The Queen is the unique symbol of the nation, her place built into its structure, while the ballot box will inevitably write Mrs Thatcher out.

Increasingly, however, the Prime Minister has borrowed some of the charismatic qualities of royalty. She rules, of course, but there is a feeling that she might also like to reign. On her visit to the Soviet Union in March 1987 the royal 'we' was heavily deployed, and there was something familiar in the progress of the small, stately woman with a handbag over one wrist, followed by Sir Geoffrey Howe walking a few yards behind with his hands clasped behind his back, and the Downing Street secretaries, like ladies-in-waiting, carrying bouquets. 'We have enjoyed ourselves immensely,' announced Mrs Thatcher, emerging radiant from a block of Moscow flats. Something rather odd seems to happen to Mrs Thatcher's English when she makes these regal pronouncements. Into the abrupt language of argument and communiqué steals a florid, rolling language reminiscent of Queen Victoria's diaries. 'We have learned so much and shall never forget the beauteous things that we have seen,' she wrote in the visitors' book of a museum.

When a British radio reporter asked if her visit was political, he was smacked down as though it were an impertinent question. 'Broaden – your – view,' she rebuked him majestically. 'I am here on an historic mission representing my country.'

Last year, the year of national disasters, she was careful to ensure that her visits to the scene were never upstaged by those of the royals. (She took to appearing at the hospital bedsides of victims of disasters and terrorist attacks so regularly that mock donor-cards went on sale, inscribed: 'In the event of an accident, I do not wish to be visited in hospital by Mrs Thatcher.') Confusion can arise. On her recent trip to Africa she was much curtsied to en route, and asked how her son Prince Charles was doing. Leaving aside the Spanish tourist who curtsied and asked for her autograph in Marks & Spencer, the story that a roomful of Conservative women curtsied to her at one of the Tory conferences, repeated by several journalists, proved apocryphal. It was, however, believed.

Ever since Falklands year, 1982, the Prime Minister has been playing a bigger role. The City of London's victory march held that October marked the pinnacle of the Prime Minister's self-glorification. No member of the royal family was present: Mrs Thatcher herself took the salute, together with the Lord Mayor. 'What a wonderful parade it has been,' she glowed later, at the Salute the Task Force lunch at the Guildhall, once more capturing the carve-it-in-marble tone of the young Victoria, 'surpassing all our expectations as the crowd, deeply moved and sensing the spirit of the occasion, accompanied the band by singing "Rule Britannia".' The Falklands war was a personal triumph for her, even if Brigadier Julian Thompson, commander of the Three Commando Brigade, was to remark soberly in an anniversary television film, 'You don't mind dying for Queen and country, but you certainly don't want to die for politicians.'

Why had royalty not taken the salute? In the Victory Parade of 1945, Churchill and Attlee were modestly placed at a distance from the royal saluting base. The Queen may have been abroad for much of that month, but other members of the royal family could have stood in for her. The press office says that the celebrations were the City's idea: 'As the royal family had attended the service at St Paul's and the Queen was away, the Palace was quite happy that the Queen was not represented.' The idea of changing the date or fielding an alternative royal was barely considered. This was to be, as everyone knew, Mrs Thatcher's day.

Even though no nuances of behaviour can change the constitution – and she remains, in Lord Pym's words, 'a bird of passage compared to the monarch' – Anthony Howard, the political commentator, says that if the Prime Minister breaks all the rules by continually being re-elected, the system breaks down: 'It was never intended to be that way. For a PM to be around for this length of time is necessarily a threat to the role the Queen is supposed to supply. Mrs Thatcher is not insular, she is a world leader . . . and God knows when the Queen was last on the cover of *Time* magazine.'

At times of government upheaval, for instance during the Profumo scandal, the monarchy has its most important role to play, reassuring the nation of stability and continuity. When the government is weakest, says Anthony Howard, the monarchy is strongest, and vice versa. 'Churchill posed an enormous threat to the monarchy because during the war he became the embodiment and personification of the nation. The King wasn't restored to his proper function until Churchill's [election] defeat.' Margaret Thatcher, who was nineteen in 1945, has told journalists that this event was one of the greatest shocks of her life.

'From time to time she appears to be cutting more of a presidential figure,' says Andrew Morton, veteran royal-watcher and author of *Theirs Is the Kingdom: The Wealth of the Windsors*. 'But face to face with the Queen she's very deferential. The curtsy, for instance, is a very deep and proper curtsy. There is a big difference between the personal attitude to the monarchy, which derives from her background, and the political aspiration to turn herself into a historical figure.'

Mrs Thatcher grew up with a deep reverence for institutions and traditions. She inherited this, together with her ambition, from a bleak, thrifty father. The Roberts family went to church four times on a Sunday. There was no drink in the house. Alderman Alfred Roberts liked to declare, 'I have to work every Sunday and I've only had two days off from business since August 1939.' Margaret Roberts, while largely ignoring her mother, adored her father, a Conservative local worthy of narrow outlook, deeply rooted in the ideas of the thirties – a world view she has been attempting to impose on everyone else ever since. There were no boyfriends and no dancing until Margaret got to Oxford, where her college principal, Dame Janet Vaughan, chillingly assessed her as 'just an average, second-class person'.

Since then she has sought to bring almost every institution into line with her vision of Britain, from the National Health to education and the BBC. Andrew Morton finds it remarkable that only one is left intact: 'The Crown Estates could well be another candidate for privatization, and it would be as logical to apply the principle of good housekeeping here as elsewhere. The estates are obviously in an administrative and legal mess. But the Queen has tenaciously quashed any attempt to alter such legislature, and Mrs Thatcher clearly draws back from any motions that would affect the monarchy.'

Caught between her idea of the Queen and the reality of the figure she confronts every Tuesday evening, the Prime Minister betrays signs of confusion. On the one hand, she perceives herself as a figure-head of the nation and a historic figure on the world stage, standing for her country above party politics. (Political columnist Hugo Young quotes her as calling herself 'a bit of an institution. And the place wouldn't be quite the same without this old institution.') On the other hand, she sees herself as a staunch and emotional royalist. Colleagues were intrigued by her instinctive reaction one day when the rehearsal for the Trooping the Colour could be heard through the open windows of Number 10. The band broke into some stirring martial music. Mrs Thatcher jumped to her feet, snapped crisply to attention and froze, remaining motionless until the end of the march. Personally, she is all emotional deference. Politically, she is expanding her role in a way that is more territorial than deferential.

The Prime Minister may play queen, but the Queen never plays prime minister. While Mrs Thatcher takes the stage, the Queen operates invisibly behind the scenes, influencing, advising and occasionally intervening. This role, though hidden from the public, is a major one. Lord Callaghan has said, 'I wouldn't accept that the Queen is powerless. You're always conscious that the monarchy has its own place in the constitution, as an essential element around which everything else revolves.'

Real disagreements between the Queen and Mrs Thatcher have only emerged occasionally from the overpowering discretion which surrounds dealings between the Palace and Number 10, but tensions were clear from the very start.

The Queen's attachment to the Commonwealth and its seventeen governors-general represents nearly forty years of contact, and she considers it a priority to attend the conferences of Commonwealth leaders. In 1979, soon after Mrs Thatcher came to power, the governors-general were to meet in Lusaka, Zambia. In the year of the Rhodesian crisis, it was all set to be a particularly tense occasion. Mrs Thatcher, stopping off at Canberra on the way home from an economic summit in Tokyo, paused to announce that she would have to consider very carefully whether she would advise the Queen to attend. 'That came through on the 8 am news,' recalls a Commonwealth source. 'By lunchtime it was firmly announced that the Queen *would* be going to Lusaka.'

By the mid-eighties, several royal interviews in the quality papers, notably with Prince Charles, indicated clearly that the traditionally paternalist, Whiggish royal family did not consider themselves converts to Thatcherism. But the critical moment, says Enoch Powell, came during the Michael Shea débâcle in July 1986, when it was reported that 'Sources close to the Queen let it be known to the *Sunday Times* ... that she is dismayed by many of Mrs Thatcher's policies.' Alarm bells rang. Such unaccustomed overtness challenged the very basis of the constitutional monarchy. 'For an instant,' Enoch Powell told me, 'The controversy appeared to broach the question of whether the Crown's conformity with its constitutional duty of action on advice was fraying at the edges.'

Both sides realized the dangers. The great and the good stepped in. The Queen's private secretary, Sir William Heseltine, wrote a rebuttal. The relaxed style of Michael Shea, the popular Buckingham Palace press secretary, was replaced with tight-lipped reticence. Both sides have been extremely careful ever since. But not everyone was convinced. Enoch Powell concluded, 'The important point was this. If it was not true, it was inadequately rebutted. If it was true, Shea should have left his job the following day, since what he was alleged to have said purported to express opinions and attitudes on which the Queen is bound to act on the advice of her advisers. Consequently the attribution to the monarch was not totally effaced.'

Mrs Thatcher's refusal to go along with comprehensive economic sanctions against South Africa has distanced her further from the monarch. And meanwhile Downing Street has remained suspicious of the bond between the Queen and Sir Sonny Ramphal, the Secretary-General who spearheaded Commonwealth sanctions against South Africa. For the Queen also has her own sources, and these can be quite different from those of the Prime Minister.

'They are the two best-informed people in the country,' says an acquaintance of the Queen. 'The nearest they would ever get to a duel of wits is a sort of assumption that their own source of information is definitive. I've heard that there can be a slight touch of "Actually, I *think* you'll find . . . ."'

On an issue of increasing importance such as green matters, the experts drawn up in the separate camps can be characteristically at odds. The Queen, who uses homoeopathic remedies and drinks only Malvern water, receives a flow of information from Prince Charles and Prince Philip, who was a patron of the World Wildlife Fund long before ecological matters were called 'green'.

'Mrs Thatcher's tendency is to define the significant issue in scientific terms,' says Robin Grove-White, head of a new environmental policy initiative at Lancaster University. 'Her view that the only problems are scientific problems, and the rest can be left to the market, is a restricted view which needs vision. Through Prince Charles the Queen has access to a broader cultural and philosophical outlook.'

In Prince Charles's circle Jonathon Porritt, formerly a state school teacher and now director of Friends of the Earth, lunches at Highgrove and can call in the relevant expert on any particular issue. Other key FoE links include its board chairman Godfrey Bradman, who funded the campaign for lead-free petrol and heads Rosehaugh, one of the biggest property developers in the country, and Andrew Thomas, who also works for the Prince's Trust. Tom Birke of the Green Lions, a small lobbying body that operates discreetly in the gap between pressure groups and the government, has lunched at Kensington Palace, as has Robin Grove-White.

Mrs Thatcher's advisers are more scientific in approach and harder-headed – men such as the industrialist George Guise and Professor Brian Griffiths, economist, Presbyterian and head of the Policy Unit. Professor David Pearce advises the Secretary of State on green economics and eco-taxes: Chris Patten himself is something of an expert on aid to third world countries. But it is Sir Crispin Tickell, ex-ambassador to the United Nations and author of a book on the impact of global climate changes, who became the key influence in the Johnny-come-lately greening of Mrs. Thatcher. He persuaded her of the worldwide consequences of the emission of carbon dioxide into the air, and acted as midwife for her first major environment speech in September 1988. This expedient speech had many consequences, leading to huge increases in Greenpeace membership, to the recognition that Nicholas Ridley was something of a liability, deflecting criticism over the development of green-field sites and convincing scientists that research might still be safe in the government's hands.

The fundamental differences between the two women shackled together as Queen and Prime Minister are illustrated by the way they dress. Whereas Mrs Thatcher cares deeply about her appearance and was quite overwhelmed to be chosen for the International Best Dressed List in 1988, providing twenty photographs when a New York publicist asked her for one, the Queen has no interest in clothes and is happy to put on whatever her dresser lays out in the morning.

These days, a bespectacled Queen battles out in all weathers with her scarf firmly kirby-gripped to her head. The Prime Minister has painstakingly evolved a successful and flattering power wardrobe. When discussing both women their admirers inevitably enthuse with repetitive rapture about their fine complexions. In her sixty-fifth year the Prime Minister is a far more attractive woman than she has ever been. Since Gordon Reece, an ex-television producer, showed her, in 1978, how to reshape her hair, lower her voice and reassess her wardrobe, she has never looked back. Always ready to call in an adviser, even when she discounts his recommendations, she has assembled a modest cabinet of fashion and beauty experts, from a Shepherd's Bush aromatherapist to a team from Aquascutum under fashion director Marianne Abrahams, and guidance from Carla Powell, wife of current chief courtier Charles. Rather like the man who knows nothing about art but knows what he likes, she has groped her way from the fashion nadir of Bri-nylon, little scarves and plonking brooches to the perfectly good suit for all occasions. Her attitude to clothes remains, for all her enthusiasm, earnest and unsubtle. Just as Sir John Pope-Hennessy noticed that on a visit to the V & A she ignored the pictures but became animated by the chemical composition of a liquid being used in picture restoration, she is invigorated by the mechanics of dress rather than its charm.

'We've been putting in shoulder pads recently,' she has said on television, and: 'People remember if you are in pink.' She's strong on manufacture, good on fibre content, a superb packer, and full of worthy, old-fashioned advice: 'Always put tissue paper under a pussy-cat bow before you put it away'; 'You never want to press your hems, because then you can't let them down.'

To say that Mrs Thatcher has drawn ahead of the Queen in the fashion stakes is to assume they are entered for the same race. Nothing could be further from the truth. The Queen does not have to compare herself to anyone. She 'doesn't notice what people wear'. The peculiar requirements of the monarch's role dictate a unique, almost abstract and mystical wardrobe: uniforms, decorations, over-dressing, pomp, allusions and references, theatrical imagery. Apart from all this, the Queen has always conformed to the French ideal of the Englishwoman – magnificent on horseback and dressed to the tens in the ballroom. In her legendary jewels and one of her pastel sparkling evening dresses she becomes the living icon her subjects hope and expect to see. Her off-duty wardrobe of cardigans and skirts, mackintoshes, wellington boots and plastic hoods testify to the existence of a separate private life: something to which Mrs Thatcher does not aspire.

When the fateful day comes and Mrs Thatcher leaves Number 10, she will have to begin that life from scratch. It is hard to know what will then become of the woman who works from 6 am through to the early hours every day, who has virtually no friends outside the job and who reads only paperback potboilers. On that day, she will be neither prime minister, nor in her prime.

On that same day, of course, the Queen will still be queen.

Correspondent Magazine, April 1990

Azzedine Alaïa: The Titan of Tight

*T*HERE are half a dozen ways Naomi Campbell could be earning tens of thousands of dollars this weekend. The presence of this sunny nineteen-year-old with a perfect body, golden eyes and a Betty Boop bob is urgently demanded in the photographic studios of four cities. But instead she has chosen to work for nothing in an obscure back street of the Marais in Paris, shacked up in the corner of a chaotic boxroom. The reason for this odd behaviour sits cross-legged at her feet, stitching a bunch of seashells on to a stiletto shoe made of string mesh.

To an ever-increasing number of women, it is as if that small, shock-headed figure were Balenciaga himself. Tina Turner says, 'Azzedine sews for Woman! I'm not talking tits and ass. I mean he gives you the very best line you can get out of your body.' Sydney Picasso says, 'Coming at the start of the eighties, after all those Japanese clothes, Alaïa gave us back our bodies.' Annie Cohen-Solal, the French cultural counsellor in New York, says, 'He changed my life. I never felt so feminine before.' Top model Tatjana says, 'Once you've worn Alaïa, you know everyone else cuts too big. You sense they don't know as much as he does. He really likes a woman's body.' Tina Turner telephones to add, 'What he does is art. Take any garment he has made. You can't drop the hem, you can't let it out or take it in. It's a piece of sculpture.'

For ten years Alaïa was the best-kept secret in Paris, his telephone number passed between a closed circle of legendary and Proustian women, the last priestesses of haute couture who bore the Holy Grail direct from the hand of Cristobal Balenciaga, Christian Dior and Jacques Fath. 'From two seasons at Guy Laroche I learned how,' says Alaïa. 'From the last elegant women in the world I learned what.'

The more you think about Azzedine Alaïa's work, the greater

becomes the stature of this diminutive figure who measures sixty-three inches in his elastic-sided cotton slippers.

What he had learned he applied to a decade of ready-to-wear, and produced the only really new contribution to fashion history since classless clothing. He worked out dress in terms of touch. He abolished all underclothes and made one garment do the work. The technique is dazzling, for just as a woman's body is a network of surface tensions, hard here, soft there, so Azzedine Alaïa's clothes are a force field of give and resistance. He did it first with stretch, and then he did it by piecing together as many as forty-three scraps of fabric in one dress, making a garment of woven cloth to hold the body like a knit.

There are no compromises. He doesn't simply choose a cloth. He flies to Venice to work with Silvia Bocchese, who also makes fabrics for Karl Lagerfeld and Yves Saint Laurent. He takes a model and an assistant and stays for days, turning wool and cotton into stretch fabrics, devising stitches, supervising the work on the machines, trying scarf-sized pieces in all directions against the model's body, pouncing on mistakes, turning them into new patterns.

The Einstein of fashion gets to his feet and picks up a hairy little dog called Patapouf. He is wearing thirty-dollar Chinese pyjamas: his wardrobe consists of 115 pairs, plus two sewn for him by Rei Kawakubo. He presses the dog to his cheek, kisses it six times, and murmurs, '*Mon petit fils! Mon bébé!*' Catching Naomi's eye, he drops his head winningly to one side, hunches his shoulders, and mimics the purse-lipped, pop-eyed expression of a woman peering into a pram.

A clown, a mimic, Harpo Marx with black hair and a voice, Alaïa has also been granted a second precious gift from heaven: women find him irresistible. Grandson of a Tunisian *gendarme*, a boy who slept in his grandmother's arms and bed until he was sixteen, he was raised, encouraged, sent to Paris, discovered, taught, and cherished on a continual wave of female affection. The relationship is passionate: instead of sex, there are clothes.

Although he helped his sister with her embroidery samples, he was excluded from the women's weekly sewing circle that he longed to join. Salvation came from his mother's midwife, Madame Pinot, who gave him *Vogue*, insisted he learn French, and sat him down at her kitchen table with paper and crayons. Later she took him to the Académie des Beaux-Arts in Tunis and lied about his age to get him accepted. Tunisian socialite Madame Menchari told him to go to Paris. Her art student daughter Leila met him there and helped him find a temporary bed. The Comtesse de Blegiers gave the Tunisian immigrant a home with her family, and Simone Zehrfuss introduced him to his future private clients, Arletty, Garbo, writer Louise de Vilmorin and socialite Cécile de Rothschild. Clients became friends, then devotees; Paloma Picasso and Andrée Putman, Tina Turner; Jacqueline Schnabel and Danielle Mitterrand, followed by the world's top models – Tatjana, Linda Evangelista, Naomi, Yasmin, Gail, Beverly, and Nadège – who break other bookings for the man who pays them in frocks, camp beds, couscous and a home away from home.

Here in Casbah Alaïa, in the early hours of the morning, down in the Rue du Parc-Royal, twenty-four hours before the showing of the spring and summer collection, Jean-Pierre has just made spaghetti. The atelier is packed with people. A whey-faced Joe McKenna, a New York stylist, is fast-forwarding through the music for the show: African music tangles with Prokofiev from the video of last year's show, watched by fourteen-year-old Beverly Peele of Los Angeles's Hawthorne High and her yawning mother. 'See them, ma? Them's my feet!' A pile of dogs snore together in a plastic filing tray. Three models, the picture of depravity, sit on the floor drinking and playing gin rummy, cigarettes are made of sugar, the drink is Coke and they are playing for peppermints. 'Play cards in our house?' asks Stephanie with a smile. 'My grandmother absolutely forbids it!'

'We played for who was gonna cook dinner and wash the floor,' says her neighbour. 'I'm telling you, I got real good!'

Christoph von Weyhe, Alaïa's gentle business partner and long-time friend, offers coffee. 'I hate coffee,' says Naomi. 'It's so gross.' She has on a tiny cotton bustier dress and a pair of cherry red boxing gloves, with which she makes feints at herself in the mirror. 'Only fourteen ounces, huh?' she murmurs to herself, checking the wristband. 'That's peanuts.'

Sylvie Sourisseau, stylist and press assistant, checks the running order. Alaïa fits trousers on his friend and model Farida Khelfa, still sparkling at 3 am, throwing back her black hair with a flash of white teeth as they gossip in Souk-Arab.

'And when you get to the end of the runway, you take off all your clothes,' Alaïa tells Tatjana over his shoulder. She folds up with laughter. 'You do it for Herb Ritts. Why not for me?'

The walls are lined with photographs of Alaïa totems and connections: Yasmin, Simon le Bon and baby; Mike Tyson, Naomi's boyfriend; a defiant Anna Magnani, a child clutched in her apron; and among the Xeroxed faces of the models with their show numbers, 'Elizabeth' above Britain's Queen Mother, in a flowered chiffon duster coat and feathered straw hat. Alaïa blows her a chef's kiss between finger and thumb: 'She comes first, above all the rest.'

Art history student Xavier Picasso sits on the floor sorting shoes. 'Azzedine made these sandals from the stomachs of stingrays,' he says. 'Me? I'm here because of a *crise d'amour*. My mother thought the Azzedine milieu would be comforting.'

And has he recovered from the heartbreak?

'I must have. Because I've just met this wonderful girl. . . .'

Round about 5 am, most people drift home. Joe, Naomi, Christoph, Stephanie and the *première* have found their beds somewhere under the roof. Alaïa, in a cloud of steam, is ironing a scrap of chiffon the colour of gasoline.

'Garbo visited me when I was at the Rue de Bellechasse,' he recalls. 'They told me she was waiting outside with Cécile de Rothschild. I said. 'Sure. Who else?' And they said, 'No, Azzedine, really.' And there she was in a sweater with a frightened look, her hair in a rubber band, shielding her eyes from the light with her hand, with a man's signet ring on her finger. She talked very quietly and quickly. She wanted a dark blue cashmere coat – big, bigger, biggest! And a huge collar to hide her neck. One pair of pants . . .. I still have the pattern.' When he delivered them to her, she thanked him 'very sweetly'. She said he had 'nice, good eyes'. Most things to all women. Alaïa is a loving son-substitute to his distinguished clients just as he is a motherly friend to his teenage models.

'Azzedine is the man in my life,' says the former Jacques Fath model Bettina Graziani with a laugh. 'Once when I was alone and unwell over a public holiday, with my maid away, Azzedine and Cristoph walked in like good angels, cleaned the house, walked the dog and brought up a delicious meal on a tray.' The Comtesse de Blegiers, who gave him a room for five years in the mid-seventies, calls him a 'child heart'.

'He made me wonderful dresses and helped with my children, who adored him. He was not exactly a disciplinarian. When we left him baby-sitting, I would come back to a pile of children in front of the television and he would say, "It's too sad to leave them alone in the dark." '

No child ever had a more entertaining companion. Life with Azzedine was a comedy sketch. No day passed without an adventure. There was the time he had to bath the baby and was discovered fully dressed in the tub with him, shoes and all. When a new maid arrived, Alaïa asked her to take a tray up to the grandmother's room, changed into a nightgown of Chantilly lace, and awaited her sitting up in bed with a pince-nez, his hair powdered white.

Farida Khelfa met him when she went to ask if she could borrow his clothes for a film of Jean-Paul Goude's. Like Alaïa, she comes from Tunisia and was raised on Egyptian movies and Oum Khalsoum records. They have two- and three-hour telephone conversations and travel together on holiday. 'These models will break any booking when Azzedine needs them,' she says. 'They know he adores them. He designs each dress specially for that girl, to make her look the most beautiful she possibly can. No one else does that. He's discreet and he never makes jokes about them. That's rare among designers.

'In some ways he's a typical Tunisian. When you're with him his house is yours. You have to eat the best he has – and finish everything on your plate. You can help yourself to clothes. But all his relationships are *passionnel*. That also means you must be careful. You do one thing to hurt him, and it's finished!'

'It's finished with *Women's Wear Daily* because they once published a feature titled 'The Rise and Fall of Azzedine Alaïa'. It's finished with Bloomingdale's because they wanted to spend too much on presentation and too little on models. It's very nearly finished with a certain member of the staff who has been very quiet since a contretemps last week.

'Does it bore you to try on clothes?' he asked suddenly, at around 2 am when she was dancing as he tried to pin a dress.

She laughed and said, 'Very much.'

Then take it off and go,' said Alaïa.

'The whole room fell quiet,' says a staff member. 'We thought she'd been sacked.'

Here in the workroom above the boutique, Alaïa takes a nap between six and seven, puts on another pair of pyjamas, and sews the wisp of ironed chiffon over a waistband of shell mosaic. Work flows on with hardly an interruption until Joe appears, rubbing his eyes, to supervise the loading of samples into the van for the trip to the Rue de la Verrerie.

Nine hours later the Alaïa circus gets under way in a charming fashion theatre under the glazed arches and palm-house gallery of the new premises. Here Alaïa is building Nirvana for the 1990s, a permanently unfinished project, 4500 square feet of what was once a nineteenth-century mattress and clock factory, with restored murals and an antique four-ton metal elevator. Up on the roof, between trees and bell towers and metal bridges, an icy moonlight breaks over the glass as Joe and Silvie assemble the first numbers three floors beneath.

'Alaïa has no respect for the demands of American buying schedules,' complains one fashion editor from the front row. 'If Azzedine didn't insist on sewing every sample himself, cutting out the pattern for every shoe and belt, his shows might not be five weeks late. Still,' she adds, looking around at the audience, 'I see we all continue to turn up – everyone but Bloomingdale's and *Women's Wear Daily.*'

As the music begins and the most beautiful girls in the world line up behind the screen, Azzedine Alaïa steps aside and takes a moment out, glancing up toward the gallery for no very obvious reason. Is he remembering for a brief instant the many women who passed him from hand to hand in order that he could be here today? Just before what will turn out to be his most acclaimed collection, is he recalling an impeccable middle-aged woman in a shady straw hat, with a little lace collar and a handbag on one gloved wrist?

Would Madame Pinot be surprised to see the boy who loved to sew acclaimed as a second Balenciaga in tomorrow's *Herald Tribune*?

American *Vogue*, March 1990

Carolyne Roehm: The Lady Who Doesn't Lunch

CAROLYNE Roehm serene in green satin and emeralds, elbow on an eighteenth-century Russian table of brass and marquetry, one slim shoulder jostling a Fabergé egg and a bunch of pink roses – proper garden roses with dew and a ladybird from her Connecticut cutting garden. Carolyne Roehm brisk in lint-covered pants and her husband's cotton shirt, smilingly helping workroom staff to goulash or salmon mousse in aspic before the all-night run-up to her show. Carolyne Roehm dashing in hacking jacket and boots, dancing her horse through the intricate steps of his dressage. Carolyne Roehm radiant in a bustle-back evening dress of blue and white chintz, on the arm of King Kravis at the entrance to the Pen dinner, walking the red carpet for the third time for the papparazzi. Carolyne Roehm calling goodbye to Henry, playing a Chopin nocturne on the 1851 Erard piano, trying to concentrate on piano teacher Rosi Grunschlag's pencil note – 'DON'T *rush*!' – aware of the Bentley ticking over, poised to deliver her to Seventh Avenue by 8.30.

And Carolyne Roehm, totally pooped, lunching in her Park Avenue apartment under the Sargent, the Gainsborough, the Reynolds and the Joseph Wright of Derby, suddenly laying down her soufflé fork on the gold vermeil flatware, head bent, cornflower eyes welling, a tear dropping on to the Venetian crystal. 'Ignore it!' she says, immediately. 'I'm always like this after the show.'

Henry Kravis rang from the private jet after they had taken off for Spain a few days later. These were to be their first few days together for as long as either could easily remember, and he was still remonstrating with his wife for bringing a briefcase of her music on board, in case she found a piano where she could practise.

'She's driven,' said the man who pulled off the biggest financial deal in history, the leveraged buy-out of RJR Nabisco. 'She's terribly hard on herself. I keep telling her, she doesn't have to be a perfectionist.' Henry Kravis frequently muses on his wife's prodigious talent and capacity for hard work. 'I sometimes wonder if she's held back because of me. Don't put that. Okay, put that. Whether, with all her gifts, she is not taken quite so seriously because she happens to be married to me.'

Carolyne Roehm talked in her office, the day after her fall collection. The walls are lined with her graphic fashion sketches, each scribbled with her bold, dramatic signature. Through the trellised windows the normal barrage of police sirens and frenzied shouting tends to drown out her light voice. She sits, as she does in her advertisements, close to vases of extraordinary flowers – bowls of sweet peas, waxy hothouse bowers and rich painterly arrangements like Dutch still-lifes. Thirty-nine, she looks, as she does in those photographs, as fresh as an Old Money debutante who's been beautifully finished in Paris: dreamy sapphire-lensed eyes, black lashes, a clear pale skin, tilted nose, crisp dark hair. She wears a Prince of Wales check suit with a sharp waist and short tight skirt. Her snowy cravat sparkles with an amber and diamond pin. Her thin wrist clatters with an amber and gold charm bracelet.

'Because I'm out in an evening gown, people don't believe the other side exists,' she says.

It does. She designs and runs her couture business with its four collections a year, fifty-six employees, twenty-two retailing accounts and its three licensees with eight more under discussion. She makes personal appearances across America and fits in the hours of preliminary trials in the search for a Roehm fragrance. As an extremely efficient President of the CFDA (Council of the Fashion Designers of America), she is committed to modernizing and redirecting the image of the fashion industry. She is currently organizing with *Vogue* the spectacular down-on-the-street Seventh on Sale event by which the fashion industry intends to raise $1 million for AIDS – and has been immediately, unanimously re-elected for another year. She masterminded the New York City Ballet gala that's still remembered for raising $750,000, became chairman of the Metropolitan Opera benefit, is a Trustee of the New York Public Library and a member of the steering committee of Carnegie Hall. And don't forget the private lessons she takes in French, cookery, wine, riding, exercise, music. With all of this I am reliably informed she never shouts or forgets staff birthdays, and her hair is always clean and shiny.

She is also her own house model for fittings and her own

advertising model for photographs taken in the Kravises' $5.5 million Park Avenue apartment. She can do this because she is a sample size 4 and five feet nine inches tall.

It's a pity she doesn't also design skiwear, because she looks so great skiing from the door of her chalet lodge at Vail – the house she and Henry designed with a local mountain architect, after they sent him on a tour of their favourite French and Swiss mountain resorts, after they showed him the Manhattan apartment and after they booked him in with Vincent Fourcade for sessions on cornices and finishing.

And it's a pity she doesn't design swimwear, because she looks neat in a big raffia hat and sunglasses (Carolyne Roehm for Classic Optical) on the deck of the Southampton house right on Shinnecock Bay, the big front room all done out in fresh blue and white Portuguese tiles, and Henry's Boston whaler bobbing alongside in the sparkling water.

And it's a terrible pity she doesn't make sportswear, because Weatherstone in Connecticut is just made for shots of Carolyne in weekend tweed jacket and pants, supervising the sixth year of the garden project or sorting out menus by a wall of eighteenth-century English sporting pictures.

'Carolyne is the best-organized woman I know,' says Henry Kravis. This is a woman who buys her Christmas tinsel in April – last year, in April in *India.* When she gives you a present – say, a beautifully bound and illustrated nineteenth-century household almanack – she hides it under a packet of home-made sand dollars in a wicker basket threaded with pine and holly and tied up with a ribboned doorknocker wreath so pretty you don't get round to opening it until January.

Henry Kravis has his own novel way of wrapping his presents to her. Once he presented her with a pair of tennis shoes. Late for a dinner in a red lace flamenco dress, she asked if she could try them another time. He insisted. She found a diamond earring in each toe. And then there was the necklace of emeralds she wore to a CFDA cocktail party.

'Where did you get that?' asked a friend.

'Under my pillow.'

'And where have you been sleeping?'

'In the right bed.'

All through the eighties, long before her husband's personal net worth shot up to $330 million, Carolyne Roehm was the very emblem of what journalist Jesse Kornbluth labelled the Working Rich. Equal amounts of print were dedicated to her husband's

business coups, her shows and her front row line-ups of friends.
Her dinner parties, galas, holidays and hoe-downs were chronicled
daily. The society weddings of the eighties were working partner-
ships, often founded on second marriages. While the men shuffled
companies and dealt themselves fortunes, the wives translated
money into visual pedigree, guided the charity cheques, chose the
houses, planned the dinners, planted the rose gardens and steered
the art collections. *Le style Rothschild* came rooting home to
Manhattan. Mostly the wives accepted the invitations and the
men went along. Wasn't this showing them? Wasn't this the
reward for all those years of grinding work and heart-rocking risk?

'We could have been out 365 days a year, four times a night,'
says Carolyne Roehm. 'And if you're a couple, people always
assume it's the woman who's keen. Actually, I want to stay home.
But Henry's the most gregarious man on earth.'

She counted the benefits in publicity to her business. As yet she
didn't fear the consequences of being branded a society queen. She
simply lived the dressing-up life most Americans would love to
have, and she was her own best advertisement.

'Actually, I wasn't so gung-ho on the idea of being in my ads. I
thought it would be perceived as egocentric. I was told it could be
a tremendous advantage. That if others could, they would. There's
been a very good response.' She pauses. She is one of the very few
people who stop to think. 'Also, people wonder if you have to be
as tall and thin as I am to wear my clothes. And of course you
don't. Our sizing is scrupulously scaled. But why don't women
say the same thing every time they see a professional model
wearing the clothes?'

In the eighties advertisers discovered that it is probably enough
to forget the clothes and show the lifestyle. But the Carolyne
Roehm advertising campaign is neither a Paloma Picasso flaunt
nor a Ralph Lauren daydream. Hovering somewhere between the
two, the image projects a suggestion of a society princess dabbling
in fashion. Which is neither true, nor fair.

'Those ads feature a concubine,' says a friend of hers. 'I've spent
whole days on Seventh Avenue with the real Carolyne Roehm.
She's not draped across a sofa in a ball gown. She's usually
working through the lunch hour for the sixth day in a row, with
a cold beer and a bucket of Kentucky fried chicken.'

Roehm's friends are always asked: 'Is she for real?'

Such questions move this normally sunny personality to
perturbation. Not to histrionics. Perplexity, yes. Anger, no.

'They can't get past the bloody candelabra!' she sighs. 'It floors me when people ask why I do this job when I'm married to a wealthy man. Where were they when I decided on my career at thirteen? Where were they when I was working for Mrs Polyester Sportswear? Where were they during the eleven years I worked in the industry before I had my own company? Where were they when I had a small high-rise apartment and didn't live this life at all?'

Carolyne Roehm pauses to receive another jumbo bouquet at her desk, reads the card and says 'Sweet' and 'I'm thrilled'. This one is a toppling herbaceous border from Saks, who liked her show so much they've reorganized their budget and extended her in-store floor space. She puts a box of jewellery on the window ledge to make a gap and we peer at each other through the foliage.

'Tell you one thing – I don't want to go to very many of those gala events any more. They're too tiring,' she says, straightening up and pouring a glass of spring water. 'Last year I started noticing how the charity circuit is managed very skilfully by women who don't work. I was heading the grouse pack.' When she laughs, her voice is deeper and louder. 'Me and the men, grumbling "It's past midnight, and they still haven't served the last course."'

This morning her husband asked her what she wanted to do, come summer, and she said stay home in her houses with the dogs and the horses.

'The era of acquiring and travelling, to me that's all over. I've got quite enough to deal with already.'

She evidently has trouble saying no. Fast forward a week and she will be getting on the plane for Madrid and Salzburg.

'I feel differently about many things. I've been thinking about the fall of Michael Milken and the demise of Drexel Burnham that stood for the junk bonds and the quick money. I read all of the criticism in the press. I thought about Donald and Ivana's divorce, and Malcolm Forbes's death. I thought about the nineties and the Bush administration. And starting in January, I vowed to stay home.'

Quite a decision for someone who has founded her $20 million business on couture ball gowns.

Organizing the CFDA Awards dinner in February, held at the Temple of Dendour inside the Metropolitan Museum, she rang decorator Philip Baloun and asked him, 'What do we do for the first big event of the decade? I want to project a different image, stylish without being extravagant.' To another friend she said, 'I don't want anyone to look at that setting and think "Nouvelle society".' The black-and-white awning-striped tables with black plates and iron candelabra tied with papyrus signalled a change in the social climate and sent out reverberations that are still being felt. The CFDA glitter evenings may never be quite the same again.

She took stock of the depressed retail climate and the changes in Japan. She asked why women were buying fewer frocks and more curtains. She remembered to remember what men like women to wear. Then she put her conclusions to work in her fall collection, with more short evening dresses and a change of silhouette with softer shoulders and wider skirts. She made easy shirtwaisters and long sweater dresses for dining at home – your apartment or mine. She cut billowing skirts in tissue taffeta you can screw up and push into an overnight case. She produced an entire collection with no black in it.

Born talented, she has expanded her view since Henry Kravis set her up in business shortly before they were married in 1985. That April she launched her label in a nightclub called the Latin Quarter. It was an elegant, confident collection and press and buyers, cheer-led by her friends in the front rows, gave her a standing ovation. Carolyne cried, Henry cried, everyone cried. She was an overnight celebrity. And immediately ran into problems of sizing, quality and shipment.

She is impatient with herself for making any mistakes, and generous in admitting them now she has battled her way through to become the promising company that Henry Kravis demands. 'I can finally say we are now shipping a quality product of the standard I've been aiming for.'

But she still needs time to build in the profit-making structure – the fragrance line and the licensees required by a company with dress prices up to $6000. 'I thought, I'm a quick study, maybe it will take two years to get the machinery rolling well. I was wrong. Ideally I wanted a Pierre Bergé to handle the business side. I didn't find him.'

Last year produced a constant series of new setbacks. 'I had collections stolen, then there were queries about honesty within the company. Fabric I desperately needed got stuck in Customs. It hurt me to see company morale so low. One evening I told Henry I didn't think I could do any more. I said, "This year has beaten the joy out of me." '

A friend, Francesca Stanfill, watched events with concern. 'Henry *is* a King Henry,' she said. 'He's a once-more-into-the-breach sort of person. He gave her the St Crispin's Day speech. He mapped out the responsibilities of the business.'

He backed the pep talk with action. He fed a corporation trouble-shooter into the system – the fearsome Lee Katz – and swept his wife off for a holiday. She weighed glamour and business values, and is now fully integrated into all parts of the company. America has proved it likes her clothes. The press hasn't been half bad. She has expanded over an entire floor on Seventh Avenue.

Hard as it's been, she is still as dedicated to glamour as ever. She brought it with her to New York when she was twenty-three, plain Jane Carolyne Smith, BFA, school teachers' daughter from Missouri, with five suitcases of clothes and a head full of Audrey Hepburn movies. Further back from there into childhood, she was given to entering rooms on the points of her ballet slippers, wearing a tutu and the $4.95 rhinestone tiara she chose at six years old from a mail order catalogue. Her loving and sometimes critical mother, Mrs Bresee, remembers the more docile of the family pets press-ganged into flower-trimmed bonnets and embroidered kerchiefs.

'Her father and I always noticed she enjoyed the meal more if it had a French name.'

Mrs Bresee thinks that only children, like her daughter, tend to pit themselves against the world rather than against a brother or sister, and demand particularly high standards of themselves. She describes her daughter as a good student, a conservative, almost staid collegiate and a lifelong Republican.

'We never had to worry about her. She intended to be quite perfect. And she was a very nice, polite child. I don't think she ever wore jeans during the sixties or seventies, and on campus she went right on wearing wool skirts and knee-socks and crisp white blouses with Peter Pan collars.'

Her ideals took a few knocks in New York's garment district, but she looks back with pride to her stint at Mrs Sportswear for Sears. The president of Kellwood still attends her shows. Tiara time began the day she took a job at Oscar de la Renta, only too eager to accept a drop in salary. It took him a little time to realize how bright she was: Miss Perfect from St Louis, a novice so awestruck that she never spoke or stirred from her seat until he turned round one day to ask, 'Don't you ever eat?'

'Oh yes, I like to eat, Mr de la Renta,' she said, humbly. 'I think I'll go get a sandwich.'

'I thought,' says Carolyne Roehm, laughing, 'if he doesn't notice me, he won't fire me.'

Rising to the ultimate compliment of the de la Renta dinner

invitations, she learnt French and cooking, read everything, boned up on art exhibitions and music.

'She's a superb girl,' says Oscar. 'She became like my own daughter.'

A third of the way through the Oscar years she married Axel Roehm, the wealthy head of a German chemical company, and briefly became a Darmstadt hausfrau. He didn't want her to work and the marriage didn't take, but years afterwards Carolyne Roehm would still be shaking her head and saying with wonder, 'I couldn't believe I could fail.' She divorced in 1981 and came back to Oscar de la Renta to design his lower-priced Miss O line. Then, at a pre-Christmas cocktail party, she ran into Henry Kravis.

Connecticut came first, a refuge where they could be together and away from New York. It is still her favourite house. Then, marriage and the duplex, home to a treasure house of ravishing French paintings. A hundred and one people came to lunch on the wedding day, and life has gone on like that, really, ever since.

Back in Missouri, Mrs Bresee is worrying about her daughter in the 'awful, awful world' of New York. She is not particularly impressed by the stupendous lifestyle. She says, 'I don't think my daughter takes the time to smell the roses. She'll have to learn to do that, or she'll be missing a lot.'

What she would really like is for Henry and Carolyne to move to Montana and raise sheep.

Even Mrs Bresee does not think this is very likely.

American *Vogue*, August 1990